Comparative Politics

Comparative Politics

A Theoretical Framework

THIRD EDITION

Gabriel A. Almond
Stanford University

G. Bingham Powell, Jr.
University of Rochester

Kaare Strøm
University of California, San Diego

Russell J. Dalton
University of California, Irvine

Longman

New York   San Francisco   Boston
London   Toronto   Sydney   Tokyo   Singapore   Madrid
Mexico City   Munich   Paris   Cape Town   Hong Kong   Montreal

Publisher: Priscilla McGeehon
Senior Acquisitions Editor: Eric Stano
Associate Editor: Anita Castro
Marketing Manager: Megan Galvin-Fak
Supplements Editor: Jennifer Ackerman
Production Manager: Joseph Vella
Project Coordination, Text Design, and Electronic Page Makeup: Shepherd, Inc.
Cover Design Manager: Wendy Fredericks
Cover Designer: Wendy Stolberg
Cover Illustration/Photo: Copyright © PhotoDisc, Inc.
Senior Manufacturing Buyer: Dennis Para
Printer and Binder: Courier—Stoughton
Cover Printer: Coral Graphics Services

Library of Congress Cataloging-in-Publication Data

Comparative politics : a theoretical framework / Gabriel A. Almond ... [et al.].—3rd ed.
   p. cm.
   Rev. ed. of: Comparative politics / Gabriel A. Almond. 2nd ed. c1996.
   Includes bibliographical references and index.
   ISBN 0-321-08453-5
   1. Comparative government. I. Almond, Gabriel Abraham, 1911-II. Almond, Gabriel
Abraham, 1911-Comparative politics.

   JF51.A575 2000
   320.3—dc21

                                                          00-059680

Please visit our website at http://www.awl.com

ISBN 0-321-08453-5

1 2 3 4 5 6 7 8 9 10—CRS—03 02 01 00

Contents

Chapter Seven   PUBLIC POLICY   **166**

Preface

Comparative Politics Today: A Theoretical Framework, Third Edition, presents in the form of a separate book, the revised and updated chapters of Parts One and Two of *Comparative Politics Today: A World View*, Seventh Edition (copyright © 2000). These theoretical chapters trace back to the original Almond and Powell, *Comparative Politics: A Developmental Approach* (Little, Brown, 1966) as revised and expanded in *Comparative Politics: System, Process, and Policy* (Little, Brown, 1978). Our purpose in making these theoretical chapters separately available is for the convenience of those teachers of comparative politics who find our approach useful, but prefer to make their own selection of exemplary reading materials from the larger literature of country and analytical studies.

In the course of these several decades, while the basic systems analysis approach has been preserved in our treatment of comparative government and public policy, there have been important changes in response to changes in the world of politics and the growth of the discipline. The twentieth century was one of the most destructive in human history. Yet, it ended with a new wave of democratization and international cooperation. We try to integrate these experiences into our comparative framework and analysis. Moreover, the Third Edition responds to the contemporary mood of questioning government authority, offering a searching exploration of the theme of why government exists and what functions it serves. We explore the debates about the costs and benefits of government in the history of philosophy, and in the contemporary exchanges among academics and politicians over the scope and performance of the state and government.

We have added two new co-authors—Professor Kaare Strom of the University of California, San Diego, and Professor Russell Dalton of the University of California, Irvine. Kaare Strom has played an important part in the new emphases in this edition; his contribution is especially evident in the chapters on Issues (1), Government and Policymaking (6), and Public Policy (7). The themes of federalism, the role of women in politics, the rule of law in transitions to democracy, and the conflicting aims of public policy are treated for the first time or in greater detail in these chapters. Russell Dalton, a specialist on European electoral politics, political culture, and the environmental movement, has improved and updated the chapters on Political Culture (3), Interest Groups (4), and Political Parties (5).

While the system, process, and policy framework has thus been substantively enriched, it has been structurally simplified. The structure and recruitment themes formerly discussed in a separate chapter have now been incorporated in the related sections in Chapter 5 on Aggregation and Political Parties and in the part of Chapter 6 that deals with the structure of government. New users of this text will find it more easily accessible, while old friends will still feel at home in its familiar logic.

The Acknowledgments in the Seventh Edition of *Comparative Politics Today: A World View* express our debts and appreciation to those who helped us prepare that edition, which is the basis of this volume also. Rather than repeat those remarks here, we wish simply to refer the reader to page xv of that text. But we do wish to reiterate explicitly our gratitude to the authors of the twelve country studies in that volume—Richard Rose (England), Martin A. Schain (France), Russell J. Dalton (Germany), Frances Rosenbluth and Michael F. Thies (Japan), Thomas F. Remington (Russia), Melanie Manion (China), Wayne A. Cornelius (Mexico), Frances Hagopian (Brazil), Ann Mosely Lesch (Egypt), Subrata K. Mitra (India), Robert J. Mundt and Oladimeji Aborisade (Nigeria), and Austin Ranney (United States)—who added once more, as they and their predecessors have many times over the years, essential content and interpretative insights to the basic theoretical framework.

Gabriel A. Almond, Stanford University
G. Bingham Powell, Jr., University of Rochester
Kaare Strøm, University of California, San Diego
Russell J. Dalton, University of California, Irvine

CHAPTER ONE

Issues in Comparative Politics

WHAT IS POLITICS?

Some people love politics. They may relish the excitement of political events, such as a presidential election, as they would an exciting athletic contest (a World Series or SuperBowl, perhaps). Others are fascinated with politics because they care about the issues and their consequences for people in their own communities and around the world. On the other hand, there are those who hate politics, either because it sets groups and individuals against each other, or because it involves abuse of power, deceit, manipulation, treachery, and violence. Finally, there are those who are indifferent to politics, who perhaps find it boring because it has little to do with the things that matter most to them. All of these reactions involve a kernel of truth, or more, about politics. Indeed, most of us react to politics with a mixture of these sentiments, which may change with time and events. Politics has many faces and can be a force for good as well as evil. The core of politics, however, is about human beings making important decisions for themselves and for others.

This book is about the comparative study of politics. In order to make political comparisons, we need to understand what is meant by politics as well as what it means to study politics comparatively. The former is the task of this chapter, whereas Chapter 2 will discuss the latter. Politics has to do with human decisions, and political science is the study of such decisions. Yet, not all decisions are political, and many of the social sciences are concerned with decisions that are of little interest to political scientists. For example, consider a situation in which you go with a friend (a date, perhaps) to an event such as a concert or a soccer match. You have a certain amount of money at your disposal. You can spend this money on your tickets (to get the best seats possible) or on food and drink, or you can save it for the future. Economists might be interested in what sorts of spending decisions you make, and perhaps in how you and your friend reach a joint decision about what to do with your money. Psychologists might wish to know why you were going with this friend and not with someone else, or who suggested going in the first place. Political scientists are not likely to want to study any of these questions, unless perhaps the event you attended turned into a riot (both soccer matches and concerts occasionally do), or the experience somehow dramatically changed your political outlook (which may occasionally happen at soccer matches and concerts, too, though you probably should not hold your breath).

The main point here is that not all choices or decisions are political. Specifically, political decisions are *public* and *authoritative*. To say that politics has to do with public decisions is to say that politics is inherently social. Politics always involves and has consequences for multiple human beings. There is no such thing as political solitaire, playing politics by yourself. Political decisions always take place within some community that we may call a *political system*. We shall discuss that concept in greater detail later.

Yet, not all social decisions are public. Most of what happens within families, among friends, or within voluntary associations belongs to the *private* sphere. Actions within this sphere are voluntary, not regulated, and do not bind anyone outside the group involved. In most societies, with whom you go to concerts and what food you buy are private decisions. When many people are indifferent to politics, it is largely because they value this private sphere, in which they may place their family life, friendships, faith, and nature, more highly than they regard the public domain. Societies vary greatly in the scope of the public versus the private sphere. In totalitarian societies, the public sphere is very large and private life very limited. In other societies, the private domain may almost crowd out the public one. To complicate things even more, the boundaries between the public and private spheres get redrawn all the time. A couple of decades ago, the sex lives of U.S. presidents or members of the British royal family were considered private matters, not to be discussed in public and certainly not by politicians. In recent years, this seems to have changed, although in other countries the traditional standards remain. On the other hand, there was a time in British history when certain religious beliefs were in themselves considered treasonous. People who held such beliefs could be executed, as was Thomas More under Henry VIII. Nowadays, religious beliefs are considered private matters in most modern democracies, though not in all parts of the world. Yet, all modern societies maintain some distinction between public and private affairs. And although politics may be influenced by what happens in the private domain, it has directly to do only with those decisions that are public.

Also, politics is authoritative. Authority means formal power that is vested in individuals or groups with the expectation that their decisions will be carried out and respected. That is to say that the choices in which we are interested are designed to be binding (compulsory) for those individuals or groups to whom they apply. In some cases, force (coercion) may be applied to ensure that they are implemented. Those who have political authority typically have access to force and to monetary resources so that they can enforce their decisions. We call such resources means of coercion. Authority does not have to be backed up by coercion, but in politics it often is. Nowadays, in most advanced democracies religious authorities, such as the Pope, have few coercive powers. They can only persuade, but rarely compel, their followers. On the other hand, tax authorities, such as the Internal Revenue Service in the United States, can typically not only exhort but also compel.

By politics we thus refer to the activities associated with the control of public decisions among a given people and in a given territory, where this control may be backed up by authoritative and coercive means. Politics refers to the processes and conflicts regarding the use of these authoritative and coercive means—who gets to employ them and for what purposes.

GOVERNMENTS AND THE STATE OF NATURE

Authority and coercive control are typically exercised by governments. **Governments** are organizations of individuals who are legally empowered to make binding decisions on behalf of a particular community. Governments thus have authoritative and coercive powers. Governments do many things. They wage war or encourage peace, cultivate or restrict international trade, open their borders to the exchange of ideas and art or close them, tax their populations heavily or lightly and through different means, allocate resources for education, health, and welfare, or leave such matters to others.

Governments may take many different forms, and they may be more or less ambitious or expansive. In the nineteenth century, most Western countries had very limited governments built on the model of the night watchman state: governments that provided basic law and order, defense, and protection of property rights, but little else (though education was also becoming a major government concern). Twentieth-century political development has produced **welfare states** with programs of social insurance, health, public education, and the like. The first such developments began in Germany in the 1880s. In response to Germany's rapid industrialization and urbanization, Chancellor Otto von Bismarck's government began offering social insurance programs that included unemployment benefits, accident and sickness insurance, and old age pensions. Bismarck initiated these policies not only because he cared about the plight of German workers but also because he wanted to stem the growth of the powerful German socialist party. His programs were soon copied by governments in many other countries. The scope and cost of welfare state programs have since grown enormously, particularly from the Great Depression of the 1930s until the 1970s. Yet, welfare state policies differ greatly from country to country. Welfare policies in the United States stress equality of opportunity through public education. In contrast, many Western European countries have given priority to social security and health programs over educational programs.

As expenditures have grown to between one-third and one-half of the national product in most industrialized democracies, problems have arisen. In some countries the increasing cost and alleged inefficiencies of the welfare state have brought about efforts to prevent further increases in programs and even to roll back some existing programs. There have been attempts to impose limits on public expenditures. Recently, the size of the government budget and its effects on savings, investment, inflation, and employment have become central issues. In effect, the government's role in providing welfare services has become more contested.

This debate over the welfare state and the regulatory state is far from new. On the contrary, it calls to mind a classic polemic in political philosophy on the nature of government. For centuries, political philosophers have debated whether governments are a force for good or evil. In the seventeenth and eighteenth centuries—the time of the English, French, and American revolutions—much of this debate was couched in arguments concerning the **state of nature.** Philosophers thought about the state of nature as the condition that would obtain if no government existed. In some cases, they may have thought that such a state had actually existed before the advent of the first governments. Whatever their conception of the state of nature, these philosophers used this idea to identify some ideal social contract (agreement) on which societies could build. We therefore often refer to them as social contract philosophers. The age of exploration, the discovery of previously unknown continents, and encounters with unfamiliar societies and cultures fed their imaginations. Even today, many political philosophers find it useful to make such a mental experiment to consider the consequences of political intervention.

Among the social contract philosophers whose reflections on the state of nature have become highly influential are Britons Thomas Hobbes and John Locke, and the Frenchman Jean-Jacques Rousseau. Though the state of nature had a similarly critical place in their respective political philosophies, their ideas about this condition varied dramatically. The contrast between Hobbes and Rousseau is most striking. Hobbes thought of the state of nature as mercilessly inhospitable, a situation of eternal conflict of all against all, and a source of barbarism and continuous fear. Referring to the state of nature, he pessimistically argued that "In such condition, there is no place for Industry; because the fruit thereof is uncertain: and consequently no Culture of the Earth; no Navigation, nor use of the commodities that may be imported by Sea; no commodious Building, . . . no Arts; no Letters; no Society; and which is worst of all, continuall feare, and danger of violent death; And the life of man, solitary, poor, nasty, brutish, and short."[1]

For Rousseau, on the other hand, the state of nature represented humanity before its fall from grace, without all the corruptions that governments have introduced. "Man is born free," Rousseau observed in *The Social Contract*, "and yet everywhere he is in chains." Rousseau saw governments as the source of power and inequality, and these conditions in turn as the causes of human alienation and corruption. "The extreme inequality in our way of life," he argued, "excess of idleness in some, excess of labor in others; . . . late nights, excesses of all kinds, immoderate ecstasies of all the passions; fatigues and exhaustion of mind, numberless sorrows and afflictions . . . that most of our ills are our own work; that we would have avoided almost all of them by preserving the simple, uniform, and solitary way of life prescribed to us by nature."[2]

Finally, John Locke, whose ideas have been particularly important for the development of Western democracies, took a position in between those of Hobbes and Rousseau. Locke did not share Hobbes's dire view of the state of nature.

Compared with Hobbes, Locke thought of human beings as more businesslike and less war prone. Yet, like Hobbes he proposed a social contract to replace the state of nature with a system of government. But whereas for Hobbes, the main task for government was to quell disorder and protect against violence and war, Locke saw the state's main role as protecting property and commerce and promoting economic growth. This it would do, in his view, by establishing and enforcing property rights and rules of economic exchange. And whereas Hobbes thought government needed to be a Leviathan, a benevolent dictator to whom the citizens would yield all their power, Locke promoted a limited government.

WHY GOVERNMENTS?

As the social contract philosophers have pointed out, there are many reasons why human beings create governments and prefer to live under such a social order. Later social theorists and politicians have come to add many items to their catalog of useful functions that governments serve. We shall discuss some of these, beginning with activities that help generate a stable community in the first place and proceeding to those that help this community prosper.

Community- and Nation-Building

One of the first purposes that governments can serve is to help create and maintain a community in which political activity can take place. While humans may be social beings, it is not always easy to build a community in which large numbers of individuals will be able to communicate, feel at home, and engage in constructive interaction such as settled family life or trade. Governments can help generate such communities in many different ways, for example by teaching a common language, instilling common norms and values, creating common myths and symbols, supporting a national identity, and so forth.

The large national communities of today have not always existed. Until about 500 years ago, Europe was a patchwork of political systems, some large and some very small, in which the residents often had no sense of citizenship or common identity. Most probably knew next to nothing about the political system to which they belonged. Since then, Europe has transformed itself into something approximating a set of nation-states, each of which contains a people with a common identity. This did not happen accidentally—indeed the governments of the emerging nation-states had a lot to do with it. They consciously strove to instill a sense of community, a common national identity, among the peoples they controlled. They did so, often heavy-handedly and with massive doses of coercion, by promoting a common language, a common educational system, and often a common religion. While we may in retrospect find many aspects of this process of *nation-building* deplorable, there is no doubt that it has produced a Europe in which the inhabitants of most states have a strong sense of community.

Many societies in the developing world today face similar challenges. Especially in Africa, the former colonial powers (particularly Britain and France) left the newly independent states with very weak national identities. In many parts of

Africa, large-scale national communities simply did not exist at the time of colonization. Even where they did exist, they were rarely reflected in the boundaries that the colonial powers drew between their possessions. These boundary lines were frequently drawn according to the strategic and military interests of the colonizers, who often knew and cared little about local identities among the populations they ruled. After independence, many new states have therefore been left with huge nation-building tasks for which strong governments often seem essential.

Nation-building activities help instill common world views, values, and expectations. Using a concept discussed at greater length in Chapter 3, we can say that such government activities can help homogenize the political cultures of their citizens. And the more homogeneous the political culture, the easier it is to live in peaceful coexistence and engage in activities for mutual gain, such as commerce.

Security and Order

Thomas Hobbes believed that governments, and only strong governments, could make society safe for its inhabitants. Providing security, law, and order are indeed among the most essential tasks that governments are called upon to perform. We often distinguish between external and internal security, both of which were important concerns to Hobbes. External security means protection against the attacks of individuals, groups, or military forces from other political systems. National defense forces, such as armies, navies, and air forces, are typically created to perform this function. Internal security means protection from theft, aggression, and violence from members of one's own society. This is in most societies the function of the police.

The provision of security and order still plays a critical role in modern states. The German social scientist Max Weber saw a monopoly on the use of force as the defining property of the modern state. Consider this issue for a moment. While governments across the world have privatized many of the services they used to perform—for example, post offices, railroads, telecommunications, health care, and pensions—it is hard to think of governments that have privatized their police or defense forces (though some U.S. states have privatized prisons).

Protecting Property and Other Rights

John Locke saw the establishment and protection of economic and political rights as the most essential purpose of government. Though Locke's greatest concern may have been with economic property rights, there are many other social and political rights that governments, and perhaps only governments, can provide. Among them are freedoms of speech and association and protection against various forms of discrimination and harassment. Nonetheless, Locke considered property rights to be particularly critical to the sustained development of nations and other communities. Without effective protection of property rights, people will not invest much of their goods or energies in productive processes. Also, unless property rights exist and credible contracts can be negotiated and enforced, people will not trust their neighbors enough to engage in much trade and commerce. Therefore, anything beyond the mere subsistence economy requires effective property rights and contracts. Effective property rights must clearly allocate ownership and use and provide security against trespass and violations. Such rights must also make the buying and selling ("alienation") of property relatively inexpensive and painless. Finally, citizens must have faith that their property rights will persist and be defended (long-term credibility). The more effective the property rights, the more people will trade, invest, and enter into other long-term agreements that generate sustained economic growth.

Promoting Economic Efficiency and Growth

Governments can thus help promote economic development by establishing and enforcing effective property rights and by facilitating trade. Particularly in the twentieth century, however, economists have come to see many other ways in which government can promote economic development. These are related to market failures in capitalist economies. Neoclassical economics shows that market economies are efficient when property rights are defined and protected, and when competition is rigorous and information freely available. When one or several of these conditions do not hold, however, market failures may result, and supply may not efficiently meet demand.

Public goods are particularly susceptible to market failure. Public goods have two defining characteristics. One is that if they are provided to one consumer, they cannot be withheld from anyone else. The second is that one person's enjoyment or consumption of the good does not detract from anyone else's. Consider clean air or national defense. It is, for most practical purposes, impossible to provide one member of a community with clean air or defense without also giving it to his or her neighbors. Moreover, my enjoyment of clean air or national security does not mean that my neighbors have any less of it. It is often argued that for these reasons, people will not pay for public goods in a market economy and that such goods will therefore be undersupplied. If anyone can benefit from such goods as public parks and lighthouses, why should I (or anyone else) voluntarily pay for them? Only government, it is argued, can by taxing its citizens step in and provide such public goods as parks, roads, lighthouses, national defense, and environmental protection.

A second type of market failures are what we call **externalities**, which occur when some economic activity produces costs that are not borne or taken into account by any of the parties. Though externalities need not be bad, some certainly are. Many forms of environmental degradation have resulted from situations in which neither those who produce the goods nor those who consume them bear all the production costs. Polluting factories, waste dumps, prisons, pornographic shops, or major highways can impose large uncompensated costs on those who live near them, and recent years have witnessed a major rise in protest activity among so-called NIMBY ("not-in-my-back-yard") groups. Governments can help protect against the imposition of obnoxious externalities or ensure that burdens are fairly shared.

So-called natural monopolies represent yet another role governments can play in promoting economic growth and efficiency. There are some goods, it is commonly held, for which efficiency dictates that there should be only one supplier. This typically occurs because there are very large start-up costs or because of the prohibitive costs of coordination between different suppliers. The government may then step in and become the monopolist, or it may tightly control a private or semipublic monopolist. In the nineteenth century, for example, many countries created railroad monopolies, which were frequently run by the government. Similarly, telecommunications have commonly been a government monopoly, as have mail services and in many countries strategic defense industries.

Social Justice

Governments can play a role not only in promoting economic growth but also in dividing the fruits of such growth equitably. Many people argue that governments are needed to promote social justice by redistributing wealth and other resources between citizens. In many countries the distribution of income is highly uneven. Land and other wealth are typically even more unequally distributed than income. Moreover, in many societies income and wealth inequalities have been getting progressively worse over time. Brazil, for example, has one of the most severe income inequalities in the world, an inequality that has grown in every decade since the 1930s.

Under such circumstances, social justice may dictate a "new deal," especially if existing inequalities deprive many individuals of education, adequate health care, and other basic needs. Government intervention may then be needed to redistribute resources from the better-off to the poor. Some theorists of distributive justice argue that such transfers should attempt to equalize the conditions of all citizens. Others would instead prefer governments to redistribute enough to "create a level playing field" and thus equalize opportunities but would then let individuals be responsible for their own fortunes. Either way, citizens in many societies would agree that there should be efforts to make the distribution of wealth and income more even. Though many private individuals, organizations, and foundations participate in voluntary efforts to help the poor, they generally do not have the capacity or authority to effect large-scale redistribution. Governments do, at least under some circumstances. Many tax and welfare policies are indeed designed to do just that, though how successful they are, or how far such redistribution should go, is often hotly disputed. But even many individuals who do not think that governments have a general responsibility to redistribute wealth would agree that they should at least provide certain minimum standards of living, a social safety net, for all citizens.

Protecting the Weak

We commonly rely on the government to protect individuals and groups, such as future generations, that are not able to speak for themselves. Such groups obviously cannot act to protect their own interests. Governments, however, can protect the interests of the unborn and prevent them from getting saddled with economic debts or environmental degradation. And in recent decades, governments have become much more involved in protecting groups that are for various rea-

---

Box 1.1   Tage Erlander and the "People's Home"

In much of Europe, social democratic parties have been a main force behind the expansion of government that has taken place in the twentieth century, and particularly from the Great Depression of the 1930s to the 1970s.
The Swedish Social Democratic Party, for example, ruled virtually without
interruption from 1932 to 1976. For most of that time Tage Erlander was
the party leader and Sweden's prime minister (1946–1969). Under his leadership, Sweden developed one of the most extensive welfare states in the
world and virtually eradicated most forms of poverty, though at the cost of
the highest tax rates in the Western world.

Tage Erlander referred to the Swedish welfare state as the "people's
home" and a "strong society," by which he meant a powerful government
guided by a sense of solidarity and community spirit. In a 1954 parliamentary speech, Erlander presented this argument:

> It is a mistake to think that the freedom of human beings, whether in the eco-
> nomic area or the political one, will diminish if they agree to join forces to do
> such things as they cannot manage by themselves. What is . . . the main part of
> our political activity other than attempts to organize such cooperation? We want
> health insurance, but nobody can manage that on his own. We must therefore
> create the opportunity for a collective solution. The same is true with respect to
> our wish to provide social security, to improve our roads, schools, defense, etc.
> All our political activities are filled with our striving to secure community cooper-
> ation to solve such tasks, which we can accomplish together, but which we cannot
> solve by ourselves. For us social democrats, it has been important to try to create
> a society in which the citizens consider the government's activities as an expres-
> sion of their own efforts.

Source: Riksdagens Protokoll, January 20, 1954, p. 169.

---

sons politically weak or unenfranchised, such as children, the old, and the infirm
or disabled, as well as nonhuman parts of the creation—from whales and birds to
trees and other parts of our natural environment.

WHEN DOES GOVERNMENT BECOME THE PROBLEM?

Although there are many reasons that governments may be called upon to inter-
vene in and regulate human affairs, such intervention is not always welcomed by
all. When and how government intervention is necessary and desirable has been
one of the greatest issues in twentieth-century politics. Over the course of this
century, the role of governments has expanded enormously. At the same time,
criticisms of many government policies have persisted and in some cases intensi-
fied. Such skepticism has been directed at virtually all government activities. Yet,

the critics of governments have been particularly insistent and influential when they have criticized the economic roles that many governments have taken on.

Critics of Government: Anarchists and Libertarians

Critics of government intervention come in many camps and political shades, but two groups are especially outspoken: anarchists and libertarians. Both groups believe that governments do many things that are unnecessary or even harmful. Both see excessive government intervention and regulation as a serious threat to basic human values. They differ, however, in the threats they see as most serious, as well as in the forms of social organization that they wish to put in the place of governments. Adherents of **libertarianism** are *individualists* who see society as composed of individual human beings with a number of fundamental rights that must be protected. Among these are property rights and the freedoms of speech and association. The main problem with government, libertarians argue, is that the more tasks it takes on, the more prone it is to violate such basic rights. While

---

Box 1.2   The Anarchist Kropotkin

Prince Petr Alekseevich Kropotkin (1842–1921), a Russian geographer and philosophical anarchist, believed that cooperation rather than competition is the norm in both animal and human life. In such a society based on cooperative norms, government would be replaced by voluntary groups. The economy would be based on need, which would leave citizens much time for leisure and creative activity. Kropotkin was imprisoned under the czars for preaching this philosophy and spent much of his later life in exile in England. His ideas are developed in a book entitled *Mutual Aid*, which was published in 1902.

The State was established for the precise purpose of imposing the rule of landowners, the employers of industry, the warrior class, and the clergy upon the peasants on the land and the artisans in the city. And the rich perfectly well know that if the machinery of the State ceased to protect them, their power over the laboring classes would be gone immediately. Socialism, we have said—whatever form it may take in its evolution toward communism—must find *its own form* of political organization. . . . This is why socialism *cannot* utilize representative government as a weapon for liberating labor. . . . A new form of political organization has to be worked out the moment that socialist principles shall enter into our life. And it is self-evident that this new form will have to be *more popular, more decentralized, and nearer to the folkmote self-government* than representative government can ever be.

Source: Petr Alekseevich Kropotkin, "Modern Science and Anarchism," in Emile Capouya and Keitha Tompkins, eds., *The Essential Kropotkin* (New York: Liveright, 1975, pp. 85–86). Emphases in the original.

adherents of **anarchism** agree that governments impose undesirable effects, they see society and the ills of governments somewhat differently. Anarchists are *communitarians*. They see societies not as collections of individuals but as communities of people who in their natural condition are equal. Governments and power corrupt such communities and lead to oppression and alienation. Anarchists see the alternative to government in voluntary cooperation and natural communities. Libertarians, on the other hand, promote a society of unfettered individuals, free to make their own choices and to seek out the groups to which they want to belong. Their differences aside, libertarians and anarchists find much to criticize in the activities of contemporary governments. Even individuals who are neither anarchists nor libertarians share many of these concerns.

Destruction of Community

Whereas some see governments as a way to build community, anarchists argue with Rousseau that governments destroy natural communities. Government, they hold, implies power and inequality between human beings. And power corrupts.

Box 1.3   The Libertarian Barry Goldwater

Some might call Barry Goldwater (1909–1998) a libertarian. A businessman and an Air Force officer, he won a seat in the U.S. Senate for Arizona (1953–1965, 1969–1987) and ran for the presidency on the Republican ticket in 1964. In his nomination acceptance address he insisted, "extremism in the defense of liberty is no vice . . . and moderation in the pursuit of justice is no virtue." He is viewed as the founder of modern Republican conservatism, though his libertarian beliefs often put him at odds with other members of his party.

For the American Conservative, there is no difficulty in identifying the day's overriding political challenge: it is *to preserve and extend freedom*. . . . Throughout history, government has proved to be the chief instrument for thwarting man's liberty. . . . The *legitimate* functions of government are actually conducive to freedom. Maintaining internal order, keeping foreign foes at bay, administering justice, removing obstacles to the free interchange of goods—the exercise of these powers makes it possible for men to follow their chosen pursuits with maximum freedom. But note that the very instruments by which these desirable ends are achieved *can* be the instrument for achieving undesirable ends—that government can, instead of extending freedom, restrict freedom. And note, secondly, that the "can" quickly becomes "will" the moment the holders of government power are left to their own devices.

Source: Barry M. Goldwater, *The Conscience of a Conservative*, Shepherdsville, KY: Victor Publishing, 1960, pp. 14–17. Emphases in the original.

In Lord Acton's famous words, "power corrupts, and absolute power corrupts absolutely." While those who have power are corrupted, those without it are degraded and alienated. According to Rousseau, only human beings unfettered by government can form bonds that allow them to develop their full human potential. By imposing an order based on coercion, hierarchy, and the threat of force, governments therefore destroy natural communities. The stronger government becomes, the more it creates inequalities of power that have such pernicious consequences. In more contemporary terms, some would argue that governments create a "client society," in which people learn to be subservient to authorities and to rely on governments to meet their needs, and in which governments patronize and pacify their citizens.

Violations of Basic Rights

At the same time that power allows governments to destroy communities, it also enables them to infringe on the rights of citizens. This is the main concern of many libertarians. Just as governments can help establish and defend many essential rights, they can also use their powers to violate these rights in the most serious manner. The twentieth century has witnessed enormous progress in the extension of political, economic, and social rights in societies all around the world. At the same time, however, basic human rights have probably never before been violated on such a gross scale. The loss of millions of lives to political persecution is only the most serious manifestation of these violations. Such horrors have happened not only in Nazi extermination camps and during Stalin's Great Terror in the Soviet Union, but also on a huge scale in China and Cambodia, and on a smaller scale in such countries as Iraq, Argentina, Guatemala, and Haiti. These extreme abuses of government power illustrate a dilemma that troubled James Madison and other founding fathers of the American Revolution: the problem of creating a government strong enough to govern effectively but not so strong that it could destroy the rights of those whom it was designed to serve.

Economic Inefficiency

Many of the most important criticisms of modern governments have come from economists. And the objections that arise out of economic scholarship and research have convinced the citizens of many countries to restrict the role of governments in the economy. Economic problems might arise even if government officials do not actively abuse their power. Some of the best-known arguments against government regulation of the economy point out that it may distort the terms of trade and lower people's incentives to produce, thus hurting overall economic performance. Further inefficiencies may arise when governments not only regulate the economy but also act as producers in their own right. This is particularly likely if the government is a monopoly producer of an important good, since monopolies generally cause goods to be undersupplied and overpriced. Moreover, government industries may be especially prone to inefficiency and complacency because management and workers often have far better job protection than those in the private sector. Therefore, they may not have to worry about losing their jobs or benefits even if their enterprises perform poorly.

Government for Private Gain

What will be the effects of government intervention if public officials are neither benevolent nor tyrannical, but simply self-interested? If politicians are rational and self-interested, we should expect them to make decisions from which they would personally profit, or to select the policies most likely to get them reelected, regardless of whether this would be the best choice for society as a whole. Such self-interested political pursuit of private gain has become known as **rent seeking.** *Rents* are benefits created through government intervention in the economy—for

---

**Box 1.4   Rent Seeking and the Case
of Mobutu Sese Seko**

The problem of rent seeking has been the particular concern of economists and political scientists in the public choice tradition, founded in the 1960s by James Buchanan and Gordon Tullock. Until that time, economists had generally assumed that governments intervened only when markets failed. They further assumed that once the government intervened, it would do so to benefit the economy as a whole. Public choice scholars ask instead, "what if government officials acted in the same ways that economics assumes other producers and consumers to behave?" That is to say, what happens if politicians use their power in their own self-interest, or to benefit individuals or groups that support them? Public choice analysts tend to see the competition of political parties and interest groups over government policy as driven by a pursuit of rents. Once in power, they argue, politicians and organizations seek to benefit themselves and their followers at the expense of their competitors. President Mobutu Sese Seko (1930–1997) of Zaire offers a tragic example of the costs that rent-seeking politicians can impose on their societies. After seizing power in a 1965 coup, Mobutu ruled the large African state of Congo (which he renamed Zaire) for more than 30 years. Mobutu banned opposition parties and ruled his country as a dictator until he was finally deposed by rebel forces under Laurent Kabila in 1997. During his long rule, President Mobutu used government funds, including aid from Western states such as the United States, to amass a huge personal fortune which he invested abroad. In addition to large sums of money, he is reported to have owned about 30 luxury residences abroad, including a number of palatial estates on the French Riviera. Meanwhile, living standards in Zaire, a poor country with large natural resources, plummeted, and the country was racked with epidemic disease and civil war. Mobutu died of natural causes shortly after his ouster in 1997.

example, tax revenue or profits created because the government has restricted competition. Rent seeking refers to efforts that individuals, groups, firms, or organizations exert in order to reap such benefits. While the terminology may sound unfamiliar, the idea behind it is really quite simple. Rent seeking occurs when people seek to use governments for their private gain.

Rent seeking is at best a game in which one person's gain is another person's loss. At worst, however, rent seeking can impose large net costs on society, because each party or group is willing to expend large resources in order to control the spoils of government. It may turn into outright corruption, when influence is traded for money or other advantage. Rent seeking may be a particularly serious problem in poor societies, in which politics is often the surest or most effective way to enrich oneself, and in which the courts, mass media, and other political actors may be too weak to constrain government officials from abusing their power. Besides, many developing societies do not have strong norms against using government for private gain. On the contrary, people often expect those in government to use their power to benefit themselves, their families, kin, and neighbors. Remember also that even in many advanced democratic societies—for example, in Britain—the line between the private property of the monarch and that of the government was not clearly drawn even in the recent past.

Vested Interests and Inertia

The fact that governments create rents also means that they are difficult to change or abolish once established. To the extent that some people enjoy the benefits of government jobs, contracts, or other benefits that they otherwise might not have enjoyed, we speak of them as having *vested interests* in the existing system of government. The larger the government and the more attractive the benefits it provides, the more likely it is that such vested interests will resist change (unless change means making their benefits even larger). Therefore, any government will foster a class of people with a vested interest in maintaining or enlarging the government itself. Such groups may become a powerful force against change and in favor of the status quo. This makes it difficult to change government policies or try to make them more efficient. Instead, once established, agencies and policies tend to live on far beyond their usefulness. When, for example, the Spanish Armada in 1588 threatened to invade, the English government posted a military observation post at Land's End in southwest England. This observation post remained in place in the late twentieth century, long after the Spanish navy had ceased to be a threat. In the United States, many federal programs created during the New Deal of the 1930s remained in place toward the end of the millennium, even though the need for them might have changed dramatically. One example is the Rural Electrification Administration, which was created in 1935 and persisted for almost 60 years, until it was finally merged into the Rural Utilities Service in 1994. The U.S. Senate maintained and staffed a Committee on Revolutionary War Claims until well into the twentieth century.

Vested interests are particularly likely to prevail in political systems that contain a lot of safeguards against rapid political change. While the checks and balances in such political systems as the United States are designed to safeguard the rights of individuals, groups, and local communities, they may also end up protecting the privileges of vested interests. Yet, even political systems that contain far fewer such checks may exhibit an excess of political inertia. Britain is an excellent example. In its House of Lords, for example, the majority of members (noblemen, bishops, and judges) represent the social groups (the "estates") that dominated British society before the Industrial Revolution more than 200 years ago. Only now have plans been introduced to reform the House of Lords and eliminate features that reflect Britain's past as a feudal and preindustrial society.

Alternatives to Government: Markets and Voluntary Coordination

To the extent that governments cannot always be trusted to solve social problems, what can take their place? Here, the answers vary substantially between different camps of government critics. Anarchists and communitarians are likely to suggest that many of the functions of large-scale governments can instead be performed either through much more local and decentralized governments, or through voluntary cooperation without any political authority. Radical anarchists reject all forms of private property as well as all formal authority. To the extent that governments have to exist, anarchists argue, they should be as close to the people as possible. That is to say that office holders should have limited terms and few privileges, that decision making should be as transparent as possible, and that ordinary citizens and groups should be given the opportunity to participate extensively in political decision making. "Green" (environmentalist) political parties, particularly in European countries such as Germany, seek to promote such political reforms.

While libertarians and market-oriented economists (such as the so-called "Chicago school") may support some of these causes (for example, government decentralization), they tend to focus their demands on a different set of reforms. Most of them tend to accept the role of governments in protecting security, individual rights, and commerce. However, they are sharply critical of government economic regulation and production. A few libertarians go further in their critique of governments and advocate draft resistance, tax resistance, and legalization of all drugs. Building on strands in modern economics, including the influential work of Ronald H. Coase, libertarians argue that much of what appears to be market failure can be solved without government intervention. Their preferred alternative to governments is to rely on free markets and individual property rights.

The debate between the proponents and critics of strong governments continues and is likely to be a key political controversy for a long time. In the past 20 years or so, there has been a clear trend away from extensive government regulation of many economic sectors. Yet, the overall size of governments in advanced industrial countries has not changed very much. Measured as a proportion of the total economy (for example, gross domestic product), the government's share has declined in some countries (e.g., Britain and New Zealand), increased in others (e.g., Japan), and stayed fairly constant in yet others (e.g., the United States). In the former Communist countries and in some developing countries, however, the government's size has shrunk much more dramatically. Since the 1970s especially, there has been a movement in many societies to privatize many economic sectors and to deregulate others, such as telecommunications, transportation (e.g., the airline industry), and banking, which many governments had previously strictly regulated. But whereas government regulation has become less extensive in some areas, it has grown in others—for example, in passing laws protecting the environment or the rights of children.

POLITICAL SYSTEMS

Politics takes place within and between political systems that interact with a setting or an environment. Since the term **political system** is the main organizing concept of this book, we shall elaborate its meaning below. Anything we call a system must necessarily have two properties: (1) it has a set of interdependent parts, and (2) it has boundaries towards the environment with which it interacts. There are many kinds of systems: mechanical systems such as automobiles, ecological systems (ecosystems) such as the plants and animals coexisting in a single habitat, and social systems such as a family. All have interdependent parts and boundaries. Political systems are a particular type of social system—namely, one involved in the making of authoritative public decisions. To put it slightly differently, the political system is a set of institutions, such as parliaments, bureaucracies, and courts, that formulate and implement the collective goals of a society or of groups within it.

Political systems mold and are molded by a domestic and an international environment. The system receives inputs from these environments and shapes them through its outputs. The boundaries of political systems are defined in terms of persons, territory, and property. Most human beings belong to, and have citizenship rights in, only one country. Similarly, territory is divided between states in ways that are meant to be mutually exclusive. A given piece of land is supposed to belong to one and only one country. Much the same is true with respect to other property rights. Of course, disputes over citizenship, territory, and property are by no means uncommon and have indeed been among the most frequent causes of international conflict all through history.

The decisions of the political system are normally backed up by legitimate coercion, and obedience may be compelled. By legitimacy we mean that those who are ruled believe that the rulers have a "right" (whether by law or by custom) to implement their decisions by force if necessary. The legitimacy of a political system may vary over time. The legitimacy of the American system was high just after World War II; it declined substantially during and after the Vietnam War but has since then recovered at least somewhat. In Germany, on the other hand, the new democratic system had little support just after World War II but has gradually gained in legitimacy since then. Low legitimacy may result in breakdowns in political organization and public policy failures. Policy failures in turn can cause declining legitimacy. The Soviet system collapsed in 1991 after its legitimacy had been undermined by a failed and costly war in Afghanistan, a nuclear power disaster in Chernobyl, corruption, and declining economic productivity. We discuss legitimacy at greater length in Chapter 3.

Governments are at the core of political systems, but the latter concept also encompasses important parts of the environment in which governments operate. There is more to politics than authoritative and coercive activities—for example, political organizations such as political parties or interest groups. Such organizations do not have coercive authority, except insofar as they control the government. Likewise, the mass media only indirectly affect elections, legislation, and law enforcement. Then there is a whole host of institutions beginning with the family and including communities, churches, schools, universities, corporations, foundations, and thinktanks, which influence political attitudes and public policy. The term *political system* refers to this whole collection of related, interacting institutions and agencies.

Comparative politics is the study of political systems, in which we try to understand these political systems not as isolated cases but through generalizations and comparisons. Chapter 2 discusses how and why we make such comparisons. In principle, comparative politics could consist of comparisons of cities, states, international organizations, klans, or even individual leaders. In practice, however, although there are important literatures comparing political institutions such as political parties, interest groups, and legislatures, comparative politics focuses on comparisons of *states,* or what we commonly refer to as countries. We shall therefore discuss states and their role in the contemporary world next.

STATES

The twelve political systems that we compare in this book are all *states*. A **state** is a particular type of political system, specifically one that has **sovereignty**—an independent legal authority over a population in a particular territory, based on the recognized right to self-determination. Sovereignty rests with those who have the ultimate right to make political decisions. We often distinguish between internal and external sovereignty. *Internal sovereignty* means the right to determine matters having to do with one's own citizens without intervention. *External sovereignty* means the right to conclude binding agreements (treaties) with other states. For example, the British government has internal sovereignty in the sense that it can impose whatever taxes it wants on British citizens. Similarly, its external sovereignty means that it can enter into treaties with other states. The city of Edinburgh does not have these rights. Nor does the county of Kent or the principality of Wales. All of them are dependent on the central British government in tax matters and foreign policy. Yet, sovereignty is never absolute, and every state in the real world faces constraints on its internal and external sovereignty. With the increasing integration of the United Kingdom (Britain) into the European Union, the British government has in fact had to give up parts of its sovereignty to that larger government, and this loss of sovereignty has been a major topic of political debate.

In the United States we confuse things a bit by calling the 50 constituent units "states," even though they enjoy much less sovereignty than Britain. The states of the United States share the power and authority of the "state" with the central government in Washington, DC. However confusing this usage is today, it does reflect what American government was once like, under the Articles of Confederation before the Constitution was signed. Since then, however, much authority has been shifted from the states to the central (federal) government.

We often think of the world as a patchwork quilt of states with sizable and contiguous territories. But even though that may seem the natural way to organize world politics, it has not always been so. Until the end of the Middle Ages, Europe was comprised of many very small political systems and a few very large ones, whose territorial possessions were not always very stable or contiguous. Nor did states always consist of people with the same national identity (on nations and nation-states, see more below). Gradually, a set of European nation-states evolved, and the 1648 Treaty of Westphalia established that principle for the political organization of Europe. The eighteenth and nineteenth centuries were the main era during which the concentration of power in the nation-state occurred. After World War II, however, power began shifting from the state downward to local governments, and upward to supranational organizations. The European Union (EU) and the North American Free Trade Agreement (NAFTA) are examples of the latter development. Most of the industrialized countries of Western Europe have, after centuries of costly and destructive wars, gradually created a common market economy and many of them in 1999 a common currency, the Euro. Originally consisting of six countries—France, Germany, Italy, Belgium, the Netherlands, and Luxembourg—the European Community has expanded to 15—adding Britain, Ireland, Spain, Portugal, Greece, Denmark, Austria, Finland, and Sweden. In addition, a number of Eastern European countries have been invited to apply.

The **United Nations (UN),** formed at the end of World War II in 1945, has acquired new responsibilities since the collapse of the Soviet Union. As of early 1994, UN forces were deployed as peacekeepers in 17 countries. Nine of these had been established since the end of the Cold War. These operations, involving more than 100,000 peacekeepers, were designed to separate combatants in domestic and international conflicts, to help settle disputes, and to form effective governing institutions. The UN has acquired increased authority over world security, constraining, supporting, and replacing the unilateral actions of individual states. But while the sovereignty of states may thus be slipping away, they are still the most important political systems around. That, of course, is the main reason that they are the subject of this, and most other, texts on comparative politics.

Old and New States

Just about the entire surface of the world today is covered by independent states. There were some 185 "member-states" of the United Nations in 1999.[3] There are also a few countries that are not members of the UN (Taiwan, Switzerland, and the Vatican), and there are some secessionary movements that, if successful, would make our figures obsolete. When the United States declared its independence in 1776, most independent states were European (see Figure 1.1). Much of the rest of the world had been parcelled out as colonies to one or another of the

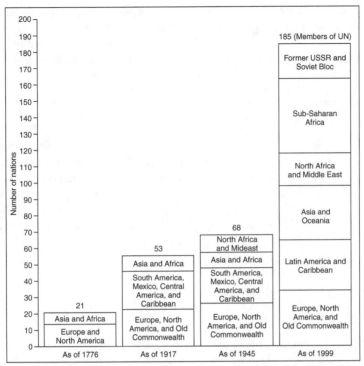

Source: For contemporary members, Information Office, United Nations. Data to 1945 from Charles Taylor and Michael Hudson, *World Handbook of Political and Social Indicators* (New Haven, CT: Yale University Press, 1972), pp. 26 ff.

FIGURE 1.1   FORMATION OF STATES SINCE 1776 *Source:* For contemporary members, Information Office, United Nations. Data to 1945 from Charles Taylor and Michael Hudson, *World Handbook of Political and Social Indicators* (New Haven, CT: Yale University Press, 1972), pp. 26 ff.

European empires. In the nineteenth and early twentieth centuries, the number of states increased, principally in Latin America where the Spanish and Portuguese empires broke up into 20 independent states. In Europe, newly independent countries emerged in the Balkans, Scandinavia, and the Low Countries. Between the two world wars, national proliferation extended to North Africa and the Middle East; and Europe continued to fragment as Poland, Finland, Czechoslovakia, and Yugoslavia gained their independence from the Russian and Austro-Hungarian empires. At the same time, the three Baltic countries—Lithuania, Latvia, and Estonia—briefly experienced independence but were again swallowed by the Soviet Union from 1939 until its collapse in 1991.

Since World War II, the development of new states has really taken off. By 1999, 117 new countries had joined the 68 states that existed in 1945. The largest group of new states are in Sub-Saharan Africa. The 1990s alone have witnessed more than 20 new countries—mostly the successor states of the Soviet Union, Yugoslavia, and Czechoslovakia. All these countries—new as well as old—share certain characteristics. They have legal authority over their territories and people; they have armies, air forces in most cases, and in some cases navies; they collect taxes and spend money; they regulate their economies, maintain public order, and pursue their general welfare. They send and receive ambassadors; most belong to several international organizations; and they do all these things through parliaments, cabinets, ministries, departments, courts, police, and prisons. But they also vary, often profoundly, in physical size, histories, institutions, cultures, religions, economies, social structures—factors that also shape their politics.

First, Second, and Third World

From the 1950s on, it became customary to divide the states of the world into three categories: the first, second, and third world. The first world consisted of the advanced capitalist democracies; the second world encompassed the communist bloc of countries, at that time led by the Soviet Union; the third world made up the remaining states of the world, those that were neither rich and Western nor communist. Indeed, most of the world's states and population fell into this third category. With the collapse of most communist states and the increasing differences between developing societies, these categories are no longer as useful as they once were. Nonetheless, it is still common to refer to the developing states collectively as the Third World.

Big and Small States

Russia is the largest country in area, encompassing more than 17 million square kilometers. China has the most people, with approximately 1.2 billion. There are many countries at the other extreme, but the smallest legally independent political entity in both respects is Vatican City, the headquarters of the Catholic Church, with less than half a square kilometer of turf and under a thousand residents. Table 1.1 reports the widely differing populations and areas of 12 countries whose

Table 1.1   AREA AND POPULATION OF SELECTED COUNTRIES

Country	Population (millions in 1997)	Average Annual Growth of Population	Area 1995 (thousands of km)
China	1,227	1.1	9,326
India	961	1.8	2,973
United States	268	1.0	9,159
Brazil	164	1.4	8,457
Russia	147	–0.1	16,889
Japan	126	0.3	377
Nigeria	118	2.9	911
Mexico	95	1.8	1,909
Germany	82	0.5	349
Britain	59	0.3	242
Egypt	60	2.0	995
France	59	0.5	550

Source: World Bank, World Development Report: 1998–1999. (New York, Oxford University Press), 1999, tables 1 and 3, pp. 192–93, 194–95.

features we consistently report in this book.[4] The political implications of these striking contrasts in population size and geographic area are not always obvious. Big countries are not always the most important and do not always prevail over the small ones. Cuba has challenged the United States for almost 40 years; Israel stands off the Arab world; and tiny Vatican City has great power and influence.

Nor do area and population size determine a country's political system. Both Luxembourg and the United States are democracies. Authoritarian regimes can be found in small, medium, or large countries. These enormous contrasts in size show only that the countries now making up the world differ greatly in their range of physical and human resources. Yet, area and population do affect economic development, foreign policy and defense problems, and many other issues of political significance. For example, with population growth rates double those of the industrialized countries, developing countries have to grow twice as fast economically just to keep from falling further behind.

A state's geographic location has important strategic implications. In the sixteenth through nineteenth centuries, a state located in the center of Europe could not avoid building a large land army to protect itself from the threats of its neighbors. Such a nation would have difficulty developing free political institutions, since it needed a strong government to extract resources on a large scale and keep its population under control. Britain has historically been protected by the English Channel and could defend itself through its navy. It could do with a smaller army, lower taxation, and less centralization of power. The United States was a similar case. The Atlantic Ocean and the relatively open continent critically shaped U.S. political institutions. Most peoples of Asia, Africa, and Latin America were dominated, and in most cases colonized, by the more powerful Western nations. Those that had the richest natural resources and the most benign climates tended to attract the largest numbers of settlers.

Whether they are old or new, large or small, most of the world's states face a number of common challenges. The first is building community. Most of the world's states do not have a homogeneous population, and instilling a sense of shared identity and interest can be a serious problem. So can creating a sense of allegiance to the government. The second is the ability to foster economic, social, and political development now and in the future, a challenge that is faced by even the wealthiest states. Finally, most states face significant challenges in the area of securing and furthering democracy and civil liberties. These challenges should be familiar from our discussion of the purposes and dangers of governments. In the remainder of this chapter, we shall discuss these challenges successively.

BUILDING COMMUNITY

One of the most important challenges facing political systems all over the world is to build a common identity and a sense of community among the citizens. The absence of such a sense of common identity can have the most severe political consequences. Conflicts over national, ethnic, or religious identities are among the most explosive causes of political turmoil, as we have recently witnessed in Northern Ireland, the former Yugoslavia, Rwanda, and elsewhere. But while building community is a pervasive challenge, some countries are in a much more favorable situation than others. Japan, for example, has relatively little to worry about. Its population is ethnically quite homogeneous and shares a language and a long political history. Large majorities of the Japanese share in the religions of Buddhism and Shintoism, and the country is separated by hundreds or thousands of miles of ocean from its most important neighbors. Nigeria, on the other hand, has an extremely diverse population of more than 100 million. The country itself is an accidental and artificial creation of British colonial rule and has no common precolonial history. The population is sharply divided between Muslims and Christians; the Christians are divided equally into Catholics and Protestants. There are some 250 different ethnic groups, speaking a variety of local languages, in addition to English. Obviously, the challenges of building community are much greater in Nigeria than they are in Japan. But although few countries face problems as complicated as those of the Nigerians, the community-building challenge is one of the most serious issues facing many states today.

States and Nations

The word *nation* is sometimes used to mean almost the same as a state, as in the name the United Nations. Strictly speaking, however, we wish to use the term **nation** to refer to a group of people with a common identity. When we speak of a "nation," we thus refer to the self-identification of a people. That common identity may be built upon a common language, history, race, or culture, or simply upon the fact that this group has occupied the same territory. Nations may or may not have their own state or independent government. In some cases, such as Japan, France, or Sweden, there is a close correspondence between the memberships of the state and the nation. Most people who identify themselves as Japanese do in fact live in the state of Japan, and most people who live in Japan identify themselves as Japanese. We call such cases, in which national identification and the scope of legal authority largely coincide, **nation-states.** In the twentieth century, we have come to think of nation-states as the natural way to organize states, and perhaps as an ideal. The national right to self-determination, the idea that every nation had a right to form its own state if it so wished, was enshrined in the Treaty of Versailles signed at the end of World War I.

But in the case of most states today or in the past, the correspondence between the nation and the state is not so neat. Nor is it obvious that it should be. In some cases, states are *multinational*—consisting of a multitude of different nations. The Soviet Union, Yugoslavia, and Czechoslovakia were multinational states that have now broken apart. On the other hand, there are some nations that are much larger than the corresponding states, such as the Germans for most of their history, or the Chinese. Some nations have been divided into two or more states for political reasons, such as Koreans today and the Germans between 1949 and 1990. Some groups with claims to be nations have no state at all, such as the Kurds, the Basques, the Jews in the past, and the Palestinians today. When states and nations do not coincide, it can cause explosive political conflict, as we shall discuss later. On the other hand, the presence of several nations within the same state can also be a source of diversity and cultural enrichment.

Nationality and Ethnicity

There is a fine line between nations and *ethnic groups,* which may also have common physical traits, languages, cultures, or history. But whereas we think of nationality as a form of primary identification, **ethnicity** may be of lesser importance to the group involved. Like nationality, ethnicity need not have any objective basis in genetics, culture, or history. In his classic introduction to sociological theory, the German sociologist Max Weber defined ethnic groups as "those human groups that entertain a subjective belief in their common descent because of similarities of physical type or of customs or both, or because of memories of colonization and migration. . . . [I]t does not matter whether or not an objective blood relationship exists."[5] Similarly, groups that are physically quite similar, but differ by language, religion, customs, marriage patterns, and historical memories (for example, the Serbs, Croats, and Muslim Bosnians) may believe themselves to be descended from different ancestors and hence genetically and physically different as well. Over centuries, originally homogeneous populations may become substantially intermixed genetically with other populations, even though the culture may continue. This is true, for example, of the Jewish population of Israel, which has come together after more than two millennia of dispersion over the globe.

Ethnic differences have been the source of a large number of political conflicts around the world. Even before the end of the Cold War, ethnic autonomy movements in parts of old countries—such as the United Kingdom (the Scots and Welsh) and Canada (the Quebecois)—sought to break free or achieve greater autonomy. And since the end of the Cold War, many states of the former Soviet bloc have been coming apart at their ethnic and religious seams. In the former Yugoslavia, secession by a number of provinces triggered several wars. The most brutal of these has taken place in Bosnia-Herzegovina, where a newly proclaimed Muslim regime faced rebellion and murderous "ethnic cleansing" by the large Serbian minority, backed by their fellow Serb majority in the remaining Yugoslavian state. Intervention by the UN, NATO, and the United States to contain Serbian aggression has thus far led to an uneasy settlement, but considerable tension remains. More recently the Serbs in Yugoslavia undertook to "cleanse" Albanians from the province of Kosovo, even though they were the ethnic majority there. After thousands of Albanians were killed and hundreds of thousands driven from their homes, NATO intervened with a bombing campaign, forcing the Serbs to withdraw their forces and permit the Kosovans to return.

In many developing countries, boundaries established by former colonial powers cut across ethnic lines. In 1947 the British withdrew from India and divided the subcontinent into a northern Muslim area—Pakistan—and a southern Hindu area—India. The most immediate consequence was a terrible civil conflict and "ethno-religious" cleansing incidental to the exchange of populations. There still are almost 100 million Muslims in India. Similarly, 30 years ago the Ibo "tribe" of Nigeria fought an unsuccessful separatist war with the rest of Nigeria, resulting in the deaths of millions of people. The Tutsi and Hutu peoples of the small African state of Rwanda have been engaged in a civil war of extermination, with hundreds of thousands of people slaughtered, and millions fleeing the country in fear of their lives.

Vestiges of imperial conquest (by Russia, Britain, France, Spain, Portugal, or the Netherlands) are one source of contemporary division. The migration of labor, forced or voluntary, across state boundaries, is another. The North and South American descendants of Africans forcefully enslaved between the seventeenth and the nineteenth centuries are witnesses of the largest coercive labor migration in world history. Voluntary migration takes the form, for example, of the many Indians, Bangladeshi, Egyptians, and Palestinians seeking better lives in the oil sheikhdoms around the Persian Gulf; of Mexican and Caribbean migrant workers in the United States; and of Turkish and Algerian migrants in Germany, France, and other European countries. Some migration is politically motivated, triggered by civil war and repression. A recent book refers to the contemporary world as living through an "Age of Migration,"[6] comparable in scale to that of the late nineteenth and early twentieth centuries.

Table 1.2 provides examples of politically significant "ethnicity," broadly defined, in our selected twelve countries. Five sets of traits are included, beginning with physical differences, then language, norms against intermarriage, religion, and negative historical memories. The table illustrates the importance of each distinction to ethnic identity. The most important bases of distinction lie in intermarriage, religion, and historical memories. Language differences are of great importance in three cases and of some importance in five; and finally, and perhaps surprisingly, physical differences are of great importance in only two cases.

Recent migration has made such previously homogeneous states as France, Japan, and Germany more multiethnic. Other countries such as the United States, Britain, and Canada have long been multiethnic and have become even more so. The political problems resulting from ethnic diversity range from demands for

Table 1.2   EXAMPLES OF ETHNICITY: ITS BASES AND THEIR SALIENCE*

	Physical Differences	Language	Norms Against Intermarriage	Religion	Negative Historical Memories
Brazil: Blacks	XX	O	XX	X	X
Britain: Scots	O	O	O	X	X
China: Tibetans	X	XX	XX	XX	XX
Egypt: Copts	O	O	XX	XX	X
France: Algerians	X	X	XX	XX	XX
Germany: Turks	X	XX	XX	XX	O
India: Muslims	O	X	XX	XX	XX
Japan: Buraku-min	O	O	XX	O	XX
Mexico: Mayan	X	X	XX	X	XX
Nigeria: Ibo	O	X	XX	XX	XX
Russia: Chechens	X	XX	XX	XX	XX
United States: African-Americans	XX	X	XX	O	XX

*Salience is estimated at the following levels: O = none or almost none; X = some; XX = much importance in affecting political differences.

civil rights and equality of treatment, through struggles for autonomy or national independence, to ethnocentric demands for ethnic cleansing.

Language

Language can be source of social division that may or may not be associated with ethnicity. There are approximately 5,000 different languages in use in the world today, and a much smaller number of language families. Most of these languages are spoken by relatively small tribal groups in North and South America, Asia, Africa, or Oceania. Only 200 languages have a million or more speakers, and only eight may be classified as world languages. English is the most truly international language. There are approximately 350 million people who speak English at home, and 1.8 billion who live in countries where it is an official language. Other international languages include Spanish (more than 300 million home speakers), Arabic (200 million), Russian (165 million), Portuguese (165 million), French (100 million), and German (100 million). The language with the largest number of speakers, though in several varieties, is Chinese (1.2 billion). The major languages with the greatest international spread are those of the former colonial powers— Great Britain, France, Spain, and Portugal.[7] Linguistic divisions can create particularly thorny political problems. It has been said that "constitutions can be blind but not dumb." That is to say that while political systems can choose to ignore racial, ethnic, or religious differences among their citizens, they cannot avoid committing themselves to one or several languages. Linguistic conflicts typically show up in controversies over educational policies, or over language use in the government. Occasionally, language regulation is more intrusive, as in Quebec, where English-only street signs are prohibited and larger corporations are required to conduct their business in French.

Religious Differences and Fundamentalism

States vary in the extent to which their citizens practice the same or different religious faiths. Religion can have various political consequences. In some countries, such as Israel, the Irish Republic, and Pakistan, it can be a source of national identity for a majority of the population. In other societies, such as Poland under communism, religious authorities can serve as a rallying point for opponents of an authoritarian government. In many Latin American countries, Catholic clergy have in recent years spoken out as advocates of the poor and critics of government brutalities. Across a wide range of countries, religious communities take a special interest in education. But religious differences can also be a source of intense antagonism, since they touch on matters of deep personal conviction on which it is often difficult to compromise. Although individuals and groups of different faiths can coexist peacefully, such differences can also be the source of particularly deeply felt divisions. Religious conflicts often materialize over issues concerning education, family life, freedom of speech, abortion and euthanasia, and the regulation of religious observances such as the sabbath. On such issues and others religious groups may clash with one another as well as with more secular groups.

Table 1.3   ADHERENTS OF ALL RELIGIONS BY SEVEN CONTINENTAL AREAS
(MID-1993, IN MILLIONS)*

	Africa	Asia	Europe	Latin America	North America	Oceania	Eurasia	Number	Total Percentage
Christian	341.0	300	410.0	443.0	241.0	23.0	112.0	1,869	34.0
Muslims	285.0	668	14.0	1.4	3.0	0.1	43.0	1,004	18.0
Nonreligious and atheists	3.0	900	73.0	22.0	26.0	3.6	135.0	1,153	21.0
Hindus	1.6	746	0.7	0.9	1.3	0.4	—	751	14.0
Buddhists	—	332	0.3	0.6	0.6	—	0.4	334	6.0
Folk and tribal	70.0	170	—	1.0	—	—	—	240	3.0
New and other	—	138	1.7	2.0	0.7	—	—	124	2.0
Sikhs	—	19	0.2	—	0.3	—	—	20	0.2
Jews	0.4	6	1.5	0.1	7.0	0.1	2.0	18	0.3
Total	703.0	3,291	502.0	475.0	282.0	28.0	30.0	5,575	99.0

*Adherents as defined in *World Christian Encyclopedia* (1982).

Christianity is the largest and most widely spread religion, having twice the numbers of the Muslims, the next most numerous group (see Table 1.3). The Christians are in turn divided into three groups—Roman Catholics, Protestants (of many denominations), and Orthodox—with the Catholics dominant in Europe and Latin America, and a more equal distribution of Catholics and Protestants elsewhere. Recent decades have witnessed the rise of left-inclined "Liberationist" Catholicism in Latin America, and the spread of Protestant denominations through missionary activities particularly in Latin America and Africa. The Muslims are almost entirely concentrated in Asia and Africa. They have been particularly successful in missionary activities in Sub-Saharan Africa.

Religious conflict often occurs in religiously divided societies, such as Northern Ireland or Nigeria. Yet, even societies in which most people ostensibly belong to the same community of faith may experience conflicts between fundamentalists and more liberal or secular groups. The rise of **religious fundamentalism** has been a recent worldwide development. The phenomenon got its name in the decades before World War I when Protestant clergymen in the United States banded together to defend the "fundamentals" of religious belief against the secularizing inroads of science and "critical" biblical scholarship. The "fundamentalists" affirmed the inerrancy (the absolute truth) of the Bible and formed enclaves to defend themselves against secularization. Orthodox Jews and pious Muslims encountering the same modernizing threats formed similar movements in Europe, the Middle East, and the United States in the decades after World War II.[8]

Christianity, Judaism, and Islam are all "religions of the book," though not exactly the same book. Each religion has experienced serious disagreement over the interpretation of these texts. Christian, Jewish, and Muslim fundamentalists all believe in the inerrancy of their respective sacred books and often organize against their own "mainstream" clergy. Islamic fundamentalists, however, pursue political power much more aggressively than do Christian fundamentalists, because there is no tradition of separation of church and state in Islamic history and culture. Though European Catholics were slow to accept the separation of church and state, Islamic fundamentalist movements such as those in Iran, Egypt, and Algeria still acknowledge no such limits to their quest to influence their societies. In Israel, Jewish fundamentalists seek to embody the Jewish canon law in marriage and divorce law, in the enforcement of dietary regulations, and in respect for the sabbath. Christian fundamentalists in the United States operate mainly as an interest group on school boards and in local governments on such issues as abortion, school prayer, and drug use; and nationally as the "Christian Right" within the Republican party.

The rise of fundamentalist movements has affected the entire world. Where they have developed into large-scale political movements, as in the Islamic countries of the Middle East and in the Hindu and Buddhist countries of South Asia, they often seek to form theocratic states, oppose such social policies as family planning, and impose religious regulations on education. Because they tend to favor traditional family life and oppose birth control and abortion, militant fundamentalist movements may inhibit population control and slow or reverse the emancipation of women. Yet, the spread of fundamentalism is limited by the fact that adherents of different faiths (e.g., Islamic and Jewish fundamentalists) are unlikely to join forces and pursue common goals. Hence fundamentalism is not an international movement comparable to socialism. Fundamentalism is politically significant mainly because it polarizes and fragments an increasing number of societies.

Cumulative and Cross-Cutting Cleavages

National, ethnic, linguistic, and religious divisions can interact in a variety of ways. When they systematically affect political allegiances and policies, we refer to such divisions as **political cleavages.** When a political system is affected by more than one such cleavage, it matters whether the different cleavages are *cumulative* or *cross-cutting*. If cleavages are cumulative, it means that they pit the same people against each other on many different issues. If, on the other hand, cleavages cross-cut, it means that groups that share a common interest on one issue are likely to be on opposite sides of a different issue. Consider the cases of Northern Ireland and the Netherlands. Both countries have traditionally had class divisions, and both are divided between Catholics and Protestants. The interaction between these cleavages is different, though. In Northern Ireland, class and religion are cumulative cleavages. If you are Catholic, you are also more likely to be poor, and very likely you have suffered a history of discrimination. In the Netherlands, on the other hand, class and religion tend to cross-cut. Catholics and Protestants are about equally likely to be poor or rich, and discrimination against Catholics is now a thing of the past. Where the cleavage lines within a country are cumulative (combining, for example, language, race and ethnicity, religion, and history), and especially where they coincide with economic inequalities, they often fuel violence and intractable political struggles. Many areas are intermittently in political flame, particularly where several social divisions mutually reinforce one another (as, for example, in Lebanon). Political conflicts and divisions based on language, ethnicity, and religion once were thought to have been subordinated or even eliminated by "modern" differences between social classes, interests, and ideologies. In the post–Cold War world though, ideological differences have often been overshadowed by ethnic and religious ones.

FOSTERING DEVELOPMENT

As important as the task of building community is, political systems cannot generally expect to satisfy their citizens unless they can foster social and economic development. Thus, as significant as nation building may be, such factors as the availability of natural resources, the level of economic and social development, and the rate of economic growth and social change are of equal, if not greater, importance. Economic development implies that citizens can enjoy new resources. On the other hand, it can often have a devastating impact on nature. For better or worse, the social changes that result from economic development transform the politics of developing countries.

Rich and Poor Countries

Figure 1.2 gives the per capita **gross national product (GNP)**—the total economic output per person—for our twelve usual nations. There are two ways to compare the economies of countries that use different currencies. The standard

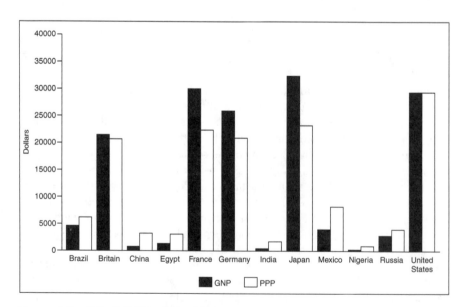

FIGURE 1.2   PER CAPITA GNP AND PPP IN SELECTED NATIONS, 1998 (IN U.S. DOLLARS) *Source:* World Bank, *World Development Report, 1999–2000.* (New York: Oxford University Press, 2000), table 1, pp. 230–31.

measure is GNP per capita computed according to the exchange rates of the national currencies. An alternative and newer measure instead uses **purchasing power parity (PPP)**, which takes into account differences in price levels from one country to another. Figure 1.2 shows that the income of developing countries turns out to be substantially higher in purchasing power parity than when we use currency exchange rates. Thus, in U.S. dollar equivalents, Mexican per capita PPP is almost twice its per capita GNP, whereas China's and India's are almost four times as high. At the opposite extreme, the economies of Japan and Germany are less impressive when we consider actual purchasing power. Thus the gap in economic wealth between the rich and the poor countries is not as great if we take into account what money actually buys. The Brazilian economy is about one-fourth that of the Japanese economy according to the purchasing power measure, as opposed to one-seventh according to the exchange rate measure. The Chinese per capita product turns out to be about one-eighth that of Japan, instead of less than one-fortieth.

Traditional official statistics have exaggerated the income inequality among nations in other respects, too. Our statistics tend to underestimate goods and services produced and consumed in subsistence agriculture, or in household production for family use. Similarly, national product estimates are not corrected for differences in the "cost of living" under different environmental conditions. As the World Development Report points out, "GNP is higher in colder countries, where people spend more money on heating and warm clothing, than in balmy climates, where people are comfortable wearing light clothing in the open air."[9]

Figure 1.3 compares the percentages of the economically active populations employed in agriculture. In comparing Figures 1.2 and 1.3 we see that the smaller the per capita GNP (or PPP), the larger is the proportion of the labor force in agriculture. The five advanced industrial countries all have agricultural labor forces in the single digits, with the United States and Britain at 2 percent each. The three poorest countries—China, India, and Nigeria—have more than two-thirds of their labor forces employed in agriculture. The middle-income countries—Mexico and Brazil—have around a third to a fifth of their labor forces in agriculture. Thus, the economies of the rich countries are predominantly industrial, commercial, and professional, while those of the poor countries are predominantly agricultural. Countries that are rich and industrialized, with a large professional service sector, also tend to have healthy, literate, and educated populations. In highly industrialized countries, practically everyone over the age of 15 can read and write. In India, Nigeria, and Egypt at most one-half the adult population has this minimal degree of education. Moreover, the countries with the fewest literate citizens also have the fewest radios and television sets—devices that do not require literacy.

Industrialization, education, and exposure to the communications media are associated with better nutrition and medical care. In the economically advanced countries, fewer children die in infancy, and the average citizen has a life expectancy at birth of about 75 years. The average Mexican has a life expectancy of 66 years; the Indian, 61 years; the Egyptian, around 60 years; and the Nigerian little more than 50 years. Material productivity, education, exposure to communications media, and

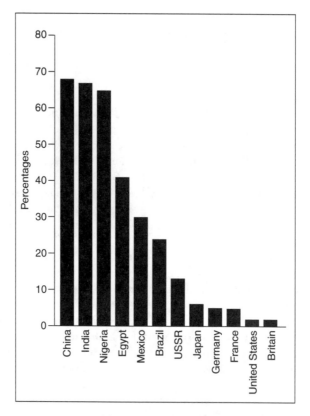

FIGURE 1.3 PERCENTAGE OF ECONOMICALLY ACTIVE POPULATION IN AGRICULTURE FOR SELECTED NATIONS (1990) *Source:* FAO, United Nations, *FAO Production Yearbook 1990* (Rome: UN, 1991), table 3.

longer and healthier lives are closely interconnected. Only economically productive countries can afford good education, communications media, and good nutrition and health care. In order to become more productive, a country needs the resources to develop a skilled and healthy labor force and build the infrastructure that material welfare requires. Preindustrial nations face most urgently the issues of economic development: how to improve the immediate welfare of their citizens yet also build and invest for the future. Typically, these are newer nations that also face the challenges of building community and effective political institutions.

Economic Inequality

It may be misleading to refer to states only on the basis of average economic measures such as per capita income, gross national product, and so on. Wealth, income, and opportunity are not evenly distributed domestically, and such inequalities are among the most serious causes of political conflict. A large gross national product may conceal significant differences in the distribution of economic and social amenities and opportunities. A high rate of national growth may benefit only particular regions or social groups, leaving large parts of the population unrewarded or even less well off than before. The "inner cities" of the United States; the older parts of such Indian cities as Delhi and Calcutta; the peripheral ramshackle settlements around the cities of Latin America; such regions as Appalachia in the United States, the Mezzogiorno (south) of Italy, and the arid northeast of Brazil—all suffer from poverty and hopelessness, while other parts of their countries experience growth and improved welfare.

A country's politics may be sharply affected by internal divisions of income, wealth, and other resources. Table 1.4 compares income distribution for our 12 countries. Clearly, there is a positive association between economic development and equality of income, at least past a certain stage of economic growth. Wealthy nations like Japan, the United States, or Germany tend to have more egalitarian income distributions than middle-income countries such as Brazil and Mexico. In Japan, the rich receive a little over four times the income going to the poor. In Mexico, a middle-income country, the ratio is closer to 10 to 1; and in Brazil it is more than 20 to 1. Yet the table also suggests that ideological and political characteristics make a difference. Particularly surprising is the inequality of income in China, the only Communist nation, where the poorest 40 percent get less of the total (15.3 percent), than the poorest 40 percent in Japan (21.9 percent).

Industrialization and high productivity have historically gone along with more equal distribution of income. This tends to be true today, too. Yet, the first stages of industrialization and modernization may actually increase income inequality by creating a dual economy—a rural sector and an urban industrial and commercial sector, both with inequalities of their own. This pattern is apparent if we contrast inequality in India with the even greater inequalities in the somewhat richer countries of Mexico and Brazil. These inequalities tend to increase as education and communication spread. This pattern helps explain the political instability of many

Table 1.4   INCOME DISTRIBUTION FOR SELECTED NATIONS

Country	Year	Wealthiest 10%	Poorest 40%	Per Capita GNP (1998)
Japan	1979	22.4	21.9	32,380
United States	1994	28.5	15.3	29,340
Germany	1989	22.6	22.5	25,850
France	1989	24.9	19.9	24,940
Britain	1986	24.7	19.9	21,400
Brazil	1995	47.9	8.2	4,570
Mexico	1992	39.2	11.9	3,970
Russia	1993	22.2	20.0	2,300
Egypt	1991	26.7	21.2	1,290
China	1995	30.9	15.3	750
India	1994	25.0	22.2	430
Nigeria	1992	31.4	12.9	300

Source: World Bank, World Development Report, 1999–2000 (New York: Oxford University Press, 2000), table 5, pp. 238–39.

developing countries, since income inequality grows at the same time that aware-ness of it is increasing. Even though inequality may tend to diminish in later stages of development, this trend cannot be taken for granted. In Brazil, income inequal-ity has increased for decades, even as the economy has developed. Nor does in-equality disappear in the most economically advanced nations. In the United States, income inequality increased substantially from the 1970s to the mid-1990s as a consequence of changes in economic structure, the increase in single-parent families, and a lowering of income taxes in the 1980s. Similar trends are evident in Britain and in many other advanced states, driven by the same factors as well as by high unemployment, immigration, and rapid salary gains among highly educated people. These developments are most dramatic in Russia and other post-commu-nist societies. Inequality is an issue that all nations must face.

Economic inequality has a very important international side. A series of stud-ies sponsored by the World Bank in the 1970s and 1980s, with the title "Redistrib-ution with Growth," proposed a variety of policy solutions to mitigate the hard-ships economic inequality causes in developing societies and specifically to avoid the extreme cases of "unequal development," such as in Brazil and Mexico.[10] In-stead, the economists involved in these studies pointed to Taiwan and South Ko-rea, which had combined rapid economic growth with a more equitable distribu-tion. In these countries early land reforms had equalized opportunity at the outset of the developmental process. Investment in education, in agricultural inputs and rural infrastructure (principally roads and water), and in labor-intensive indus-tries, and an emphasis on export-oriented growth, produced remarkable results for several decades. Their comparative advantage in cheap and skilled labor enabled these countries to compete effectively in international markets. Thus it is possible to identify growth policies with lesser inequalities, but it can be very difficult to put them into practice, especially where substantial inequalities already exist.

Population Growth, Economic Development, and the Environment

While the goal of economic growth for the world's lower-income economies is generally accepted and fostered by such international agencies as the UN, the World Bank, and the International Monetary Fund, as well as the by the foreign aid programs of advanced industrial nations, it has an ominous "downside." The advanced economies have only begun to pay for the environmental costs of their industrial development. Despoiled forests, depleted soils and fisheries, polluted air and water, nuclear waste, endangered species, and a threatened ozone layer now burden their legislative dockets. Some of these environmental problems—for example, deforestation—are even more acute in developing countries. With in-creasing industrialization and urbanization in the developing world, many envi-ronmental problems could get dramatically worse.

Thus economic development can impose serious environmental costs. The book *The Population Explosion* drew attention to the great environmental burden that had resulted from the population growth and industrial development of the nineteenth and twentieth centuries.[11] Our arable soil, our forests, the quality of our air and water, the welfare of our plant and animal life, and the continuity of our climate have been seriously damaged by the combination of economic and demographic growth. In addition to the challenge of combining economic growth with equity, we must now find a way to counteract the environmental degradation caused by the combined growth of the economy and the population.

Table 1.5 puts the second dilemma in sharp relief. The table divides world population into three strata: low-income economies, middle-income economies, and high-income economies. In 1992 the low-income countries had a population total of more than 3 billion, or 60 percent of the total world population; the middle-income group had roughly one-fourth of the total population, and the high-income population had 15 percent. Projections are that world population in 2025 will increase to 8 billion and that the poorer countries will still see a more rapid growth of population. Rapid economic growth in the developing world would result in great burdens on the environment indeed.

These frightening prospects have produced a mixed literature of both light and heat. Economist Amartya Sen warns of a "danger that in the confrontation between apocalyptic pessimism on one hand, and a dismissive smugness, on the other, a genuine understanding of the nature of the population problem may be lost."[12] He points out that the first impact of "modernization" on population is to increase it rapidly, as new sanitation measures and modern pharmaceuticals reduce the death rate. As an economy develops, however, public policies and changing incentives tend to reduce fertility. With improved education (particularly of women), health, and welfare, the advantages of lower fertility become clear, and population growth declines. This happened in Europe and North America as they underwent industrialization and appears to be taking place in the developing world. Thus annual population growth in the world has in the last two decades declined from 2.2 percent to 1.7 percent. The rate of population growth in India, for example, rose to 2.2 percent in the 1970s and has since declined. Latin America peaked at a higher rate and then came down sharply. The great problem area is Sub-Saharan Africa with an average growth rate of more than 2.7 percent each year during the 1990s.[13] Tragically, the fertility rate in Africa has most potently been counteracted by a rising death rate from the epidemic spread of AIDS.

Table 1.5   POPULATION BY ECONOMIC DEVELOPMENT LEVEL IN 1992 AND PROJECTED TO 2025 (IN MILLIONS US $)

Economic Development Level	In 1992		Projected to 2025	
	Number	Percentage	Number	Percentage
Low-income economies	3,191	59	5,062	62
Middle-income economies	1,416	26	2,139	27
High-income economies	828	15	922	11
Total	5,437	100	8,123	100

Source: World Bank, *World Development Report 1994* (New York: Oxford University Press, 1994), tables 1 and 25.

But while the trend is in the desired direction, population growth and its geographic incidence leaves us with very serious problems. China has confronted this problem with a coercive policy of abortion and contraception, which in urban areas has produced dramatic results at great costs. India and other countries have had some success with what Sen calls a "collaborative" approach, involving governmental intervention in influencing family choices, as well as counting on the market and education to affect family choices.[14] Kerala in southern India is a dramatic example of what can be accomplished by the "collaborative" approach, where expanding education particularly among women, and otherwise improving conditions, has reduced fertility more than in China, or even Sweden, the United States, or Canada. Amartya Sen tells us that humankind can resolve these dilemmas by drawing on our knowledge and experience, without heavy coercion. To avoid the irreversible catastrophes prophesied by the "Apocalyptic pessimists," however, requires sacrifices and foresight. These are difficult to mobilize in a world divided into almost 200 independent countries, where powerful interests support the status quo.

SECURING DEMOCRACY, HUMAN RIGHTS, AND CIVIL LIBERTIES

Democracy is the form of government to which most contemporary countries, more or less sincerely and successfully, aspire. A **democracy,** briefly defined, is a political system in which citizens enjoy a number of basic civil and political rights, and in which their most important political leaders are elected in free and fair elections and accountable under a rule of law. Democracy literally means "government by the people." In small political systems, such as local communities, it may be possible for "the people" to share directly in debating, deciding, and implementing public policy. In large political systems, such as contemporary states, democracy must be achieved largely through indirect participation in policymaking. Elections, competitive political parties, free mass media, and representative assemblies make some degree of democracy, some degree of "government by the people," possible. This indirect, or representative, democracy is not complete or ideal. But the more citizens are involved and the more influential their choices, the more democratic the system.

The most important general distinction in classifying political systems is between democratic systems and authoritarian systems. Nondemocracies, which we usually speak of as *authoritarian,* lack one or several of the defining features of democracy. In democracies, competitive elections give citizens the chance to shape the entire policymaking process through their selection and rejection of key policymakers. In authoritarian systems the policymakers are chosen by military councils, hereditary families, dominant political parties, and the like. Citizens are either ignored or pressed into symbolic assent to the government's choices. In **oligarchies,** literally "rule by the few," important political rights are withheld from the majority of the population. South Africa until the abolition of apartheid in the early 1990s was a good example. **Totalitarian systems,** such as Nazi Germany or the Soviet Union under Stalin, are a subtype of nondemocracies in which the government constricts the rights and privacy of its citizens in a particularly severe and intrusive manner. All totalitarian systems are authoritarian, but most authoritarian systems are not totalitarian.

As political systems become more complex, richer, and more technologically advanced, the probability of citizen involvement increases. At the same time the freedom of this participation may become more problematic. In the past century most Western states have been transformed from authoritarian regimes, or oligarchies with limited voting rights, to democracies. And during the past century, the power of the state has increasingly been used to meet popular needs and demands. Yet, in a modern society the government can try to control and manipulate the flow of information and communication, the formation of attitudes and culture, and the choices—if any—offered to citizens. Thus more developed political systems, especially in industrial societies, have greater potential for authoritarian control of citizens on a mass scale. On the other hand, independent social and political groups and organizations can exert autonomous influence on politics. High levels of education and information can contribute to a participant political culture.

Democracy is not an all-or-nothing question. No democracy is perfect, and we can speak of shades or gradations of democracy. Nor does democracy typically come about overnight. It often takes time to establish democratic institutions and to have citizens recognize them and comply with the rules of the democratic process. One of the most hopeful developments of the past couple of decades is the large number of countries that have undergone or are undergoing a transition to democracy. Transitions toward democracy have been a major feature of world politics in the last 20 or 30 years. Many transitions have been relatively peaceful, as authoritarian rulers have negotiated a solution in response to citizen pressures. Military forces have frequently stood aside or even supported the citizens against the dictators. Authoritarian regimes have lost legitimacy everywhere, especially since the model (and support) of the Soviet Union has collapsed.

Samuel P. Huntington speaks of the recent move toward democracy as a "Third Wave" of worldwide **democratization.** The first of these waves began in the nineteenth century and culminated with the establishment of many new democracies after World War I. But this wave reversed itself in the next 20 years, when many democracies collapsed or were conquered by authoritarian states. After World War II a second democratic wave, which lasted from 1943 until the early 1960s, saw both newly independent states (such as India and Nigeria) and defeated authoritarian powers (such as Germany and Japan) set up the formal institutions of democracy. While quite a number of countries became formally democratic in these years, most of them quickly lapsed into authoritarianism. Many of these would-be democracies failed in their first decade; another "reverse wave" in the 1960s and early 1970s swept away some older democracies (Chile, Greece, and Uruguay, for example) as well. The third wave, beginning in 1974, has involved Southern Europe, East Asia, Latin America, and recently Eastern Europe, the successor states to the Soviet Union, and a number of African states.

It can be difficult to consolidate democracies, especially in less economically developed societies. Not all of the newly democratizing countries are succeeding beyond the first few years. In some, democratic processes fail to produce stable institutions and effective public policies and give way to some form of authoritarianism. In Nigeria, a democratic-leaning regime installed in 1979 was overthrown by a military coup in 1983, and a partial movement toward redemocratization was again aborted by the military in 1993. Nigeria is by no means unique. Transition can move in either direction, toward or away from democracy. While today's Third Wave of democratization is supported by the more favorable environments of more modernized societies and the very fact that there are now more democracies in the world, it remains to be seen how long the democratic gains will last.

Even when states democratize, there is no guarantee that they will grant human rights and civil liberties to all their people. In some countries, majority rule turns into a "tyranny of the majority" against ethnic or religious minorities. Therefore, democracies always have to find a balance between respecting the will of the majority and protecting the rights of the minority. But even when political rulers sincerely try to promote human rights and civil liberties (which is by no means always the case), they do not always agree what those rights should be. Although the United Nations has tried to secure agreement on a range of rights and liberties that all individuals should enjoy, different governments and cultures seriously disagree about the implementation of such protections. Some societies believe that freedom of speech should not be protected when it is used for blasphemy, or to denigrate particular social groups. Governments in Western industrial societies tend to want gender equality policies to go further than what is considered appropriate in many Muslim countries. In most developing societies and most states in the United States, capital punishment is considered an acceptable penalty for particularly severe crimes. Most Western European societies, however, do not permit such punishment and consider it inhumane.

Community-building, development, and democratization cannot be dealt with in isolation from one another. On the contrary, progress in one of these areas can create new opportunities, but also new problems, in another. Economic development, for example, can reinforce (but also ameliorate) ethnic strife and destabilize political institutions. While development has obvious positive consequences for productivity and welfare, it can disrupt social life. The growth of technology and the service economy coupled with the spread of market economies results in growing wealth and income inequality. This trend has in recent decades become quite noticeable in advanced industrial societies, and it tends to affect the developing economies even more sharply. Increasing inequality of income and wealth can sharpen class antagonisms and partisanship.

The political effects of these developments vary from country to country, depending on economic resources, demography, geography, historical experience, and the like. Environmental deterioration, growing economic inequality, economic dislocation, and migration as well as ethnic and religious mobilization can cause political fragmentation and polarization and make it more difficult to form stable governments. A more affluent and information-driven citizenry impairs the effectiveness of political parties, interest groups, parliaments, and political executives. It is more difficult to structure political alternatives when party and interest group leaders can no longer effectively muster and discipline their followers, and when political leaders are losing control of the political agenda to such new forces as the electronic media. In subsequent chapters, we examine in more detail the ways in which these challenges constrain and inform the political choices of citizens and policymakers.

KEY TERMS

anarchism

civil liberties

democracy

democratization

ethnicity

European Union (EU)

externalities

government

gross national product (GNP)

human rights

income and wealth inequality

libertarianism

nation

nation-state

oligarchies

political cleavages

political system

privatization

public goods

purchasing power parity (PPP)

religious fundamentalism

rent seeking

service economy

sovereignty

state

state of nature

totalitarian systems

United Nations (UN)

welfare state

SUGGESTED READINGS

Chenery, Hollis, et al. *Redistribution with Growth.* New York: Oxford University Press. 1981.

Cornelius, Wayne, et al., eds. *Controlling Immigration: A Global Perspective.* Stanford, CA: Stanford University Press, 1995.

Dahl, Robert A. *Democracy and Its Critics.* New Haven: Yale University Press. 1989.

Diamond, Larry, ed. *Developing Democracy: Towards Consolidation.* Baltimore: Johns Hopkins. 1999.

Ehrlich, Paul, and Anne Ehrlich. *The Population Explosion.* New York: Simon and Schuster, 1990.

Hoffman, Stanley, and Robert Keohane, eds. *The New European Community.* Boulder, CO: Westview, 1991.

Horowitz, Donald. *Ethnic Groups in Conflict.* Berkeley: University of California Press, 1985.

Huntington, Samuel. *The Third Wave: Democratization in the Late Twentieth Century.* Norman, OK: University of Oklahoma Press, 1991.

Lijphart, Arend. *Patterns of Democracy.* New Haven: Yale University Press, 1999.

Linz, Juan, and Alfred Stepan, eds. *Problems of Democratic Transitions and Consolidation.* Baltimore: Johns Hopkins. 1996.

Marty, Martin, and Scott Appleby. *Fundamentalism Observed.* Chicago: University of Chicago Press, 1991.

Putnam, Robert. *Making Democracy Work: Civic Traditions in Modern Italy.* Princeton, NJ: Princeton University Press, 1993.

Weiner, Myron. *The Global Migration Crisis: Challenge to States and to Human Rights.* New York: HarperCollins, 1995.

World Bank. *World Development Report.* New York: Oxford University Press, annual editions.

NOTES

1. Thomas Hobbes, *Leviathan,* ed. C. B. Macpherson (New York: Penguin, 1968, p. 186).
2. J. J. Rousseau, *Second Discourse On Inequality, The First And Second Discourses* (New York: St. Martin's, 1964), pp. 109–10.
3. The Vatican and Switzerland are not members of the UN but maintain permanent observer missions at the UN headquarters. Taiwan was expelled from the UN in 1971 to accommodate mainland China (the People's Republic).
4. More detailed discussions of the politics of each of these 12 countries are found in the chapters written by country specialists in Gabriel A. Almond, G. Bingham Powell, Jr., Kaare Strom, and Russell J. Dalton, eds., *Comparative Politics Today: A World View* (New York: Longman, 2000).
5. Max Weber, *Economy and Society,* ed. Guenther Roth and Claus Wittich (Berkeley: University of California Press, 1978), p. 389.
6. Stephen Castles and Mark J. Miller, *The Age of Migration: International Population Movements in The Modern World* (New York: Guilford, 1994).
7. Erik V. Gunnemark, *Countries, Peoples, and Their Languages: The Geolinguistic Handbook* (Gothenburg, Sweden: Lanstryckeriet, 1991).
8. See, among others, Martin Marty and Scott Appleby, *Fundamentalism Observed* (Chicago, IL: University of Chicago Press, 1991).
9. World Bank, *World Development Report* (New York: Oxford University Press, 1994), p. 230.
10. Hollis Chenery et al., *Redistribution with Growth* (New York: Oxford University Press, 1981).
11. Paul and Anne Ehrlich, *The Population Explosion* (New York: Simon and Schuster, 1990).
12. Amartya Sen, "Population: Delusion and Reality," *New York Review of Books,* Sept. 22, 1994, pp. 62ff.
13. World Bank, *World Development Report, 1998–1999* (New York: Oxford University Press, 1999).
14. Sen, "Population: Delusion and Reality."

CHAPTER TWO

Comparing Political Systems

WHY WE COMPARE

The great French interpreter of American democracy, Alexis de Tocqueville, while on his travels in America in the 1830s, wrote to a friend about how his ideas about French institutions and culture entered into the writing of *Democracy in America*. Tocqueville wrote "Although I very rarely spoke of France in my book, I did not write one page of it without having her, so to speak, before my eyes."[1] On a more general note about the comparative method, he offered this comment: "Without comparisons to make, the mind does not know how to proceed."[2]

Tocqueville was telling us that comparison is fundamental to all human thought. We add that it is the methodological core of the humanistic and scientific methods as well. It is the only way we can fully understand our own political system. Comparing the past and present of our nation and comparing our experience with that of other nations deepen our understanding of our own institutions. Examining politics in other societies permits us to see a wider range of political alternatives and illuminates the virtues and shortcomings of our own political life. By taking us beyond our familiar arrangements and assumptions, comparative analysis helps expand our awareness of the possibilities of politics.

Comparison is the methodological core of the scientific study of politics. Comparative analysis helps us develop explanations and test theories of the ways in which political processes work and in which political change occurs. Here the logic and the intention of the comparative methods used by political scientists are similar to those used in more exact sciences. Political scientists cannot normally design experiments to control and manipulate political arrangements and observe the consequences, especially when dealing with large-scale events that drastically affect many people. For example, researchers cannot and would not want to start a social revolution to see its effects. Nor would they want to initiate military escalation to see if it leads to war. It is possible, however, to use the comparative method to describe and explain the different combinations of political events and institutions found in different societies. More than two thousand years ago, Aristotle in his *Politics* contrasted the economies and social structures of the many Greek city-states in an effort to determine how the social and economic environment affected political institutions and policies.

A contemporary political scientist, Robert Dahl, in his studies of democracy, compares the economic characteristics, cultures, and historical experiences of many contemporary nations in an effort to discover the combinations of conditions and characteristics that are associated with that form of government.[3] Other theorists, in their attempt to explain differences between the processes and performance of political systems, have compared constitutional regimes with tyrannies, two-party democracies with multiparty democracies, parliamentary with presidential regimes, and stable governments with unstable ones.

The end of the Cold War has left a world engaged in vast experiments in different approaches to economic growth, different strategies for transition to democracy, differing ways of controlling and using the powers of government. Governments today are grappling with new issues of preserving our environment, old issues of opportunity and economic security for citizens, and ancient issues of conflicts of ethnic identities and religious beliefs. In a world made ever smaller by instantaneous communication and interdependent economies, these problems and achievements spill across national boundaries. Comparative analysis is a pow-

---

Box 2.1   Aristotle's Library

There is historical evidence that Aristotle had accumulated a library of more than 150 studies of the political systems of the Mediterranean world of 400–300 B.C. Many of these these had probably been researched and written by his disciples.

While only the Athenian constitution survives of this library of Aristotelian polities, it is evident from the references to such studies that do survive, that Aristotle was concerned with sampling the variety of political systems then in existence, including the "barbarian" (Third World?) countries such as Libya, Etruria, and Rome: "the references in ancient authorities give us the names of some 70 or more of the states described in the compilation of 'polities.' They range from Sinope, on the Black Sea, to Cyrene in North Africa; they extend from Marseilles in the Western Mediterranean to Crete, Rhodes, and Cyprus in the East. Aristotle thus included colonial constitutions as well as those of metropolitan states. His descriptions embraced states on the Aegean, Ionian, and the Tyrrhenian Seas, and the three continents of Europe, Asia, and Africa."

Source: Ernest Barker, ed., *The Politics of Aristotle* (London: Oxford University Press, 1977), p. 386.

erful and versatile tool. It enhances our ability to describe and understand political processes and political change in any country by offering concepts and refer-
ence points from a broader perspective. The comparative approach also stimu-
lates us to form general theories of political relationships. It encourages and
enables us to test our political theories by confronting them with the experience of
many institutions and settings. The primary goal of this book is to provide access
to this powerful tool for thought and analysis.

HOW WE COMPARE

We study politics in several different ways: we describe it; we seek to explain it;
and sometimes we try to predict it. These are all parts of the scientific process, and
in each of them we may use the comparative method. The first stage in the study
of politics is description. If we cannot describe a political process or event, we
cannot really hope to understand or explain, much less predict what might happen
next, or in similar situations. In order to describe political phenomena, we need a
set of concepts that are clearly defined and well understood. We speak of this as a
conceptual framework or apparatus. The easier this set of concepts is to understand, and the more generally it can be applied, the more helpful it is to the study
of politics. Conceptual frameworks are not generally right or wrong, but they may
be more or less useful to the task at hand.

Once we are able to describe political phenomena with the help of the conceptual framework that we choose, the next task is to explain these phenomena.
What we mean by explaining political phenomena is seeking to identify relationships between them. For example, we might be interested in the relationship between democracy and international peace. Are democratic states more peaceful
than others? If so, are they peaceful because they are democratic, are they democratic because they are peaceful, or are they perhaps both peaceful and democratic because they are more prosperous than other states?

These questions show that we often want explanations to go beyond associat-
ing one thing with another. Ideally we want to put many political relationships in
causal terms, so that we can say that one political relationship is the cause of another, and the latter is the effect of the former. For example, a theory may state
that countries are peaceful because they are democratic. There are different kinds
of causal statements that we can make about this relationship between war and
form of government. One such statement might be "only authoritarian governments start wars"; in other words, authoritarianism is necessary to starting wars.
Another statement might be, "all democracies are peaceful"; in other words,
democracy is sufficient to guarantee peacefulness. A third statement might express only a tendency or probability, such as "authoritarian governments tend to
be more warlike than democracies."

Theories are statements about causal relationships between general classes of
events—for example, about what causes democracy, war, or political development. Theories are always tentative; they are always subject to modification or fal-
sification as our knowledge improves. And theories need to be testable. A good

theory is one that holds up after continued trials and experiments, that can be confirmed or modified as we test the theory again and again. The number of cases that political scientists have to generalize about varies from problem to problem. Similarly, the number of cases that are examined when we test theories can vary dramatically.

Researchers in political science distinguish between studies based on large numbers (large "*n*") and small numbers (small "*n*"). Large "*n*" studies are usually referred to as *statistical studies*, small "*n*" as *case studies*. Large "*n*" studies have a

---

Box 2.2   Statistical Methods

A popular contemporary research program known as *democratic peace research* illustrates the pros and cons of statistical and case study research. It has been of primary interest to international relations scholars, who took the diplomatic history of the Cold War period and asked whether democratic countries are more peaceful in their foreign policy than authoritarian and nondemocratic ones. Many scholars in the democratic peace research group took the statistical route. They counted each year of interaction between two states as one case, and with roughly half a century of diplomatic history involving a state system of 100 countries or more, they had a very large number of cases, even after eliminating the many irrelevant cases of countries that never, or rarely, had any relations with one another. Political scientists Andrew Bennett and Alexander George drew these conclusions after surveying the statistical research:

> Statistical methods achieved important advances on the issue of whether a non-spurious inter-democratic peace exists. A fairly strong though not unanimous consensus emerged that: (1) democracies are not less war-prone in general; (2) they have very rarely if ever fought one another; (3) this pattern of an inter-democratic peace applies to both war and conflicts short of war; (4) states in transition to democracy are more war prone than established democracies; and (5) these correlations were not spuriously brought about by the most obvious alternative explanations.

There is a consensus now that statistical studies are not as good as are case studies at answering "why" questions. Case studies make clinical depth possible, revealing causal interconnections in individual cases. Careful repetition of these causal tracings from case to case strengthens confidence in these relationships. Thus Bennett and George concluded that the best research strategy to follow is to use statistical and case study methods together, with each one of the methods having its own strengths.

Source: Andrew Bennett and Alexander George, "An Alliance of Statistical and Case Study Methods: Research on the Interdemocratic Peace," *APSA-CP: Newsletter of the APSA Organized Section in Comparative Politics* 9, no. 1: 6.

sufficient number and variety of cases to enable the researcher to examine the relation among the variables (variables being the dimensions or the parameters on which our cases differ—for example, "form of government: democracy or dictatorship," or "income per capita"). Small "n" studies permit investigators to go deeply into a case, identify the particularities of it, get the clinical details, and examine each link in the causal process. In this manner, political scientists may come to know not only whether democracies are more peaceful than dictatorships but more precisely why democratic leaders behave in the way that they do.

It is now generally recognized that these methods are complementary. Large "n" statistical studies allow us to be more certain and precise in our explanations. On the other hand, we need the depth that case studies provide in order to formulate insightful hypotheses for statistical testing in the first place. Also, case study methods can be used to examine in detail some aspects of cause-and-effect relations better than large "n" studies.

An example may suggest how you might go about theorizing in comparative politics, going beyond "just mastering the facts." In international relations there is just one global system in existence at any given time. While we can ask precise questions about it, and while we can observe the interaction of its parts, it would be better if we could compare it with other cases to try to rule out coincidence or spurious correlation (which means that something that looks like a relationship between two variables, such as democracy and peace, is in fact caused by a third factor that they have in common, such as, for example, affluence). We can improve on the one contemporary case problem by adding historical cases—for example the "Cold War" international system (1946–1989), the "Interwar" system (1918–1939), the nineteenth century "Balance of Power" system (1871–1914), and the like; or we may gain additional cases by comparing one international region with another—the European subsystem, the Latin American, the East Asian, the Middle Eastern, and the like.

SYSTEMS: STRUCTURE AND FUNCTION

Comparative Politics: A Theoretical Framework suggests that we approach the comparison of political systems with a structural-functional system framework. To do so, we need to discuss in some detail these three general concepts that we use throughout this book: (1) system, (2) structure, and (3) function. **System,** as we defined it in Chapter 1, suggests an object having moving parts, interacting with a setting or an environment. The **political system** is a set of institutions and agencies concerned with formulating and implementing the collective goals of a society or of groups within it. **Governments** or **states** are the policymaking parts of political systems. The decisions of governments are normally backed up by legitimate coercion, and obedience may be compelled. We discuss legitimacy at greater length in Chapter 3.

Governments do many things—from establishing and operating school systems, to maintaining public order, to fighting wars. In order to carry on these many activities, governments have specialized agencies, or **structures,** such as parliaments, bureaucracies, administrative agencies, and courts, which perform

functions, which in turn enable the government to formulate, implement, and enforce its policies. The policies reflect the goals; the agencies provide the means.

Another useful term enabling us to describe the historical variation of governments over time is political regime. The political regime is the structural-functional-policy configuration governments take on at different times. We can generate and test hypotheses about the causes and consequences of political change by comparing countries at different historical periods just as we can compare the institutions of different countries in our search for political theories. Tocqueville's study of the French Revolution contributed to a general theory of revolution by comparing pre- and postrevolutionary France.[4] Theda Skocpol based her theories of the causes of revolution on a comparison of the "old regimes" of France, Russia, and China with their revolutionary and postrevolutionary regimes.[5]

Some writers have argued that structural functionalism is an approach to politics that is conservative in its methodology, that it is biased in favor of the status quo, since it describes a set of institutions at a particular time. However, to describe political institutions precisely and comprehensively at some particular time is not to praise or defend them but to try to comprehend them. We would use the structural-functional approach to compare Nazi Germany, which we reject with horror, with democratic, peaceful, and prosperous states such as Sweden and Switzerland, which many of us may admire. Moreover, we recognize the need to supplement the structural-functional approach with a dynamic developmental approach, since we want to know not only how a political system functions, but why as well. A structural-functional approach does not in itself tell us why Germany or France developed as they did in the 1930s and 1940s. It tells us what changes occurred in these regimes. The explanation of why they changed requires that we bring in the economic, social, cultural, and international context in a historical way. We may speak of the structural-functional mapping of government and politics that we do in the theoretical chapters that follow, as a "comparative statics," a way to understand how different political processes interact at any one time, and of the analysis of political development and change as a "political dynamics."

Figure 2.1 tells us that a political system exists in both a domestic and an international environment, molding these environments and being molded by them. The system receives **inputs** from these environments and attempts to shape them through its outputs. In the figure, which is quite schematic and simple, we use the United States as the central actor, and we include some other countries as our environmental examples—Russia, China, Britain, Germany, Japan, Mexico, and Egypt. Exchanges among countries may vary in many ways. For example, they may be "dense" or "sparse"; United States–Canadian relations exemplify the dense end of the continuum, while United States–Nepalese relations would be at the sparse end. Relationships between political systems may be of many different kinds. The United States has substantial trade relations with some nations and relatively little trade with others. Some countries have an excess of imports over exports, whereas others have an excess of exports over imports. With such countries as the NATO nations, Japan, South Korea, Israel, and Saudi Arabia, military exchanges and support have been of great importance to the United States. The interdependence of nations—the volume and value of imports and exports, transfers of capital, the extent of foreign travel and international communication—has in-

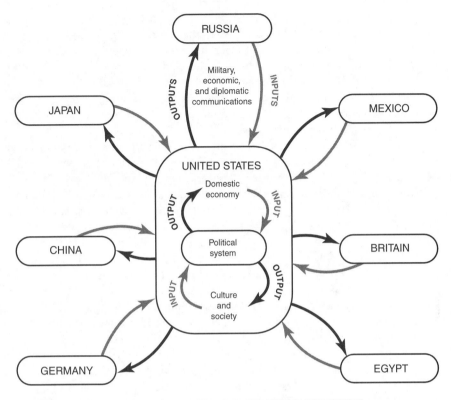

FIGURE 2.1   THE POLITICAL SYSTEM AND ITS ENVIRONMENTS

creased enormously in the last decades. We might represent this process as a thickening of the input and output arrows in Figure 2.1. Fluctuations in this flow of international transactions and traffic attributable to depression, inflation, protective tariffs, war, and the like may wreak havoc with the economies of the nations affected.

The interaction of the political system with its domestic environment may be illustrated in the American case by the rise of the "high-tech information-based economy" and the enormous increase in international trade. The composition of the American labor force, and consequently its citizenry, has changed dramatically in the last century. Agriculture has declined to under 3 percent of the gainfully employed. Employment in heavy extractive and manufacturing industries has decreased substantially, and the newer, high-technology occupations, the professions, and the service occupations have increased sharply as a proportion of the labor force. The last half-century has also witnessed significant improvements in the educational level of the American population, although the quality of education particularly at the primary and secondary levels has come in for very serious criticism in recent years. These and other changes in American social structure have transformed the social bases of the party system. There are now as many independents among American voters as loyal Democrats and Republicans. Workers of the older, primarily European, ethnic stocks have ceased being a solid support for the Democratic Party, and they now tend to divide their votes almost equally between the two parties. On the whole, these changes in the labor force have been associated with a more conservative trend in economic policy and with efforts to cut back welfare and other expenditures. A more educated and culturally sophisticated society has become more concerned with the quality of life, the beauty and healthfulness of the environment, and similar issues. In input-output terms, socioeconomic changes have transformed the political demands of the electorate and the kinds of policies that it supports.

Thus a new pattern of society results in different policy outputs, different kinds and levels of taxation, changes in regulatory patterns, and changes in welfare expenditures. The advantage of the system-environment approach is that it directs our attention to the interdependence of what happens within and between nations, and it provides us with a vocabulary to describe, compare, and explain these interacting events. If we are to make sound judgments in politics, we need to be able to place political systems in their environments, recognizing how these environments both set limits on and provide opportunities for political choices. This approach keeps us from reaching quick and biased political judgments. If a country is poor in natural resources and lacks the skills necessary to exploit what it has, we cannot fault it for having a low industrial output or poor educational and social services. Similarly, a country dominated and exploited by another country with a conservative policy cannot be condemned for failing to introduce social reforms.

The policies that leaders and political activists can follow are limited by the system and its institutions. However, in this era of rapid change, if the goals of the leadership and the political activists change, one set of political institutions may quickly be replaced by another. One of the most dramatic illustrations of such an institutional transformation was the breakdown of control by the Communist parties in Eastern Europe, and their replacement by multiparty systems when the leadership of the Soviet Union lost its confidence in the Soviet system and the future of socialism. Once the Soviet leadership lost confidence in the legitimacy of the Soviet Communist Party, it had no choice but to adopt a permissive and conciliatory policy toward its former satellites. The notion of interdependence goes even further than this relationship between policy and institutions. The various structural parts of a political system are also interdependent. If a government is based on popularly elected representatives in legislative bodies, then a system of election must be instituted. If many people enjoy the right to vote, then the politicians seeking office will have to mobilize the electorate and organize political parties to carry on election campaigns. As the policymaking agencies of the political system enact laws, they will need administrators and civil servants to implement these laws, and they will need judges to determine whether the laws have been violated and to decide what punishments to impose on the violators.

STRUCTURES AND FUNCTIONS

Figure 2.2 locates within the political system six types of political structures—political parties, interest groups, legislatures, executives, bureaucracies, and courts. Such structures are found in almost all modern political systems. One

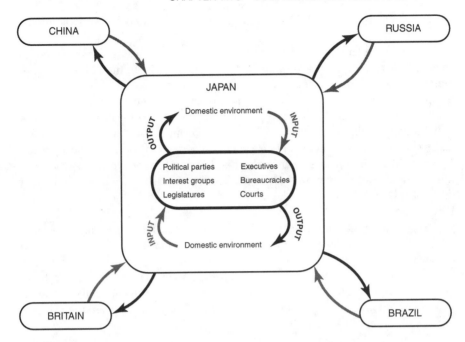

FIGURE 2.2   THE POLITICAL SYSTEM AND ITS STRUCTURES

might therefore think that if we understand how such structures work in one political system, we can apply this insight to any other system. Unfortunately that is not always the case, and this sixfold classification will not carry us very far in comparing political systems with each other. The problem is that similar structures may have very different functions across political systems. Britain and China have all six types of political institutions, at least in name; however, these institutions are organized differently in the two countries, and they function in dramatically different ways. Britain has a monarch—currently Elizabeth II—who performs ceremonial functions, like opening Parliament and conferring knighthoods and other honors. China does not have a specialized ceremonial executive. There is, however, a president, elected by the National People's Congress, who performs the ceremonial functions as well as some political functions. The political executive in Britain consists of the prime minister, the ministers assigned to the Cabinet, and the larger ministry, which consists of all the heads of departments and agencies. All these officials are usually selected from Parliament. There is a similar structure in China, called the State Council, headed by a premier and consisting of the various ministers and ministerial commissions. But while the British prime minister and Cabinet have substantial policymaking power, the State Council in China is closely supervised by the general secretary of the Communist Party, the Politburo, and the Central Committee of the party.

Both Britain and China have legislative bodies—the House of Commons in Britain and the National People's Congress in China. But while the House of Commons is a key institution in the policymaking process, the Chinese Congress meets for only brief periods, ratifying decisions made mainly by the Communist Party authorities.

There are even larger differences between political parties in the two countries. Britain has a competitive party system. The majority in the House of Commons and the Cabinet are constantly confronted by an opposition party or parties, competing for public support and looking forward to the next election when they may unseat the incumbent majority, as happened most recently in 1997, when the Labour Party replaced the Conservatives in government. In China the Communist Party controls the whole political process. There are no other political parties. The principal decisions are taken in the Politburo and to some extent in the Central Committee of the Communist Party. The governmental agencies implement the policies, which have to be initiated and/or approved by the top Communist Party leaders.

British interest groups are autonomous organizations that play important roles in the polity and the economy. Chinese trade unions and other professional organizations have to be viewed as parts of the official apparatus, dominated by the Communist Party, that perform mobilizing, socializing, and facilitating functions. Thus an institution-by-institution comparison of British and Chinese politics that did not spell out functions in detail would not bring us far toward understanding the important differences in the politics of these countries.

Figure 2.3 shows how we relate structure to function and process to policy and performance. (The functions and processes shown in the figure are discussed in greater detail in Chapters 3 through 7.) In the center of Figure 2.3 under the heading "Process functions" are listed the distinctive activities necessary for policy to be made and implemented in any kind of political system: interest articulation, interest aggregation, policymaking, and policy implementation and adjudication. We call these process functions because they play a direct and necessary role in the process of making policy. Before policy can be decided, some individuals and groups in the government or the society must decide what they want and hope to get from politics. The political process begins as these interests are expressed or articulated. The many arrows on the left of the figure show these initial expressions.

To be effective, however, these demands must be combined (aggregated) into policy alternatives—such as higher or lower taxes or more or less social security benefits—for which substantial political support can be mobilized. Thus the arrows on the left are consolidated as the process moves from interest articulation to interest aggregation. Alternative policies are then considered. Whoever controls the government backs one of them, and authoritative policymaking takes place. The policy must be enforced and implemented, and if it is challenged or violated, there must be some process of adjudication. Each policy may affect several different aspects of a society, as reflected in the many arrows for the implementation phase. These process functions that we have been describing are performed by such political structures as parties, legislatures, political executives, bureaucracies, and courts. The structural-functional approach stresses the point that while a particular institution such as a legislature may have a special relationship to a particular function such as law-making or rule-making, it does not have a

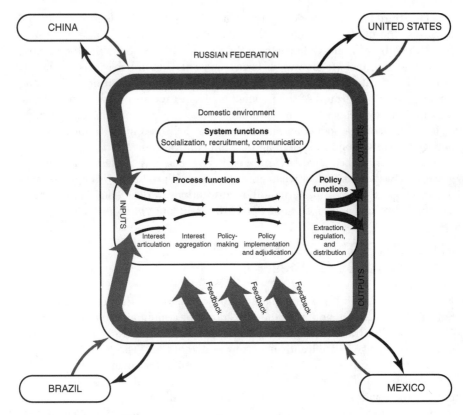

FIGURE 2.3   THE POLITICAL SYSTEM AND ITS FUNCTIONS

monopoly on this function. Presidents and governors may share in the legislative function (veto powers), as do the higher courts (judicial review of statutes for their constitutionality).

The three functions listed at the top of the figure—socialization, recruitment, and communication—are not directly involved in making and implementing public policy but are of fundamental importance to the political system. We refer to these three functions as **system functions,** because they determine whether or not the system will be maintained or changed—for example—whether policymaking will continue to be dominated by a single authoritarian party or military council, or whether competitive parties and a legislature will replace them. The arrows leading from these three functions to all parts of the political process suggest their crucial role in underpinning and permeating the political process. **Political socialization** involves families, schools, communications media, churches, and all the various political structures that develop, reinforce, and transform attitudes of political significance in the society. **Political recruitment** refers to the selection of people for political activity and government offices. **Political communication** refers to the flow of information through the society and through the various structures that make up the political system.

The third set of functions, listed at the right of the figure, treats the **outputs**—the implementations of the political process. We call these the **policy functions,** the substantive impacts on the society, the economy, and the culture. These functions include the various forms of **regulation** of behavior, **extractions** of resources in the form of taxes and the like, and **distribution** of benefits and services to various groups in the population. The **outcomes** of all these political activities, in a cyclical fashion, result in new inputs, in new demands for legislation or for administrative action, and in increases or decreases in the amount of support given to the political system and incumbent officeholders. These functional concepts describe the activities carried on in any society regardless of how its political system is organized, or what kinds of policies it produces. Using these functional categories, we can determine how institutions in different countries combine in the making and implementation of different kinds of public policy.

AN ILLUSTRATIVE COMPARISON: RUSSIA IN 1985 AND 1998*

Figures 2.4 and 2.5 offer a simplified graphic comparison of structures and functions in Russia before and after the breakdown of communist rule in the Soviet Union. They illustrate the use of the comparative method to assess the way a political regime changed significantly in a short period of time. The point here is to illustrate how we can use the tools of political analysis, rather than the details of the Russian case. The figures depict the changes in the functioning of the major structures of the political system brought about by the collapse of communism. These include two revolutionary changes: the end of the single-party political system dominated by the Communist Party of the Soviet Union, which held together the vast, multinational Soviet state, and the dissolution of the Soviet Union itself as a state into its 15 member republics. As a result of these two remarkable events, Russia, the republic that was the core republic of the old union, became an independent noncommunist state.

In June 1991, Boris Yeltsin, a bitter rival to the Soviet president, Mikhail Gorbachev, was elected President of Russia. Six months later, the Soviet Union collapsed and Gorbachev gave up his office. In December 1993, voters were called upon to ratify a new Constitution, which provided for a powerful executive presidency and at the same time elected a new parliament dominated by a diverse range of political parties.

In the new Russia of 1998, democratic tendencies competed with pressures for authoritarian rule. Overall the system was a mixture of pluralism with vestiges of the old, bureaucratically run, state socialist order. The major political parties were represented in Parliament and were developing national political bases of support for the next elections, while the reborn Communist Party—called the Communist Party of the Russian Federation—regularly denounced Yeltsin and

---

*Figures 2.4 and 2.5 and the text of "An Illustrative Comparison: Russia in 1985 and 1998" were contributed by Thomas Remington.

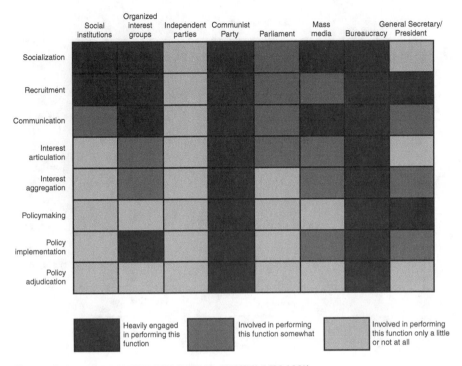

FIGURE 2.4   THE SOVIET POLITICAL SYSTEM IN 1985

called for the restoration of a strong state and more social protection. Parliament, now called the Federal Assembly, had become a meaningful site for policy debate and decision making. The mass media were no longer tightly controlled by the Communist Party. New organized interest groups, such as business associations and labor unions, were actively involved in policymaking. The bureaucracy remained a powerful central player in the political process, however, with substantial continued control over the economy.

These changes are reflected in the differences between the two figures. In 1985 (the year that the reform leader Mikhail Gorbachev came to power), the Soviet Union was a communist regime. Its Communist Party ruled the country. The top leader of the country was the General Secretary of the Communist Party. Although the country had the formal trappings of democracy, power actually flowed downward from the decision-makers at the top to government and society. Figure 2.4 therefore shows how the basic functions of the political system were performed in 1985, when the Communist Party was the dominant political institution of the country, overseeing schools and media, the arts and public organizations, government and courts. For this reason, all the cells of the chart in the column marked "Communist Party" are shaded dark, as are the cells under the column marked "Bureaucracy." Although social institutions such as the family, workplace, arts, and hobby groups exercised some influence over such system-level functions as socialization, recruitment, and communication, it was the Communist Party and state

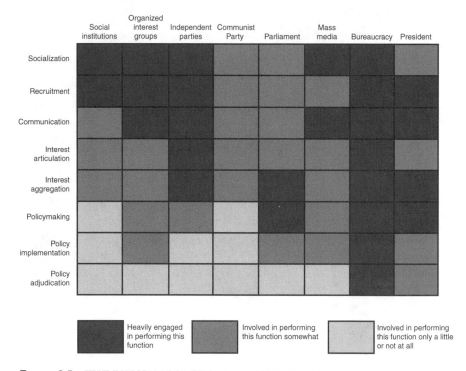

FIGURE 2.5   THE RUSSIAN POLITICAL SYSTEM IN 1998

bureaucracy that dominated process-level functions. Under their tutelage, the mass media in 1985 were a key agent of communist political socialization and communication while Parliament was a compliant instrument for ratifying decisions made by the party and bureaucracy. No other parties could exist beside the Communist Party, and the only organized interest groups were those authorized by the party. The party's General Secretary was the most powerful official in the country, since there was no state presidency.

By 1998 the political system had undergone fundamental change, as shown in Figure 2.5. Many more structures played a role in the political process, as is immediately evident by the larger number of cells that are heavily shaded. In particular, Parliament, independent political parties, and regional governments all acquired important new powers in policymaking. The freedom enjoyed by ordinary citizens to articulate their interests and to organize to advance them had expanded enormously. The Communist Party, no longer an official or monopolistic party, had declined substantially in power and was playing by the rules of the parliamentary game. The state bureaucracy remained an important element in the political system, although adapting itself to the new trend of movement toward a market economy by adopting quasi-commercial forms. The presidency, occupied by Boris Yeltsin, was a dominant policymaking institution. The Parliament, although fairly representative of the diversity of opinion in the country, was frustrated in its policymaking and oversight roles by the inertia of the vast state bureaucracy, its inability to compel compliance with its laws, its weak links with the electorate, and Yeltsin's power to make policy by decree. Nevertheless, it played a crucial role in aggregating interests and making policy.

The brief comparisons presented here are meant to illustrate the use of the structural-functional approach, an approach that enables us to examine how similar functions are performed in different countries, or in the same country, at two different points in time. Similarly, we may examine changes or contrasts in the functions performed by the same structures over time or across different political systems. In a country undergoing as rapid and dramatic transition as Russia in the 1990s, this framework helps us to analyze changes in the distribution of power among the major institutions making up the political system. Neither the analysis of structures nor that of functions is complete without the other. A structural analysis tells us the number of political parties, or the organization of the legislature, and how the executive branch, the courts, the bureaucracy, the mass media, interest groups, and other elements of the political system are set up and by what rules or standards they operate. A functional analysis tells us how these institutions and organizations interact to produce and implement policies. In Part 2 of this book we deal more specifically with the functions of the various political institutions, with the variety of interest groups and their functions, and with the structural-functional properties of party systems, legislatures, executives, and cabinets. Here we have only illustrated the method and its advantages.

THE POLICY LEVEL: PERFORMANCE, OUTCOME, AND EVALUATION

The important question is what these differences in structure and function do for the interests, needs, and aspirations of people. Looking again at Figures 2.1 and 2.3, we see a reflection of the relationship between what happens in politics and in the society, and between what happens in the society and the international environment. The structural-functional differences determine the give-and-take between politics and environment, and the importance of that give-and-take for such goals and objectives as welfare, justice, freedom, equality, peace, and prosperity. At the left of Figure 2.3 are arrows signifying inputs of demands and supports from the society and the international system and inputs from the independent initiatives of political leaders and bureaucrats. At the right are arrows signifying outputs and outcomes, the end products of the political process, the things a government does for and to its people.

We have to distinguish between the efforts—the things a government does—and the actual outcome of these efforts. Governments may spend equal amounts on education and health, or defense, but with different consequences. Not only government efficiency or corruption but the underlying cultural, economic, and technological level, as well as changes in its environment, play a role in the effectiveness of politics. Americans spend more per capita on education than any other people in the world, but their children perform less well in important subjects than do children in some other countries that spend substantially less. The United States and the Soviet Union spent enormous sums on defense in the last decades, and yet both countries were held at bay by small countries resolved to resist at all costs, and because of these failed efforts, they were weakened internally. The outcome of public policy is never wholly in the hands of the people and their leaders in the various nations of the world. Conditions in the internal environment, conditions and events in the larger external world, and simple chance may frustrate the most thoughtfully crafted programs and plans. We call the outputs of a political system—its extractions, distributions, regulations, and symbolic acts—its performance.

Finally, we must step even further back to consider the whole situation of political system, process, and policy, and the environment, to evaluate what political systems are doing. Evaluation is complex because people value different things and put different emphasis on what they value. We will refer to the different things people may value as political "goods." In Chapter 7 we discuss goods associated with the system level, such as the stability or adaptability of political institutions; goods associated with the process level, such as citizen participation in politics; and goods associated with the policy level, such as welfare, security, and liberty. To evaluate what a political system is doing, we must look at each of these areas and assess performance and outcomes. We must also be aware of how outcomes affect individuals and subgroups in the society, of specific changes that may often be overlooked in presenting averages, and of the continuing problem of building for the future as well as living today. This last problem affects both poor nations, which wish to survive and alleviate suffering today but also improve their children's lot tomorrow, and rich nations, which must deal with the costs to their children of polluted and depleted natural resources as the result of the thoughtless environmental policies of the past.

KEY TERMS

adjudication	media of communication	political socialization
communication	outcomes	political system
distribution	outputs	process functions
extraction	policy functions	regime
function	policymaking	regulation
government	political communication	states
implementation	political performance	structure
inputs	political recruitment	structural-functional approach
institution	political regime	symbolic functions
interest aggregation	political socialization	system
interest articulation	political regime	system functions

SUGGESTED READINGS

Collier, David. "The Comparative Method," in Ada W. Finifter, ed., *Political Science: The State of the Discipline* II. Washington: American Political Science Association, 1993.

Dogan, Mattei, and Dominique Pelassy. *How to Compare Nations: Strategies in Comparative Politics.* Chatham, NJ: Chatham House, 1990.

Goodin, Robert E., and Hans-Dieter Klingemann. *A New Handbook of Political Science.* New York: Oxford University Press, 1996, chs. 2 and 3, and part 4.

King, Gary, Robert O. Keohane, and Sidney Verba. *Scientific Inference in Qualitative Research.* New York: Cambridge University Press, 1993.

Lichbach, Mark, and Alan Zuckerman. *Comparing Nations: Rationality, Culture, and Structure.* New York: Cambridge University Press, 1997.

Przeworski, Adam, and Henry Teune. *The Logic of Comparative Social Inquiry.* New York: Wiley, 1970.

NOTES

1. Alexis de Tocqueville to Ernest de Chabrol, October 7, 1831, and Louis de Kergolay, October 18, 1847, in *Alexis de Tocqueville: Selected Letters on Politics and Society,* ed. Roger Boesche (Berkeley: University of California Press, 1985), pp. 59 and 191.
2. See also George Wilson Pierson, *Tocqueville and Beaumont in America* (New York: Oxford University Press, 1938).
3. Robert A. Dahl, *Polyarchy: Participation and Opposition* (New Haven, CT: Yale University Press, 1971).
4. Alexis de Tocqueville, *The Old Regime and the French Revolution,* trans. Stuart Gilbert (New York: Doubleday, 1955).
5. Theda Skocpol, *States and Social Revolutions* (New York: Cambridge University Press, 1979).

CHAPTER THREE

Political Culture and Political Socialization

POLITICAL CULTURE

Americans' strong feelings of patriotism, the Japanese deference toward political elites, and French proclivity toward dissent and protest are all examples of how cultural norms shape politics. Our attitudes and values inevitably affect how we act, and it is the same with politics. The functioning of political institutions at least partially reflects the attitudes, norms, and expectations of the citizenry. Thus the English use their constitutional arrangements to sustain their liberty, while the same institutions were turned into instruments of repression in South Africa and Northern Ireland. In times of systemic change, a supportive public can facilitate the development of a new political system, while the lack of public support may erode the foundations of a political system. To understand the tendencies for present and future behavior in a nation, we must begin with public attitudes toward politics and their role within the political system—what we call a nation's **political culture.**

Political culture does not explain everything about politics. Even people with similar values and skills will behave differently when they face different opportunities or problems. Nor is political culture unchangeable. New experiences can change the attitudes of individuals; for example, peasants who migrate to the city learn new ways of urban life. But cultural norms typically change slowly and reflect enduring patterns of political action. This means that political culture is a critical element in understanding politics across countries or across time. If we do not take it into account, we will not understand how politics really functions.

This chapter begins by mapping the important parts of political culture. Then, we discuss **political socialization:** how individuals form their political attitudes and thus, collectively, how citizens form their political culture. We conclude with observations about the trends in political culture in world politics today.

MAPPING THE THREE LEVELS OF POLITICAL CULTURE

A nation's political culture includes its citizens' orientations toward three levels: the political system, the political and policymaking process, and policy outputs and outcomes (Table 3.1). The *system* level involves the citizens' and leaders' views of the values and organizations that hold the political system together. Do citizens identify with the nation and accept the general system of government? The *process* level includes expectations of how politics should function, and individuals' relationship to the political process. The *policy* level deals with citizens' and leaders' policy expectations from the government. What are the government's policy goals and how are they to be achieved?

The System Level

Orientations toward the political system are important because they tap basic commitments to the political system and the nation. Feelings of national pride are a revealing example of this aspect of the political culture (Figure 3.1). National pride seems strongest in nations with a long history that has emphasized feelings of patriotism—the United States is a prime example. Such a common sense of identity and national history is often what binds a people together in times of political strain. In contrast, national pride is low in Japan and Germany, two nations that have avoided nationalist sentiments in reaction to the pre–World War II regimes and their excesses. In other cases ethnicity, language, or history divide the public, which may strain national identities and ultimately lead to conflict and division.

The **legitimacy** of the political system also provides a foundation for a successful political process. When citizens believe that they ought to obey the laws, then legitimacy is high. If they see no reason to obey, or if they comply only from fear, then legitimacy is low. Because it is much easier for government to function when citizens believe in the legitimacy of the political system, virtually all governments, even the most brutal and coercive, try to make their citizens believe that the laws ought to be obeyed. A political system and a government with high legitimacy will be more effective in making and carrying out policies and more likely to overcome hardships and reversals.

Table 3.1   THE ASPECTS OF POLITICAL CULTURE

Aspects of Political Culture	Examples
System	Pride in nation
	National identity
	Legitimacy of government
Process	Role of citizens
	Perceptions of political rights
Policy	Role of government
	Government policy priorities

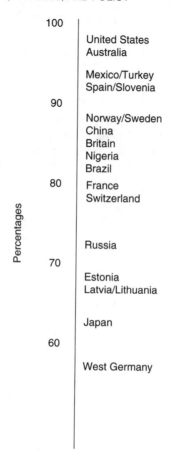

FIGURE 3.1   FEELINGS OF NATIONAL PRIDE (IN PERCENT)   *Source:* Selected nations from the 1995–1998 *World Values Survey;* the French and British data are from the 1990 *World Values Survey.* Figure entries are the percentage "very proud" and "proud."

Citizens may grant legitimacy to a government for different reasons. In a traditional society, legitimacy may depend on the ruler's inheriting the throne or on the ruler's obedience to religious customs, such as making sacrifices and performing rituals. In a modern democracy, the legitimacy of the authorities will depend on their selection by voters in competitive elections and on their following constitutional procedures in their actions. In other political cultures, the leaders may base their claim to legitimacy on their special grace, wisdom, or ideology, which they claim will transform citizens' lives for the better, even though the government does not respond to specific demands or follow prescribed procedures.[1]

Whether legitimacy is based on tradition, ideology, citizen participation, or specific policies, the basis of legitimacy defines the fundamental understanding between citizens and political authorities. Citizens obey the laws—and in return the government meets the obligations set by the terms of its legitimacy. As long as the government meets its obligations, the public is supposed to comply, be supportive, and act appropriately. If legitimacy is violated—the line of succession is broken, the constitution is subverted, or the ruling ideology is ignored—then the government may expect resistance and perhaps rebellion.

In systems with low legitimacy or where the claimed bases for legitimacy are not accepted, people often resort to violence to solve political disagreement. Legitimacy may be undermined where the public (1) disputes the boundaries of the political system, as in Northern Ireland or the parts of the former Yugoslavia; (2) rejects the current arrangements for recruiting leaders and making policies, as when Filipinos took to the streets and demanded the ouster of Ferdinand Marcos and free elections; or (3) loses confidence that the leaders are fulfilling their part of the political bargain in making the right kinds of laws or following the right procedures, as when Indonesians protested the deterioration of living conditions under the Sukarno regime.

The Soviet Union disintegrated in the early 1990s because all three kinds of legitimacy problems appeared. After Communist ideology failed as a legitimizing force, there was no basis for a national political community in the absence of common language or ethnicity. Similarly, the general loss of confidence in the Communist Party as the dominating structure for the political system led many people to call for new arrangements. Finally, shortages of food and consumer goods caused people to lose faith in the government's short-term economic and political policies. Soviet President Mikhail Gorbachev failed in his efforts to deal with all three problems at the same time.

In the early twentieth century a variety of political systems divided the world. Fascism was on the rise in Europe, communism was establishing itself in the Soviet Union, colonial administrations governed large parts of the world, monarchical or authoritarian governments ruled other parts of the world, and Western Europe and North America strained to maintain democracy in this sea of conflicting currents.

Today, many of these forms of governance are no longer widely accepted. Communism still has strongholds in China and Cuba, but it has lost its image as a progressive force for global change. Some nations of the world still accept autocratic or religiously based systems of government. However, the global wave of democratization in the 1990s has raised democratic principles to a position of prominence. Most of the people in the world today seem to favor democratic principles even if they differ in how those principles should be applied.[2]

The Process Level

The second level of the political culture involves what the public expects of the political process. If you are English or Nigerian, what do you think about the institutions of your political system and what is expected of you as a citizen?

Broadly speaking, three different patterns describe the citizens' role in the political process.[3] **Participants** are involved as actual or potential participants in the political process. They are informed about politics and make demands on the polity, granting their support to political leaders based on performance. **Subjects** passively obey government officials and the law, but they do not vote or actively involve themselves in politics. **Parochials** are hardly aware of government and politics. They may be illiterates, rural people living in remote areas, or simply people who ignore politics and its impact on their lives.

As shown in Figure 3.2, in a hypothetical modern industrial democracy a sizable proportion (for instance, 60 percent) are participants, another third are simply subjects, and a small group are parochials. Such a distribution provides enough political activists to ensure competition between political parties and sizable voter turnout, as well as critical audiences for debate on public issues by parties, candidates, and pressure groups. At the same time, not all citizens feel the need to be active or concerned about the political system.

The second column in Figure 3.2 depicts the pattern we expect in a largely industrialized authoritarian society, such as the former communist nations of Eastern Europe. A small minority of citizens are involved in one-party systems, which penetrate and oversee the society, as well as decide its policies. Most other citizens are mobilized as subjects by political institutions: political parties, the bureaucracy, and government-controlled mass media. People are encouraged and even forced to cast a symbolic vote of support in elections and to pay taxes, obey regulations, and accept assigned jobs. Thanks to the effectiveness of modern social organization and mass communications and the efforts of the authoritarian power structure, few citizens are unaware of the government and its influence on their lives. If such a society suddenly attempts democratization of its politics, many citizens must learn to become participants as well as democrats.

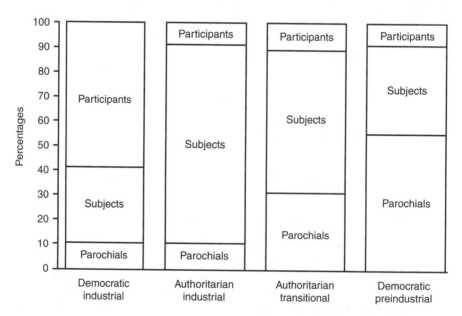

FIGURE 3.2 MODELS OF POLITICAL CULTURE: ORIENTATIONS TOWARD INVOLVEMENT IN THE POLITICAL PROCESS

The third column shows an authoritarian system in a society that is partly industrial and partly modern, such as in Egypt and Thailand. In spite of an authoritarian political organization, some participants—students and intellectuals, for example—oppose the system and try to change it by persuasion or more aggressive acts of protest. Favored groups, like business people and landowners, discuss public issues and engage in lobbying. Most people in such a system are passive subjects, aware of government and complying with the law but not otherwise involved in public affairs. The parochials—poor and illiterate slum dwellers, peasants, or farm laborers—have little conscious contact with the political system.

Our fourth example is the democratic preindustrial system, perhaps one like India, which has a predominantly rural, illiterate population. In such a country there are few political participants, chiefly educated professionals, business people, and landowners. A much larger number of employees, workers, and perhaps independent farmers are directly affected by government taxation and other official policies. The largest group of citizens are illiterate farmworkers and peasants, whose knowledge of and involvement with national politics is minimal. In such a society it is a great challenge to create a more aware citizenry that can participate meaningfully and shape public policies through democratic means.

In summary, the distribution of these cultural patterns is related to the type of political process that citizens expect and support. For instance, we normally identify democracy with a more participatory political culture. Authoritarian states are more likely to endure when the public is characterized by subjects and parochials—although authoritarian states can come in many forms, ranging from communism, to dictatorships, to religion-based regimes.

Another critical feature of the process culture is people's beliefs about other groups and themselves as group members. Do individuals trust their fellow citizens? Do they see the society as divided into social classes, regional groups, or ethnic communities? Do they identify themselves with particular factions or parties? How do they feel about groups of which they are not members? When people trust others they will be more willing to work together for political goals, and group leaders may be more willing to form coalitions.[4] Governing a large nation requires forming large coalitions, and there must be substantial amounts of trust in other leaders to keep bargains and ensure honesty in negotiations.

The converse of trust is hostility, which can destroy intergroup and interpersonal relations. The tragic examples of ethnic, religious, and ideological conflict in many nations—such as the conflicts in Rwanda, Lebanon, Northern Ireland, and the former Yugoslavia—show how easily hostility can be converted into violence and aggressive action. Respect for human life and dignity is sometimes in too short supply in the contemporary world.

The Policy Level

The politics of a country are also influenced by public images of what constitutes the good society and how to achieve it. At one level, the political culture includes expectations of the government's overall involvement in society and the economy. Should government manage the economy, or should private property rights and market forces guide economic activity? Should the state be interventionist in addressing societal issues, or follow a minimalist strategy? The ongoing debates over "big government" versus "small government" in democratic states, and between socialist and market-based economies reflect these different images of the scope of government (see Chapter 1).

Figure 3.3 illustrates the extent of cross-national differences in public expectations about whether it is the government's role to ensure that everyone is provided for. The range in opinions is considerable, from nearly two-thirds believing this is a government responsibility in Chile and Latvia, to only one-sixth of Americans. In general, such sentiments are more common in developing nations and in

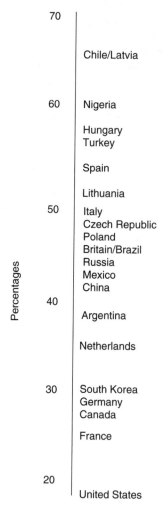

FIGURE 3.3   PERCENTAGE AGREEING THAT THE GOVERNMENT SHOULD ENSURE EVERYONE IS PROVIDED FOR *Source:* Selected nations from the 1990–1991 *World Values Survey.*

the formerly communist nations in Eastern Europe—reflecting both the socioeconomic context and political ideologies. There are some Western nations, such as Britain and Spain, where traditions also include a large role for the government. When the public expects a larger role for government, it is likely that the policies of the government will grow to meet the public's expectations.

Policy expectations also involve specific policy demands.[5] Some policy goals, such as material welfare, are valued by nearly everyone. Concern about other policy goals may vary widely across nations because of the nation's circumstances and because of cultural traditions. People in developing countries are more likely to focus on the government's provision of basic services to ensure public well-being. Advanced industrial societies provide for basic needs, and in these nations people may be more concerned with quality of life goals, such as preservation of nature and even government support for the arts. One of the basic measures of government performance is its ability to meet the policy expectations of its citizens.

Another set of expectations involves the functioning of government. Some cultures put more weight on the policy outputs of government, such as providing welfare and security. Other cultures also emphasize how the process functions, which involves values such as the rule of law and procedural justice. Among Germans, for example, the rule of law is given great importance; in many developing nations political relations are personally based, and there is less willingness to rely on legalistic frameworks.

Finally, the combination of learned values, strategies, and social conditions may lead to quite different perceptions about how to achieve desired social outcomes. For instance, one study showed that 73 percent of the members of the Italian Parliament strongly agreed that a government wanting to help the poor would have to take from the rich in order to do it. Only 12 percent of the British Parliament members took the same strong position.[6]

Cultural Congruence

At the heart of our discussion of political culture is the belief that political structures and political cultures are mutually reinforcing in stable political systems. It is difficult to sustain democracy in a nation lacking participatory democrats, just as it is difficult to sustain an authoritarian state if the citizens become politically sophisticated and want to participate. Indeed, one of the major political issues in the world today is whether the democratic transitions in Eastern Europe, Latin America, and East Asia that began in the 1990s can be sustained. The political culture in these nations will provide a significant part of the answer.

Figure 3.4 illustrates the relationship between history and political culture. The figure displays public satisfaction with the functioning of democracy for three groups of nations; each oval in the figure represents a separate nation. One can readily see that satisfaction with democracy is higher in the first group of stable and very democratic nations; these are largely the established democracies of Western Europe and North America. Political satisfaction is lower in the second group of recently formed nations that have highly developed democratic structures—several Latin American and East European nations fall into this category.

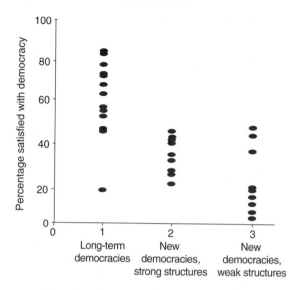

FIGURE 3.4   THE RELATIONSHIP BETWEEN DEMOCRATIC EXPERIENCE AND POLITICAL SUPPORT   *Source:* Calculated from data on system age from Ted Gurr, *Polity III* dataset; the 1996 democracy rating from the Freedom House; satisfaction with the functioning of democracy is from Hans-Dieter Klingemann, "Mapping Political Support in the 1990s: A Global Analysis," in Pippa Norris, ed. *Critical Citizens: Global Support for Democratic Government* (Oxford, England: Oxford University Press, 1999), table 2.10.

Finally, political satisfaction is lowest in the third group—nations with new political systems having weak democratic structures, such as the states of the former Soviet Union. Structure and culture do overlap in these nations.[7]

One may ask whether democracies create a satisfied and democratic public, or whether such a political culture leads to a democratic political system. Obviously it works both ways. For example, immediately after World War II Germans were less supportive of democracy, but the political culture was transformed by political institutions and political experiences over the generation.[8] At the same time, democracy endured in Britain during the strains of the Great Depression and World War II at least in part because the British public was supportive of the democratic process. The important conclusion is that there is normally a relationship between political culture and political structures.

Consensual or Conflictual Political Cultures

We have described political culture as a characteristic of a nation, but values and beliefs also vary within nations. Political cultures may be consensual or conflictual on issues of public policy and, more fundamentally, on views of legitimate governmental and political arrangements. In a **consensual political culture,** citizens tend to agree on the appropriate means of making political decisions and to agree on the major problems facing the society and how to solve them. In a **conflictual political culture,** the citizens are sharply divided, often on both the legitimacy of the regime and solutions to major problems.

When a country is deeply divided in political attitudes and these differences persist over time, distinctive **political subcultures** may develop. The citizens in these subcultures may have sharply different points of view on at least some critical political matters, such as the boundaries of the nation, the nature of the regime, or the correct ideology. Typically, they affiliate with different political parties and interest groups, read different newspapers, and even have separate social clubs and sporting groups. Thus they are exposed to quite distinctive patterns of learning about politics. Such organized differences characterize the publics in India and Russia today, or Italy and the Netherlands in the past.

Where political subcultures coincide with ethnic, national, or religious differences, as in Northern Ireland, Bosnia, and Lebanon, the divisions can be enduring and threatening. The fragmentation of the Soviet empire, the breakup of Yugoslavia, and the impulses toward autonomy and secession among ethnically distinct regions (such as in Scotland or separatist movements in Africa) all reflect the lasting power of language, culture, and historical memory to create and sustain the sense of ethnic and national identity among parts of contemporary states. Samuel Huntington has predicted that the places in the world where the major traditional cultures collide will be major sources of political conflict in the next century.[9]

POLITICAL SOCIALIZATION

Political cultures are sustained or changed as people acquire their attitudes and values. We use the term *socialization* to refer to the way in which political values are formed and the political culture is transmitted from one generation to the next. Most children acquire elementary but distinctive political attitudes and behavior patterns at a relatively early age.[10] Some of these attitudes will evolve and change through life, but others may remain part of the political self throughout life.

At any specific time, an individual's political self will be a combination of several feelings and attitudes. At the deepest level, there are general identifications and beliefs such as nationalism, ethnic or class self-images, religious and ideological commitments, and a fundamental sense of rights and duties in the society. Divisions between ethnic or religious groups often generate such attachments because they are based on deep self-images. At an intermediate level, individuals acquire less intense emotional attitudes toward politics and governmental institutions. Finally, there are more immediate views of current events, policies, issues, and personalities. All these levels of attitudes can change, but those in the first group usually were acquired earliest, have been most frequently reinforced, and tend to be the most durable.

Three general points about political socialization and learning need to be emphasized. First, there can be either **direct** or **indirect socialization.** Socialization is direct when it involves the explicit communication of information, values, or feelings toward politics. Civics courses in public schools are direct political socialization, as are the efforts of Islamic fundamentalist movements to indoctrinate children in such countries as Iran and Pakistan. Communist political systems also heavily use indoctrination programs. Political socialization is indirect when political views are inadvertently molded by our experiences. Such indirect political socialization may have particular force in a child's early years. For example, the child's relationships to parents, teachers, and friends are likely to affect the adult's posture toward political leaders and fellow citizens in later life. Or, growing up in a time of deprivation and hardship may leave the future adult more concerned about economic well-being.

Second, socialization continues throughout an individual's life. Early family influences can create an individual's initial values, but subsequent life experiences—becoming involved in new social groups and roles, moving from one part of the country to another, shifting up or down the social ladder, becoming a parent, finding or losing a job—may change one's political perspectives. More dramatic experiences, such as immigration to a new country or suffering through an economic depression or a war, can sharply alter even quite basic political attitudes. Such events seem to have their greatest impact on young people just becoming involved in politics, such as first-time voters, but most people are affected to some degree.

Third, patterns of socialization in a society can either be *unifying* or *divisive*. Some events, such as international conflict or the loss of a popular public figure, can affect nearly the entire nation similarly. In contrast, subcultures in a society can have their own distinctive patterns of socialization. Social groups that provide their members with their own newspapers, their own neighborhood groups, and perhaps their own schools can create distinctive subcultural attitudes. These divisive patterns of socialization can have a momentous impact on the society.

AGENTS OF POLITICAL SOCIALIZATION

Individuals in all societies are affected by **agents of political socialization:** institutions and organizations that influence political attitudes. Some, like civics courses in schools, are direct and deliberate sources of political learning. Others, like play and work groups, are likely to affect political socialization indirectly.

The Family

The direct and indirect influences of the family—the first socialization source that an individual encounters—are powerful and lasting. The family has distinctive influences on attitudes toward authority. Participation in family decision making can increase a child's sense of political competence, providing skills for political interaction and encouraging active participation in the political system as an adult. By the same token, unquestioning obedience to parental decisions may predispose the child to a role as a political subject. The family also shapes future political attitudes by locating the individual in a vast social world; establishing ethnic, linguistic, class, and religious ties, affirming cultural values, and directing occupational and economic aspirations.

A revolution in women's resources and expectations in recent decades has profoundly affected the politics of advanced industrial nations. The trend toward gender equality in education, occupation, and profession has transformed the structure of the family. The lessening of gender differences in self-images, in parental roles, and in relations to the economy and the political system is significantly affecting patterns of political recruitment, political participation, and public policy. A more open family, equality of parenting, and the early exposure of children to child care and preschool group experiences have modified the impact of the family in the socialization process in ways that are still being assessed. Especially in the developing world, the changing role of women may have profound influences in modernizing the society.[11]

Schools

Schools provide children and adolescents with knowledge about the political world and their role in it and with more concrete perceptions of political institutions and relationships. Schools also transmit the values and attitudes of the society. They can play an important role in shaping attitudes about the unwritten rules of the political game, instilling the values of public duty, and developing informal political relations. Schools can reinforce affection for the political system and provide common symbols, such as the flag and pledge of allegiance, that encourage emotional attachments to the system. When a new nation comes into being, or a revolutionary regime comes to power in an old nation, it usually turns immediately to the schools as a means to supplant "outdated" values and symbols with new ones more congruent with the new ideology.

In some nations educational systems do not provide unifying political socialization but send starkly different messages to different groups. Until recently, one

---

Box 3.1 Socializing Values

Communist East Germany had a special ceremony for eighth graders that marked their passage to adulthood. The heart of the ceremony was the endorsement of the following four pledges:

- As young citizens of our German Democratic Republic, are you prepared to work and fight loyally for the great and honorable goals of socialism, and to honor the revolutionary inheritance of the people?
- As sons and daughters of the worker-and-peasant state, are you prepared to pursue higher education, to cultivate your mind, to become a master of your trade, to learn permanently, and to use your knowledge to pursue our great humanist ideals?
- As honorable members of the socialist community, are you ready to cooperate as comrades, to respect and support each other, and to always merge the pursuit of your personal happiness with the happiness of all the people?
- As true patriots, are you ready to deepen the friendship with the Soviet Union, to strengthen our brotherhood with socialist countries, to struggle in the spirit of proletarian internationalism, to protect peace and to defend socialism against every imperialist aggression?

of the main goals of the South African educational system was to perpetuate differences between the races. The apartheid culture was supported both by creating attitudes of separateness and by providing different skills and knowledge to whites and nonwhites. There was no mixing of white and black children. White children learned early that their parents and other siblings treated blacks as inferior people. As they grew older they learned that whites were different and superior to blacks. White children in South Africa were required by law to attend primary and secondary school, where the environment was racially exclusive. The school experience usually confirmed and strengthened the attitudes acquired by white children at home.

Education for the black majority was very different. A separate government department provided segregated elementary education for black children. Even in the 1980s, the government still spent many times more per student on white education.[12] Black dissatisfaction with the quality of education, as well as with the unsuccessful government efforts to force the use of Afrikaans (the native language of most white South Africans) as the medium of instruction, was one of the major stimulants of the unrest that challenged white-dominated politics in the 1990s. Today the new South African government is committed to a huge task: to alter profoundly (with a limited budget) the role of the school system from a perpetuator of difference to a provider of unifying symbols and equal skills to children of all races.

Education also affects the political skills and resources of the public. Educated persons are more aware of the impact of government on their lives and pay more attention to politics. The better-educated have mental skills that improve their ability to interpret and act on new information. They also have more information about political processes and undertake a wider range of political activities. These effects of education appear in studies of political attitudes in many nations.[13]

Religious Institutions

The religions of the world are carriers of cultural and moral values, which often have political implications. The great religious leaders have seen themselves as teachers, and their followers have usually attempted to shape the socialization of children through schooling, preaching, and religious services. In contrast to the pattern in the United States, in most nations there are formal ties between the dominant religion and the government. In these instances, religious values and public policy inevitably overlap. Catholic nations, for instance, are less likely to have liberal abortion policies, just as Islamic governments enforce strict moral codes.

Where the churches systematically teach values that may be at odds with the controlling political system—as in the conflict between Islamic fundamentalists and secular governments in Algeria and Egypt, or in the efforts of American fundamentalists to introduce prayer in the schools—the struggle over socialization can be of the greatest significance in the society. In these nations religious subcultures may oppose the policies of the state, or even the state itself.

The emergence of aggressive religious fundamentalism in recent decades has had a major impact on the society and politics of countries as diverse as the United

States, India, Israel, Lebanon, Iran, Pakistan, Algeria, and Nigeria. Such fundamentalism is often a defensive reaction against the spread of scientific views of nature and human behavior, and the libertarian values and attitudes that accompany these views. Fundamentalism usually defines a world in which believers must engage in the great struggle between the forces of spiritual goodness and evil.[14] While the influence of fundamentalism has been most visible in the Middle East and among Muslim countries, it is important in Christian countries as well. There are both Protestant and Catholic versions of fundamentalism in the United States, Europe, and Latin America. Versions of fundamentalism are also to be found, combined with ethnic and nationalist tendencies, among the Confucian, Buddhist, and Hindu countries of Asia. Broadly speaking, fundamentalism seeks to raise conservative social, moral, and religious issues to the top of the contemporary policy agenda.

Of course, religious institutions of many kinds offer valuable moral and ethical guidance that individuals often need to make choices in complex societies. Religious affiliations are often important sources of partisan preferences and can guide people in making other political choices. Thus even though the frequency of church attendance is declining in many nations, the political relevance of religion continues.

Peer Groups

Peer groups are important social units that shape political attitudes. They include childhood play groups, friendship cliques, school and college fraternities, and small work groups, in which members share relatively equal status and close ties, and they can be as varied as a group of Russian mothers who meet regularly at the park, a street gang in Brazil, or a group of Wall Street executives who are members of a social club.

A peer group socializes its members by motivating or pressuring them to conform to the attitudes or behavior accepted by the group. Individuals often adopt the views of their peers because they like or respect them or because they want to be like them. An individual may become interested in politics or attend a political demonstration because close friends do so.[15] In such cases, the individual modifies his or her interests and behavior to reflect those of the group in an effort to be accepted by its members. The international youth culture symbolized by rock music, T-shirts, and blue jeans may have played a major role in the failure of communist officials to mold Soviet and Eastern European youth to the "socialist personality" that was the Marxist-Leninist ideal. Likewise, groupings such as the "skinheads" that have sprouted up among lower-class youth in many Western countries have adopted political views that are based on peer interactions.

Social Class and Gender

Most societies have significant social divisions based on class or occupation. Individuals live in different social worlds defined by their class position. For instance, industrialization created a working class in Britain that was concentrated in particular neighborhoods and developed its own forms of speech, dress, recreation, and entertainment and its own organizations, including trade unions and political parties. Similarly, in many less-developed nations the life experience of the rural peasantry is radically different from urban dwellers. In many instances these social divisions are politically relevant: identifying oneself as a member of the working class or the peasantry leads to distinct political views about what issues are important and which political groups best represent one's interest.

Gender is another important pattern of social and political learning. From birth, nature and society ascribe different patterns of behavior to males and females. Traditionally these social divisions have carried over to politics, defining politics as a male activity and focusing the interests of women on social and family issues. In many less-developed nations these gender roles still exist today. In many industrial nations, however, gender roles are changing. The rise of the women's movement and self-help groups have encouraged women to become active and provided social cues about how women should relate to politics.

Mass Media

Much of the world has become a single audience, exposed to the same information and moved by the same events. There is virtually no part so remote that its inhabitants lack the means to be informed almost simultaneously about events elsewhere: mass-produced and inexpensive transistor radios are omnipresent, even in Third World villages far removed from political power centers. The mass media—newspapers, radio, television, magazines—play an important part in internationalizing attitudes and values around the globe.

Television, enlisting the senses of both sight and sound, can have a powerful emotional impact on large public audiences. Watching war on television—such as the live broadcasts provided by CNN during the war in Kosovo—gives a reality to the news, just as people's feelings were touched by media coverage of Princess Diana's death in 1997. The mass media can also transcend national boundaries and ideological divides. The movements for democracy throughout Eastern Europe were partially created by the image of another way of life that came through the international media. As these democratic revolutions spread in the late 1980s, they fed on the knowledge of the tactics and successes of others, given extra impact through newspapers, television, and radio newly free to report these exciting events.

In addition to providing specific and immediate information about political events, the mass media also convey, directly or indirectly, the major values on which a society agrees. The media can portray certain events as symbolizing the nation—for example, national holidays or traditional government activities—and the events take on a specific emotional color. Mass media controlled by an authoritarian government can be a force in shaping political beliefs. However, citizens will soon ignore reports that are inconsistent with their personal experiences, and word-of-mouth transmission of inconsistent attitudes is often a powerful antidote to the effectiveness of government-controlled mass media.

Interest Groups

Interest groups, associations, economic groups, and similar organizations also shape political attitudes. Among economic groups, trade unions may have had the most important consequences for politics. In most industrial countries, the rise of trade unions transformed political culture and politics, created new political parties, and ushered in new social benefit programs. Other occupational and professional associations, such as groups of peasants and farmers, manufacturers, wholesalers and retailers, medical societies, and lawyers can also influence political attitudes in modern and modernizing societies. These groups ensure the loyalty of their members by defending their economic and professional interests. They can also provide valuable political cues to nonmembers, who might identify with a group's interests or political ideology.

Also important in political socialization are the public groups that define a civil society; this might include ethnic organizations, fraternal associations, civic associations (such as parent-teacher associations), and policy groups (such as taxpayers' associations or environmental groups). Such groups provide valuable political cues to their members and try to reinforce distinct social and political orientations. In addition, these groups—using the media and the mails—send out large quantities of information on political, social, and economic issues to the public and elites.

Political Parties

As specialized political structures that exist in democratic and nondemocratic systems, political parties play an important role in political socialization. Political parties attempt to mold issue preferences, arouse the apathetic, and find new issues to mobilize support. Party leaders and party spokespersons provide the public with a steady flow of information on the political issues of the day. Party organizations regularly contact voters by mail or phone, and in many nations party activists visit voters at home. And every few years there is an election in democratic systems, in which parties present their past accomplishments and discuss the nation's political future. Elections can serve as national civics lessons, and parties are the teachers.

In competitive party systems, partisan socialization can be also be a divisive force. In their efforts to gain support, leaders may appeal to class, language, religion, and ethnic divisions and make citizens more aware of these differences. The Labour and Conservative parties in Britain, for example, draw heavily on traditional symbols of class to attract supporters. Similarly, the Congress Party in India tries to develop a national program and appeal, but other minor parties emphasize the ethnic and religious divisions. Leaders of preindustrial nations often oppose competitive parties because they fear such divisiveness. Although this is sometimes a sincere concern, it is also self-serving to government leaders, and is becoming increasingly difficult to justify against widespread contemporary demands for multiparty systems.

Authoritarian governments often use a single party to attempt to inculcate common attitudes of national unity, support for the government, and ideological agreement. The combination of a single party and controlled mass media is potent: The media present a single point of view, and the party activities reinforce that perspective by directly involving the citizen. Yet, as demonstrated in Eastern Europe in 1989, years of directed socialization by media and party cannot compete with citizens' personal experiences in shaping basic attitudes.

Direct Contact with Governmental Structures

In modern societies, the wide scope of governmental activities brings citizens into frequent contact with various bureaucratic agencies. One study found that 72 percent of adult Americans had interacted with at least one government agency in the preceding year; about a third had interacted with more. The most frequent contacts were with tax authorities, school officials, and the police.[16] The degree of government intervention in daily life, and hence the necessity for contacts with government, is greater in many Western European nations than in the United States, and it is greater yet in the remaining communist countries.

These personal experiences are powerful agents of socialization, strengthening or undercutting the images presented by other agents. No matter how positive the view of the political system that has been taught in school, citizens who face a different reality in everyday life are likely to change their early-learned views. Indeed, the contradictions between ideology and reality proved to be one of the weaknesses of the communist systems in Eastern Europe.

In their study of citizen attitudes in five nations, Almond and Verba found marked differences across countries in the expectations that citizens had of their treatment by police and bureaucrats.[17] Italians, and particularly Mexicans, had quite dismal expectations as to equality and responsiveness of treatment. African Americans also reported quite negative expectations in these 1960 interviews. It is likely that these expectations were in large measure a response to actual patterns of treatment by government.

TRENDS IN CONTEMPORARY POLITICAL CULTURES

A political culture exists uniquely in its own time and place. Citizens' attitudes and beliefs are shaped by personal experiences and by the agents of political socialization. Yet, in any historical period there may be trends that change the culture in many nations. Such trends reflect two kinds of factors: similar environmental conditions or exposure to the same historic events. The major social trends of our time—modernity and secularism, postmaterial values, fundamentalism and ethnic awareness, democratization, and marketization—reflect both general societal developments and specific historic events.

The major cultural trend that has transformed the world and public values has been **modernization.** For almost two centuries now, the secularizing influences of science and control over nature have altered economic and social systems and shaped political cultures, first in the West and increasingly throughout the world. This trend toward cultural modernization continues to have powerful effects as it penetrates societies (or parts of societies) that have been shielded from it. Exposure to modernity through work, education, and the media shapes an individual's personal experiences and sends messages about modernity in other societies. It encourages citizen participation, a sense of individual equality, the desire for improved living standards and increased life expectancy, and government legitimacy based on policy performance. It also frequently disrupts familiar ways of life, traditional bases of legitimacy, and political arrangements that depend on citizens remaining predominantly parochials or subjects. Alex Inkeles and David Smith's study of the development of modern attitudes emphasized how factory experience can create an awareness of the possibilities of organization, change, and control over nature (see Box 3.2).

A by-product of socioeconomic modernization appears in the nations of North America, Western Europe, and Japan that have developed the characteristics of a postindustrial society. Younger generations who grew up under conditions of international peace and economic prosperity are now less concerned with material well-being and personal security than their parents.[18] Instead, the young are more likely to emphasize **postmaterial values:** social equality, environmental protection, cultural pluralism, and self-expression. Postmaterial values have spawned new citizen groups, such as the environmental movement, the women's movement, and other public interest associations. These changing values have also reshaped the policy agenda of industrial democracies; more citizens are asking government to restore the environment, expand social and political freedoms, and emphasize policies to ensure social equality. Politicians in these democracies are struggling to balance these new policy demands against the continuing policy needs of the past.

A much different response to modernization has been the resurgence of **ethnicity,** or ethnic identities, in many parts of the world.[19] As citizen skills and self-confidence have increased, formerly suppressed ethnic groups have begun to express their identities and demand equal treatment. Development of education and communication skills may encourage a flourishing of literature in a local language whose previous tradition has been informal and oral. This development can further

Box 3.2   Becoming Modern

Inkeles and Smith report how one Nigerian worker replied to a question about how his new work made him feel. "Sometimes like 9 feet tall with arms a yard wide. Here in the factory I alone with my machine can twist any way I want a piece of steel that all the men in my home village together could not begin to bend at all." Such experiences, and the parallel changes in educational levels and access to information can create a more modern political culture.

Source: Alex Inkeles and David Smith, *Becoming Modern* (Cambridge, MA: Harvard University Press, 1974), p. 158.

intensify awareness of common symbols and history. While resurgence of distinctive local cultures enriches the global society, clashes between cultures and subcultures can also be particularly deadly bases of political conflict. Moreover, the migration of peoples into new areas, made possible by easier transportation and encouraged by wars, political conflicts, and the desire for economic betterment, can seem to threaten the way of life of the host society. The exposure to values from other cultures may intensify one's own self-image, which may increase cultural tensions. Although such exposure may eventually lead to greater tolerance, there is no guarantee of this outcome.

In the last decade the major new development has been the trend toward democracy in Eastern Europe, East Asia, and other parts of the developing world. This **democratization** trend reflects long-term responses to modernity as well as immediate reactions to current events. Modernization gradually eroded the legitimacy of nondemocratic ideologies, while the development of citizens' skills and political resources made their claim to equal participation in policymaking (at least indirectly) more plausible. Thus many studies of political culture in Eastern Europe and the former Soviet Union uncovered surprising support for democratic norms and processes among the citizenry as the new democratic system formed.[20]

Ironically, as democratic values have begun to take root in Eastern Europe, citizens in many Western democracies have become increasingly skeptical about politicians and political institutions. In 1964, three-quarters of Americans said they trusted the government; today only a third of the public say as much—and the malaise is spreading to Western Europe and Japan.[21] Recent research shows that citizen support for democratic norms has not waned; in fact, democratic norms and values have strengthened over time as democracy has developed in the West. Instead, people are critical about how democracy functions. Western citizens expect democracy to fulfill its ideals and are critical of politicians and political parties when they fall short of these ideals. Although this cynicism is a strain on democratic politicians, it presses democracy to continue to improve and adapt, which is ultimately democracy's greatest strength.

Another cultural trend in recent years has been a shift toward **marketization**—that is, a greater public acceptance of free markets and private profit incentives, rather than a government-managed economy. The movement appeared in the United States and many Western European nations in the 1980s, where economies had experienced serious problems of inefficiency and economic stagnation. Margaret Thatcher in Britain and Ronald Reagan in the United States rode to power on waves of public support for reducing the scale of government. Public opinion surveys showed that people in these nations felt that government had grown too large (see again Figure 3.3). The political victories of Reagan and Thatcher gave further prestige to efforts to roll back government involvement.

Just as Western Europeans began to question the government's role in the economy, the political changes in Eastern Europe and the Soviet Union added a new dimension to the discussion. The command economies of Eastern Europe were almost exclusively controlled by state corporations and government agencies. The government set both wages and prices and directed the economy. Today, the collapse of these systems raises new questions about public support for marketization.

Public opinion surveys generally find that Eastern Europeans support a capitalist market system.[22]

Support for market economies has also apparently grown in the developing world. In the past decade, many developing nations had difficulties in modernizing their economies through government-controlled economic development; this made freer markets a plausible alternative. The successes of the Asian "tigers" of South Korea, Taiwan, and Singapore in achieving rapid economic growth in a structure of government encouragement of marketization encouraged this movement, which even affected policy directions in the People's Republic of China. It is difficult to disentangle the fundamental political economy issues here from the effects of contemporary events. The trend toward marketization is a response to a long period of increased government intervention in economies. At the moment, no particular mixture of free market and government intervention seems ideal. We expect much further experimentation; the current trend to marketization may also encounter reversals or countertrends in the future.

Clearly, political culture is not a static phenomenon. Our understanding of political culture must be dynamic. It must encompass how the agents of political socialization communicate and interpret historic events and traditional values. It must juxtapose these with the exposure of citizens and leaders to new experiences and new ideas. We must understand also that the gradual change of generations means continuing modification of the political culture as new groups of citizens have different experiences on which to draw.

KEY TERMS

agents of political socialization

conflictual political culture

consensual political culture

democratization

direct and indirect socialization

ethnicity

fundamentalism

legitimacy

marketization

modernization

parochials

participants

political culture

political socialization

postmaterial values

subjects

SUGGESTED READINGS

Aberbach, Joel D., Robert D. Putnam, and Bert A. Rockman. *Bureaucrats and Politicians in Western Democracies.* Cambridge, MA: Harvard University Press, 1981.

Almond, Gabriel A., and Sidney Verba. *The Civic Culture.* Princeton, NJ: Princeton University Press, 1963.

———, eds. *The Civic Culture Revisited.* Boston: Little Brown, 1980.

Brown, Archie, and Jack Gray. *Political Culture and Political Change in Communist States.* New York: Holmes and Meier, 1977.

Eckstein, Harry. "A Culturalist Theory of Political Change." *American Political Science Review* 82 (Sept. 1988): 789–804.

Horowitz, Donald. *Ethnic Groups in Conflict.* Berkeley: University of California Press, 1985.

Inglehart, R. *Modernization and Postmodernization.* Princeton, NJ: Princeton University Press, 1997.

Inkeles, Alex, and David H. Smith. *Becoming Modern.* Cambridge, MA: Harvard University Press, 1974.

Jennings, M. Kent, and Richard Niemi. *The Political Character of Adolescence.* Princeton, NJ: Princeton University Press, 1974.

Klingemann, Hans Dieter, and Dieter Fuchs. *Citizens and the State.* Oxford, England: Oxford University Press, 1995.

Norris, Pippa, ed. *Critical Citizens: Global Support for Democratic Government.* Oxford, England: Oxford University Press, 1999.

Putnam, Robert. *The Beliefs of Politicians.* New Haven, CT: Yale University Press, 1973.

———. *Making Democracy Work: Civic Traditions in Modern Italy.* Princeton, NJ: Princeton University Press, 1993.

Pye, Lucian W., and Sidney Verba, eds. *Political Culture and Political Development.* Princeton, NJ: Princeton University Press, 1965.

Rochon, Thomas. *Culture Moves: Ideas, Activism and Changing Values.* Princeton, NJ: Princeton University Press, 1998.

Sears, David O. "Political Socialization." In F. I. Greenstein and N. W. Polsby, *Handbook of Political Science,* vol. 2, ch. 2. Reading, MA: Addison-Wesley, 1975.

NOTES

1. This concept of legitimacy and its bases in different societies draws upon the work of Max Weber. For example, see Max Weber, *Basic Concepts in Sociology,* trans. H. P. Secher (New York: Citadel Press, 1964), chs. 5–7.
2. Pippa Norris, ed., *Critical Citizens: Global Support for Democratic Government* (Oxford, England: Oxford University Press, 1999).
3. These terms were developed in Gabriel A. Almond and Sidney Verba, *The Civic Culture: Political Attitudes and Democracy in Five Nations* (Princeton, NJ: Princeton University Press, 1963).
4. On the importance of trust, see Almond and Verba, *Civic Culture,* ch. 10; Ronald Inglehart, *Culture Shift in Advanced Industrial Society* (Princeton, NJ: Princeton University Press, 1990), ch. 1; and Robert D. Putnam, *Making Democracy Work: Civic Traditions in Modern Italy* (Princeton, NJ: Princeton University Press, 1993), especially chs. 4 and 6.
5. Ole Borre and Elinor Scarbrough, eds., *The Scope of Government* (Oxford, England: Oxford University Press, 1995).
6. Robert Putnam, *The Beliefs of Politicians* (New Haven, CT: Yale University Press, 1973), p. 108.
7. Also see, Putnam, *Making Democracy Work.*
8. Kendall Baker, Russell Dalton, and Kai Hildebrandt, *Germany Transformed* (Cambridge, MA: Harvard University Press, 1981).
9. Samuel P. Huntington, *The Clash of Civilizations and the Remaking of World Order* (New York: Simon and Schuster, 1996).
10. See Almond and Verba, *Civic Culture,* ch. 12; M. Kent Jennings, Klaus R. Allerbeck, and Leopold Rosenmayr, "Generations and Families," in Samuel H. Barnes, Max Kaase, et al., *Political Action* (Beverly Hills, CA: Sage, 1979), chs. 15 and 16.
11. Martha Nussbaum and Jonathan Glover, eds., *Women, Culture, and Development: A Study of Human Capabilities* (New York: Oxford University Press, 1995).
12. Leonard Thompson and Andrew Prior, *South African Politics* (New Haven, CT: Yale University Press, 1982), p. 119.

13. For example, see Sidney Verba, Norman H. Nie, and Jae-on Kim, *Participation and Political Equality: A Seven-Nation Study* (New York: Cambridge University Press, 1978); Barnes, Kaase, et al., *Political Action,* ch. 4.

14. See, among others, Martin Marty and Scott Appleby, *Fundamentalism Observed* (Chicago: University of Chicago Press, 1991).

15. Richard E. Dawson, Kenneth Prewitt, and Karen Dawson, *Political Socialization,* 2nd ed. (Boston: Little, Brown, 1977), ch. 9.

16. Robert G. Lehnen, *American Institutions: Political Opinion and Public Policy* (Hinsdale, IL: Holt, Rinehart, and Winston, 1976), p. 183; see also Charles Goodsell, *The Case for Bureaucracy,* 3rd ed. (Chatham, NJ: Chatham House, 1994), ch. 2.

17. Almond and Verba, *Civic Culture,* pp. 108–109.

18. Ronald Inglehart, *Culture Shift in Advanced Industrial Society* (Princeton, NJ: Princeton University Press, 1990); Ronald Inglehart, *The Silent Revolution: Changing Values and Political Styles among Western Publics* (Princeton, NJ: Princeton University Press, 1977).

19. Donald Horowitz, *Ethnic Groups in Conflict* (Berkeley: University of California Press, 1985).

20. Arthur Miller, William Reisinger, and Vicki Hesli, eds., *Public Opinion and Regime Change* (Boulder, CO: Westview Press, 1993); William Mishler and Richard Rose, "Trajectories of Fear and Hope: Support for Democracy in Post-communist Europe," *Comparative Political Studies* 28 (1995): 553–581. Compare to Robert Rohrschneider, "Institutional Learning Versus Value Diffusion," *Journal of Politics* 58 (1996): 442–466.

21. Norris, *Critical Citizens.*

22. See Raymond Duch, "Tolerating Economic Reform," *American Political Science Review* 87 (1993): 590–608; Richard Rose et al., *New Democracies Barometer 1994* (Glasgow, Scotland: University of Strathclyde, 1994). Russian support for marketization noticeably lags behind that of most Eastern Europeans.

CHAPTER FOUR

Interest
Articulation

Every political system has some way for citizens and social groups to express their needs and demands to the government. This process of **interest articulation** can take many forms. The most basic might be an individual making a request to a city council member or other government official, or, in a more traditional system, to the village head or tribal chieftain. Collective action by groups of citizens is also an essential part of the articulation process. In larger political systems, individuals working together as a formal interest group are a prime tool in promoting political interests.

During the last hundred years or so, as societies have become internally more complex and the scope of government activity has widened, the quantity and variety of different forms of interest articulation have grown proportionately. Citizens work together to address local and national needs, ranging from the provision of clean water in a village to the passage of national clean water standards. Social movements involve the public in issues as diverse as protecting the rights of indigenous people in the Amazon to debating nuclear power. Interest group headquarters, in large numbers, are found in capitals like London, Washington, Tokyo, and Rome. Some of these headquarters are in buildings as imposing as those housing major governmental agencies. In countries with powerful local governments, interest groups are active at the provincial or local level as well.

This chapter considers the multiple ways that political interests might be expressed and represented in political systems. We discuss both the informal and direct forms of citizen action, as well as more institutionalized forms of articulation. For example, in most countries that allow them, labor unions, manufacturers' associations, farm groups, and associations of doctors, lawyers, engineers, and teachers form to represent these interests. And in the end, most political systems rely on all of these forms of interest articulation to determine what the public and social groups desire of their government.

CITIZEN ACTION

Before political institutions and political processes come into play, we are first members of a society. We interact with family and friends throughout our lives, we

78

express our interests and needs, and we work with others to achieve our goals. These human patterns of social interaction carry over to politics.

In interest articulation, citizens can use a variety of methods to make requests, demands, and pleas for policies (Table 4.1). The most common form of citizen participation is voting in an election—something found even in many authoritarian political systems. Elections provide a basis for the public to express their interests and to make a collective choice about the government's past progress and the future policies for the nation. Even though elections select political elites, they often have a blunt policy impact because elections involve many different issues, and between elections officeholders may stray from the voters' preferences.

Another form of interest articulation occurs when people work with others in their community to address common social or political needs, as when parents work to better the local schools or residents express a concern about how the community is developing. These activities tend to be very policy focused and to exert direct pressure on decision-makers. Such group activity can be found in democratic and authoritarian systems, although nondemocracies may limit the methods of expression to ones that do not openly confront authorities.

Some interest articulation involves only an individual and his or her family, as when a veteran writes to his congressman for help in getting his benefits approved, or when a homeowner asks the local party precinct leader to get her driveway snowplowed regularly. These are **personal interest contacts,** and they are universal in all kinds of political systems including the authoritarian ones. However, the interests being expressed tend to be limited to those of a specific individual or a small group of people.

Often the expression of interests and political demands may extend beyond the bounds of conventional politics to involve protests or other forms of direct action. The spontaneous gathering of outraged ghetto dwellers, the public protests that overthrew the communist governments of Eastern Europe, and the environmental protests of Greenpeace are all examples of how political protest can focus political interests and influence. Protests and other direct actions tend to be high-pressure activities that can both mobilize the public and directly pressure elites; these activities can also be very focused in their political content.

Table 4.1   FORMS OF CITIZEN INTEREST ARTICULATION

Form	Scope of Interests	Degree of Pressure on Elites
Voting in elections	Broad, collective decision on government leaders and their programs	Modest pressure, but unfocused
Informal group, social movement	Collective action focused on a common interest	High pressure
Direct contact	Normally deals with specific, personal problem	Low pressure
Protest activity	Highly expressive support for specific interests	High pressure

In summary, citizens have many routes available to them in expressing their political interests, and each of these routes has particular characteristics associated with it.

How Citizens Participate

The amount of citizen participation in politics varies greatly according to the type of activity and the type of political system. Table 4.2 shows some examples of different types of citizen participation in five countries: the United States, Britain, Germany, France, and the former USSR. The table reveals that common forms of political participation revolve around elections: turning out to vote, trying to convince others how to vote, or working with political parties. Because elections are the most common form of public involvement in the political process, they are important in the interest articulation process. During elections, citizens speak their minds on current issues through conversations, attending meetings, contributing to campaigns, and even expressing their opinions to pollsters. Ultimately, individuals express their preferences in their ballot choices. At the same time, however, elections perform many other functions: the aggregation of political interests (see Chapter 5), the recruitment of political elites, and even the socialization of political values and preferences through the campaign process.

Democracies are remarkable in that competitive elections offer important political resources to all citizens. Among the democracies, the United States stands out for its rather low levels of national voting participation: both Europeans (with

Table 4.2   CITIZEN PARTICIPATION IN FIVE NATIONS (PERCENTAGE)

Type of Participation	United States	(West) Germany	Britain	France	USSR
Voter turnout in most recent national elections	49%	82%	72%	68%	64%
Persuaded others how to vote	32	25	17	39	31
Worked for party or candidate	27	9	8	—	9
Worked with others to solve a community problem	34	12	14	—	—
Contacted local officials	24	—	21	—	27
Signed a petition	70	55	75	51	27
Participated in peaceful protest demonstration	15	25	13	21	4

Sources: United States: Sidney Verba, Kay L. Schlozman, and Henry E. Brady, *Voice and Equality* (Cambridge, MA: Harvard University Press, 1995), p. 72; *Britain:* Geraint Parry, George Moser, and Neil Day, *Political Participation and Democracy in Britain* (Cambridge, England: Cambridge University Press, 1992), p. 44; *Germany:* Russell Dalton, *Politics in Germany* (New York: HarperCollins, 1993), ch. 6; *France:* Russell Dalton, *Citizen Politics* (Chatham, NJ: Chatham House, 1996, chs. 4 and 5); *USSR:* provided by Raymond M. Duch and James L. Gibson, based on their 1990 survey in European USSR in conjunction with the Institute of Sociology, USSR Academy of Sciences; petition and protest estimates from the 1990–1993 *World Values Survey;* election turnout data from most recent national election.

their long democratic experience) and Russians (who are new to democratic elections) vote more frequently than Americans. However, as the table shows, Americans' low level of election turnout does not simply reflect apathy. Americans are much more likely to try to persuade others how to vote than are their British counterparts, and they are much more likely to work for a party or candidate than either Britons or Germans.

Public efforts to express political interests and influence public policy extend beyond elections. Grassroots politics, people working together to address a common problem, represents a very direct method for articulating political interests and attempting policy influence. Alexis de Tocqueville considered such grassroots community action as the foundation of democratic politics. Today such activities are often identified with middle-class participation in affluent societies—PTA groups, community associations, public interest groups—but group activity can be a form of political participation in any nation.[1] Indian villagers working together to build a communal latrine or to develop rural electricity, or indigenous people protecting their land rights are other examples of community action.

Table 4.2 also indicates that group activity has become a frequent form of political expression in the advanced industrial democracies. Nearly a third of Americans had worked with others to address a community problem, and significant numbers are active in European polities as well. Indirect evidence from the developing world suggests that these activities are regularly used, albeit less frequently than in more developed nations.

Perhaps the most expressive and visible form of citizen action involves participation in **protests,** demonstrations, or other direct actions. What better way to articulate one's interest in preventing pollution than to hang an environmental banner from a polluting smokestack, stage a mass demonstration outside of parliament, or boycott polluters? Participation in political protests can arise for two quite different reasons. On the one hand, protest and direct action is often used by individuals and groups that feel they lack access to legitimate political channels. The mass demonstrations in Eastern Europe in the late 1980s and the public rallies and marches of black South Africans against apartheid illustrate protests as the last resort of the disadvantaged. On the other hand, peaceful protests are also increasingly used by the young and better-educated citizens in Western democracies. To many democratic citizens, protest is the continuation of "normal" politics by other means.

A majority in most nations have signed a petition, a form of political action that has become so common that it no longer can be described as unconventional (see again Table 4.2). Roughly 10 to 15 percent of the citizens in the United States, Britain, and Germany have at some time participated in a legal demonstration. Protests are now used by many sectors of society.[2] France has had far more protest involvement than the other established democracies, with more than a quarter of the population reporting participation at some point. These numbers reflect both French traditions of popular protest and the difficulties citizens have often found in getting the attention of majoritarian governments of both right and left. In the Soviet Union, only 4 percent of citizens reported having participated in protests, reflecting the strong government repression of such activities before the

---

Box 4.1   Protest Politics in Action

The Dutch Greenpeace had launched a campaign to protest the dumping of toxic wastes into the North Sea. When calls to end this dumping were ignored, a Greenpeace ship attempted to block the activities at sea. The Belgian navy seized the Greenpeace vessel and impounded it in the Antwerp harbor, which generated extensive media coverage. But Greenpeace's campaign had just begun.

Late one night, camouflaged Greenpeace activists "rescued" their ship from its internment in Belgium, and took backwater canals and waterways to escape to Dutch territory. The entire escape was filmed by an independent Dutch film crew. The event caused an official protest from Belgium, and a public relations coup for Greenpeace. The film of the escape was shown during a Greenpeace telethon on Dutch television, and Greenpeace received millions of guilders in new contributions. These activities also contributed to an eventual decision to stop the dumping of waste at sea.

Source: Russell Dalton, *The Green Rainbow* (New Haven, CT: Yale University Press, 1994), p. 189.

---

late 1980s. Given their current circumstances of serious discontent, substantial education, the absence of regularized party competition, and much looser government controls, we may expect to see future increases in protest actions in Russia and other successor states to the old Soviet Union, such as Ukraine and Belarus.

Citizen participation thus reflects the way that people with various participant attitudes utilize the opportunities existing within a political system. In nations with active political parties and competitive elections, many citizens may be mobilized to participate in the electoral process; in nations where such activities are limited, people may turn to group-based activity or protest in order to express their preferences.

Cross-national research shows that the better-educated and higher social status individuals are more likely to use the various opportunities for participation. These individuals tend to develop attitudes that encourage participation, such as feelings of efficacy and a sense of civic duty,[3] and they possess the personal resources and skills that are easily converted into political involvement when duty calls or need arises. Skill and confidence are especially important in complicated activities like organizing new groups or rising to be a leader in an organization. This pattern is less pronounced for easier activities, such as voting participation and personal contacting. The tendency for the better-off to dominate in the arenas of participation is also more pronounced in societies, such as the United States, with weak party organizations, weak working-class groups (such as labor unions), and a lack of parties appealing distinctively to the interests of the lower classes. In nations with stronger working-class parties and labor unions, organizational networks may develop that to some extent counterbalance the greater information and awareness of the more affluent citizens.

INTEREST GROUPS

A more institutionalized form of interest articulation occurs through the activities of social or political groups that represent the interests of their constituents. In contrast to individual citizen action, interest groups normally have an enduring organizational base, and they often have professional staffs to provide the group with expertise and representation. In addition, interest groups often participate within the political process, serving on government advisory bodies and testifying at parliamentary hearings. Interest groups vary in structure, style, financing, and support base, and these differences may greatly influence a nation's politics, its economics, and its social life.

Anomic Groups

Anomic Groups are generally spontaneous groups that form suddenly when many individuals respond similarly to frustration, disappointment, or other strong emotions. They are flash affairs, rising and subsiding suddenly. Without previous organization or planning, frustrated individuals may suddenly take to the streets to vent their anger as news of a government action touches deep emotions or as a rumor of new injustice sweeps the community. Their actions may lead to violence, although not necessarily. Particularly where organized groups are absent or where they have failed to obtain adequate representation in the political system, smoldering discontent may be sparked by an incident or by the emergence of a leader. It may then suddenly explode in relatively unpredictable and uncontrollable ways.

Some political systems, including those of the United States, France, Italy, India, and some Arab nations, report a rather high frequency of violent and spontaneous anomic behavior.[4] This often involves spontaneous public demonstrations or acts of violence, rather than the planned and orchestrated protests of institutionalized political groups. Other countries are notable for the infrequency of such disturbances. Traditions and models of anomic behavior help turn frustration into action.

In France, for example, protests have become part of the tradition of politics. In the late 1960s, for example, the French government nearly collapsed as the result of protests that began when university students were not allowed to have members of the opposite sex visit their dorm rooms. Soon other disenchanted French men and women joined the students' protest. Anger over the assassination of a popular political leader or other catastrophic event can also stimulate a public outburst. For instance, one commonly sees relatively spontaneous public demonstrations when one nation makes a hostile action toward another nation. Wildcat strikes (spontaneous strike actions by local workers, not organized actions by national unions), long a feature of the British trade union scene, also occur frequently in such continental European countries as France, Italy, and Sweden.

Sometimes anomic groups are a subset of autonomous individuals drawn from a larger social grouping, such as a racial or ethnic group. For instance, in 1992 there was rioting and looting by some residents in minority neighborhoods of Los Angeles following the acquittal of police officers accused of excessive violence in the beating of an African-American suspect. Similarly, in 1992, riots broke out in Algeria when some Muslim fundamentalists protested the government's invalidation of the recent election. We treat these as anomic group actions because there is no structure or planning to the event, and the individuals involved disperse after the protest ends.

From 1988 to 1990, pro-democracy rallies, protests, and riots spread rapidly across Eastern Europe. Long-suppressed discontent burst forth relatively spontaneously in many places as citizens realized that the Soviet Union would no longer support repressive local regimes and that many of the Eastern European governments had lost the will and military support to crush dissent. News of other protests stimulated more protests and provided a model for similar action; each new success provided further encouragement.

We must be cautious, however, about characterizing as anomic political behavior what is really the result of detailed planning by organized groups. For instance, the demonstrations of French and British farmers at the European Union headquarters in Brussels have owed much to indignation but little to spontaneity.

Nonassociational Groups

Like anomic groups, **nonassociational groups** rarely are well organized, and their activity is episodic. They differ from anomic groups because they are based on common interests and identities of ethnicity, region, religion, occupation, or perhaps kinship. Because of these continuing economic or cultural ties, nonassociational groups have more continuity than anomic groups. Subgroups within a large nonassociational group (such as blacks or workers) may act as an anomic group, as in the spontaneous 1992 Los Angeles riots. Throughout the world, ethnicity and religion, like occupation, are powerful identities that can be a basis for collective activity.

There are two especially interesting kinds of nonassociational groups. One is the very large group that has not become formally organized, although its members perceive, perhaps dimly, their common interests. Many ethnic, regional, and occupational groups fit into this category. It can be very difficult to organize such groups. Several members may share a problem, but none of them may find it sufficiently rewarding to commit the effort and time needed to organize other group members. Moreover, if large collective benefits—for example, ending discriminatory legislation or cleaning up water pollution—are achieved, they will be shared even by those who did not work to achieve them, the so-called "free riders." Thus many may prefer to wait for the rewards without sharing the cost or risk of action. The study of such **collective action problems** is valuable in understanding why some groups (including governments and revolutionary challengers) become organized and others do not, and why and under what circumstances the obstacles to collective action can be overcome.[5]

A second type of nonassociational group is the small village or economic or ethnic subgroup whose members know each other personally. The small, face-to-face group has some important advantages and may be highly effective in some political situations. If its members are well connected or its goals unpopular or illegal, the group may prefer to remain informal or even inconspicuous. Examples of the action of such groups include work stoppages and petitions demanding better support and training by students, requests made by large landowners asking a bureaucrat to continue a grain tariff, and the appeal of relatives of a government tax collector for favored treatment for the family business. As the last two examples suggest, personal interest articulation may often have more legitimacy and be put on a more permanent basis by invoking group ties and interests.

Institutional Groups

Political parties, business corporations, legislatures, armies, bureaucracies, and churches often support separate political groups or have members with special responsibility for representing a group's interests. **Institutional groups** are formal and have other political or social functions in addition to interest articulation. Either as corporate bodies or as smaller groups within these bodies (legislative blocs, officer cliques, groups in the clergy, or ideological cliques in bureaucracies), such groups express their own interests or represent the interest of other groups in the society. The influence of institutional interest groups is usually derived from the strength of their primary organizational base—for instance, their soldiers or their business income. A group based on a governmental institution has direct access to policymakers.

In industrial democracies, bureaucratic and corporate interests use their great resources and special information to affect policy. In the United States the military-industrial complex consists of the combination of personnel in the Defense Department and defense industries who join in support of military expenditures. Political parties represent one of the most active institutional participants in the policy process of most democracies. And as in most societies, government bureaucracies do not simply react to pressures from the outside; in the absence of political directives they often act as independent forces of interest representation.

Nonpolitical institutional groups can also become involved in the political process. In Italy, for example, the Roman Catholic Church has been an institutional interest group with great influence in Italian politics. A major form of intervention has been religious education. In electoral politics, the Church used to admonish Catholics to use their votes to defeat the Communists. Less overtly, the Church seeks influence by having members of the clergy call on officeholders to express opinions on matters of concern to the Church. In Islamic countries fundamentalist clergy pursue a similar role, prescribing what morals public policy should follow, actively lobbying governmental officials, and sometimes participating in the governing process.

In authoritarian regimes, which prohibit or at least control explicit political groups, institutional groups can still play a large role. Educational officials, party officials, jurists, factory managers, officers in the military services, and government bodies representing other social units had significant roles in interest articulation in Communist regimes.[6] In preindustrial societies, which usually have fewer associational groups and where such groups usually fail to mobilize much support, the prominent part played by military groups, corporations, party factions, and bureaucrats is well known. Even where the military does not seize power directly, the possibility of such action often forces close government attention to military requests.

Associational Groups

Associational groups are formed explicitly to represent the interests of a particular group. This includes trade unions, chambers of commerce and manufacturers' associations, ethnic associations, and religious associations. A special subset of associational groups includes civic groups, voluntary associations, and other groups formed to represent a policy interest or political perspective. These organizations have orderly procedures for formulating interests and demands, and they usually employ a full-time professional staff. Associational groups are often very active in representing the interests of their members in the policy process. For instance, in recent debates about health care in the United States there has been an enormous mobilization of pressure groups and lobbyists—from representatives of doctors and health insurance organizations to consumer groups and the like—in efforts to influence legislation.

Associational interest groups—where they are allowed to flourish—affect the development of other types of groups. Their organizational base gives them an advantage over nonassociational groups, and their tactics and goals are often recognized as legitimate in society. Labor unions, for example, are often central political actors because they represent the mass of the working class; in the same way, business associations often speak for the corporate interests of the nation. By representing a broad range of groups and interests, they may limit the influence of anomic, nonassociational, and institutional groups.

Another type of associational group is composed of citizens who are united not by a common economic or individual self-interest but by a common belief in a political ideology or a policy goal.[7] The environmental movement, many women's groups, and other civic groups are examples of this kind of associational group. In some of these issue groups the members may seldom interact directly and not even share common social characteristics (such as employment or ethnicity), but are bound together by their support of a political organization, such as Greenpeace or Amnesty International. On the organizational side, many of these new social groups have sought more fluid and dynamic organizations, with frequent turnover in both leadership and membership. On the tactical side, they have used a wide range of approaches, often discounting the value of partisan campaigning and conventional lobbying in favor of unconventional protests and direct actions.

Civic associations represent another way for citizens to directly and explicitly articulate their policy goals by supporting groups that advocate their preferred positions. Such groups have proliferated in most advanced industrial democracies in the past generation, and they have begun to spread to the developing world.

A social interest can manifest itself in many different groups. We can illustrate this point with examples of different groups that might involve members of the working class:

> *Anomic group:* a spontaneous group of working-class individuals living in the same neighborhood

Nonassociational group: the working class as a collective
Institutional group: the labor department within the government
Associational group: a labor union

Civil Society

In recent years there has been increasing attention to whether an extensive network of interest groups and public participation in these groups creates a **civil society**—a society in which people are involved in social and political interactions free of state control or regulation. Community groups, voluntary associations, and even religious groups, as well as access to free communication and information through the mass media and (now) the Internet, are important parts of a civil society.[8] Participation in associational and institutional groups socializes individuals into the types of political skills and cooperative relations that are part of a well-functioning society. People learn how to organize, how to express their interests, and how to work with others to achieve common goals. They also learn the important lesson that the political process is equally as important as the immediate results. Thus a system of active associational groups can lessen the development of anomic or nonassociational activity. Group involvement can also be an important route into politics for citizens with fewer individual resources. Group activity can help citizens to develop and clarify their own preferences, provide important information about political events, and articulate the interests of citizens more clearly and precisely than parties and elections.[9] Thus, an active public involved in a diversity of interest groups provides a fertile ground for the development of democratic politics.

As political and economic conditions become interdependent across nations, there is also increasing attention directed toward the development of a global civil society to parallel these political and economic developments. Individuals and groups in one nation are connected to groups with similar concerns in other nations, and jointly reinforce their individual efforts. Environmental groups in the developed democracies, for example, assist environmental groups in developing nations with the expertise and organizational resources to address the issues facing their country. National groups meet at international conferences and policy forums, and the network of social relations, as well as the electronic Internet, extends across national borders. This is another sign of how the international context of domestic politics is growing throughout the world.

One of the problems faced by the nations of Eastern Europe and other newly democratizing nations is building a rich associational group life in societies in which organized groups have long been suppressed or controlled. These nations were dominated for over 40 years by the Communist Party and the government bureaucracy, and associational life was controlled by the government to pursue its goals. The process of building new, independent associational groups to articulate the specialized interests of different citizens is underway and will be important to the democratic process. Similarly, many less economically developed nations face an urgent need to develop a civil society of associational groups to involve citizens in the political process and represent their interests if democratization is to have a chance for success.

Interest Group Systems

Research in comparative politics has drawn attention to systematic connections between interest groups and government policymaking institutions. The differences in the types of connections allow us to talk of different interest group systems in modern societies. All modern societies have large numbers of interest groups, but the patterns of relationships differ. Interest group systems are classified into three major groupings: (1) pluralist, (2) democratic corporatist, and (3) controlled.[10]

Pluralist interest group systems are characterized by several features that involve both how interests are organized and how they participate in the political process:

- Multiple groups may represent a single societal interest.
- Membership in groups is noncompulsory and limited.
- Groups often have a loose or decentralized organizational structure.
- There is a clear separation between interest groups and the government.

For instance, not only are there different groups for different social sectors, such as labor unions, business associations, and professional groups, but there may be many multiple labor unions or business associations within each sector. These groups compete among themselves for membership and influence, and all simultaneously press their demands on policymakers and the bureaucracies. The United States is the best-known example of a strongly pluralist interest group system; Canada and New Zealand are also typically cited as examples. Despite its greater labor union membership and somewhat greater coordination of economic associations, Britain tends to fall on the pluralist side in most analyses, as do France and Japan.

Democratic corporatist interest group systems are characterized by a much more organized representation of interests:

- A single peak association normally represents each societal interest.
- Membership in the peak association is often compulsory and nearly universal.
- Peak associations are centrally organized and direct the actions of their members.
- Groups are often systematically involved in making and implementing policy.

For instance, in a corporatist system there may be a single peak association that represents all the major business or industrial interests; a pluralist system may have a wide diversity of business groups that act autonomously. Equally important, interest groups in corporatist systems often regularly and legitimately work with the government agencies and/or political parties as partners in negotiating solutions to policy problems. The best-studied democratic corporatist arrangements have been in the area of economic problems. Countries with large and unified peak associations of business and labor that negotiated with each other and the government have better records than more pluralist countries in sustaining employment, restraining inflation, and increasing social spending.[11] The most thoroughly corporatist interest group systems are in Austria, the Netherlands, Norway, and Sweden. Substantial democratic corporatist tendencies are also found in Germany and Denmark. Some developing nations also follow a corporatist pattern.

Because different sectors of a society may vary in their organized interest groups and in their government relations, we must be cautious about generalizing too much about interest group systems. However, Figure 4.1 shows the striking differences in organization of the labor movements in some industrialized societies. The countries are arrayed along the horizontal axis in terms of the percentage of the total labor force that belongs to a labor union. The vertical axis displays the degree or organizational unity within the labor union movement. In Sweden, for example, about 90 percent of the nonagricultural workforce is organized into unions, and the movement is highly centralized and united on most labor-related issues.

In Britain less than half the labor force is unionized, but these unions are not as highly coordinated as those of the corporatist countries. The member unions in the British Trades Union Congress have strong traditions of individual autonomy and are themselves relatively decentralized. Moreover, the influence of the labor unions on government policymakers has waned over the past two decades. The Thatcher government moved away from direct negotiation with labor, and thus away from corporatism in the 1980s, and even the Labour Party distanced itself from the labor unions in the 1990s. Germany has about the same level of union membership, but the German unions are relatively well coordinated and negotiate national wage policies with representatives of business and government. The United States is the polar opposite to Sweden; only about a sixth of the labor force is unionized, and the unions maintain a great deal of independence.

Figure 4.1 also shows that union membership in Japan and France is relatively low, with only about one worker in four or fewer belonging to a union.

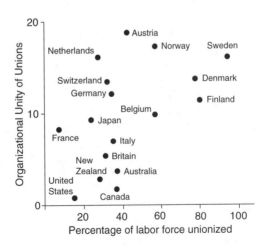

FIGURE 4.1 INTEREST GROUP SYSTEMS OF LABOR UNIONS *Sources:* Data for the percentage of the labor force unionized is from Organization for Economic Cooperation and Development, *Employment Outlook, July 1997* (Paris: OECD, 1997), p. 71; the unity of unions is from Arend Lijphart and Marcus Crepaz, "Corporatism and Consensus Democracy in Eighteen Countries," *British Journal of Political Science* 21 (1991): pp. 235–256.

Moreover, the union movements themselves are relatively fragmented and decentralized. In these countries there are few traditions of "social partnership" between government, unions, and employer associations. In the area of labor policy, at least, these are highly pluralist, not corporatist, interest group systems. However, corporatist-type arrangements among individual industries, trade associations, and governmental bureaucracies (without organized labor involvement) are found in Japan.

In some democratic systems—for example, in France and Italy—some interest groups such as trade unions and peasant associations have been controlled by the Communist Party or the Roman Catholic Church. Usually, these groups mobilized support for the political parties or social institutions that dominated them. This lack of autonomy had serious consequences for politics. Denial of independent expression to interest groups may lead to outbreaks of violence, and the subordination of interest group interests may limit the adaptability of the political process. However, these restrictive structures seem to be breaking down, particularly with the reorganization and weakening of the formerly Communist parties.

Finally, the pattern of interest groups is completely different in **controlled interest group systems:**

- There is a single group for each social sector.
- Membership is often compulsory.
- Each group is normally hierarchically organized.
- Groups are controlled by the government or its agents in order to mobilize support for government policy.

The most important factor is the last: Groups exist to facilitate government control of society. The best examples are the traditional Communist systems in which the dominating party organizations penetrate all levels of society and exercise close control over all the associational groups that are permitted to exist. Unions and youth associations, for example, are completely subordinated to the Communist Party, and they are only rarely permitted to articulate the interests of their members. This control was exercised in the Soviet Union and Eastern Europe; it continues today in China, North Korea, Vietnam, and Cuba. The political systems of several non-Communist nations, such as Brazil and Mexico, also encourage highly controlled interest groups. These nations limit interest articulation to leaders of institutional groups, who can use their positions in political institutions as a base for expressing their demands. As we have already noted, numerous institutional interest groups do emerge in these societies, especially from parts of the party and bureaucracy, such as the military, as do informal nonassociational groups.

ACCESS TO THE INFLUENTIAL

To be effective, interest groups must be able to reach key policymakers through **channels of political access.** Groups may express the interests of their members and yet fail to have an impact on policymakers. Political systems vary in the ways they respond to political interests. Interest groups vary in the tactics used to gain access to the resource holders. Their tactics are shaped in part by the opportunities offered by the structure of policymaking, as well as by their own values and preferences.

It is useful to distinguish between legitimate and constitutional channels of political access (such as the mass media, parties, and legislatures) and illegitimate, coercive access channels. These channels correspond to the two major types of political resources that can be used to influence elites. The first type is established by the legitimate structures of the government, which designate the resources to be used in policymaking. In a democratic political system, the appropriate resources may be votes in the national assembly. Various groups may attempt to control legislative votes by influencing the parties that win elections, or the voters who choose them, or through bargaining, persuasion, or promises of support to incumbents. However, direct action remains as a second type of resource, a coercive channel of influence for individuals and groups who feel that they are otherwise powerless.

If only one major legitimate channel of political access is available, as in a political system dominated by a single party, it is difficult for all groups to have access. Demands transmitted through that channel may be distorted as they work their way to key decision-makers. The leadership thus may be prevented from getting information about the needs and demands of important groups. Over the long run, such misperceptions can easily lead to miscalculations by the leadership and to unrest among the dissatisfied groups, who may turn to violence. Thus a system with multiple channels of access is usually more efficient in responding to societal interests.

Legitimate Access Channels

An important means of reaching political elites in all societies is through personal connections—the use of family, school, local, or other social ties. An excellent example is the information network among the British elite based on old school ties originating at Eton, Harrow, or other "public" schools, or in the colleges at Oxford and Cambridge universities. Similarly, in Japan many alumni of the University of Tokyo Law School hold top positions among the political and bureaucratic elites and are able to act in concert because of these personal ties. Although personal connections are commonly used by nonassociational groups representing family or regional interests, they serve other groups as well. Face-to-face contact is one of the most effective means of shaping attitudes and conveying messages. Demands communicated by a friend or neighbor carry much more weight than a formal letter from a stranger. In modern nations personal connections are usually cultivated with special care. In Washington, the business of advising interest groups and individuals on access to politicians has become an increasingly lucrative profession (and, increasingly a target of government regulation). These activities are often carried on by former officeholders who use their personal governmental contacts for their lobbyist clients.

The **mass media**—television, radio, newspapers, and magazines—are another important access channel in democratic societies. Many interest groups spend a great deal of effort hiring skillful public relations specialists and purchasing direct advertising, trying to see that their interests receive favorable attention in the media. Interest groups, such as senior citizens organizations, encourage media reports on their needs as well as coverage of their views on specific policies. When a cause receives national media attention, the message to policymakers has added weight because they know that millions of voters have been sensitized to the issue. Moreover, groups believe that in an open society, "objective" news coverage will have more credibility than sponsored messages. However, the confusion created by the number of messages and by their lack of specific direction can limit the effectiveness of the mass media for many less important groups.

The mass media can also mobilize support for interest group efforts, leading to donations of time and money, as well as stimulating similar demands from sympathizers. The loosening of government control from the media in the communist regimes of Eastern Europe and the former Soviet Union gave a huge boost to democracy movements. There is a story that when asked what caused the democratic revolution in Poland, Lech Walesa pointed to a television and said "that did." Media reports on the failures in communist government policy and the lifestyles in the West undermined the legitimacy of the incumbent regimes. As democratic protests spread across Eastern Europe in 1989 and 1990, stories of successful protests in other parts of the country, or in other countries, enhanced the confidence of demonstrators everywhere. The multitude of spontaneous, as well as coordinated, actions encouraged by mass media reports helped convince the ruling groups that their support had vanished.

Political parties are another important legitimate channel of access. Democratic political parties often rely on interest groups for financial and voter support, and serve as institutional representatives of these interests within government. In a nation like Britain, the various components of the party organization, particularly parliamentary committees, are important channels for transmitting demands to the cabinet and the party in power. In other cases there are factors that may limit the role of parties as interest representatives. For instance, highly ideological parties with a hierarchical structure, such as most Communist parties, are more likely to control affiliated interest groups than to communicate the interest groups' demands. Decentralized party organizations, like those in the United States, whether inside or outside the legislative organization, may be less helpful than individual legislators in providing access.

Legislatures are a common target of interest group activities. Standard lobbying tactics include appearances before legislative committees, providing information to individual legislators, and similar activities. In the United States political action committees raise campaign contributions for individual members of Congress and can usually be sure of some political attention in exchange. In Britain and France the strong party discipline in the legislature and in its committees lessen the importance of members of Parliament (MPs) and parliamentary committees as access channels for interest groups. In Germany and many other European democracies, the presence of strong committees and/or power divided among multiple parties encourage interest groups to use them as access channels. The combination of loose party discipline and decentralized committees as a source of much legislation makes the U.S. Congress a major target of group efforts.

Government bureaucracies are major access channels in most political systems. Contacts with the bureaucratic agencies may be particularly important where the bureaucracy has been delegated policymaking authority, or where interests are narrow and directly involve few citizens. A bureaucrat sympathetic to a group may try to respond to its demands without leaving bureaucratic channels, by exercising administrative discretion. A government official may also help to gain consideration of a problem, or may help to frame an issue in a way more likely to receive a sympathetic hearing by policymakers. Thus a study of access channels used by groups in Birmingham, England, showed that on broad issues involving class, ethnic, or consumer groups, interest groups tended to work through the political parties. On narrower issues, involving few other groups and less political conflict, the groups tended to turn to the appropriate administrative department.[12]

Protest demonstrations, strikes, and other forms of nonviolent but dramatic and direct pressure on government may be regarded by authorities as legitimate or illegitimate tactics, depending on the political system. Demonstrations may be either spontaneous actions of an anomic group or a planned use of unconventional channels by an organized group. In democratic societies, demonstrations may attempt to mobilize popular support—eventually electoral support—for the group's

---

Box 4.2   The Velvet Revolution

On November 17, 1989, a large group of students staged a sit-in in the center of Prague to urge democratic reform. They placed lighted candles on the ground, and sang the Czech version of "We Shall Overcome." Confronted by this civil disobedience, the police beat the students and several bystanders. This was the spark that set the Czech democracy movement on fire. The students went on strike and called for a general strike by the workforce. The public demonstrations grew day by day, and the government entered into negotiations with Vaclav Havel and representatives of the Civic Forum reform movement. By November 25, half a million protestors assembled in a demonstration against the regime, and the government was struggling under the weight of the general strike. A television broadcast showing tapes of the November 17 protest mobilized further support for the reformers. By mid-December the regime capitulated: communism had come to an end, its demise marked by large celebrations in the city center. In less than a month, people had seized power in order to establish democracy in Czechoslovakia.

Source: Timothy Garton Ash, *The Magic Lantern: The Revolution of 1989* (New York: Random House, 1990), ch. 5.

cause. The gay rights and environmental demonstrations in the United States are examples of such activity, as are the continuing pro-life and pro-choice rallies on the Mall in Washington. In nondemocratic societies, such demonstrations are more hazardous and represent perhaps more extreme dissatisfaction with alternative channels.

Protest demonstrations have been described as a tactic of society's powerless, those who do not have access or resources to influence policymakers through conventional channels. As a tactic of the powerless, protest activity is especially attractive to young people and minority groups, who are not among the elite. Protests have also been a favored tactic of groups whose ideological commitments focus on challenging the established social and political order.[13] Yet, since the 1970s protest demonstrations have increasingly been used as a channel for interest articulation by organized and accepted interests who feel that disciplined parties and bureaucratic agencies are deaf to their complaints. Protests can supplement other channels, especially in gaining the attention of the mass media in an age when television comes to every household. Thus we find doctors in Paris, civil servants in Sweden, and "gray panthers" (the elderly) in Germany using a tactic once limited to the poor and minorities.

Coercive Access Channels and Tactics

Most scholars see acts of collective violence as closely associated with the character of a society and the circumstances that prevail there. In his studies of civil strife, Ted Robert Gurr has developed the concept of relative deprivation to explain the frustration or discontent that motivates people to act aggressively. Gurr defines relative deprivation as a "discrepancy between people's expectations about the goods and conditions of life to which they are entitled, on the one hand, and, on the other, their value capabilities—the degree to which they think they can attain these goods and conditions."[14] The sense of relative deprivation leads to frustration and anger; aggressive violence releases those feelings.

Feelings of relative deprivation are a source of frustration, discontent, and anger. The more such discontent and anger persist, the greater the chance of collective violence. But other conditions are important also. People will tend to turn to violence if they believe it is justified and if they believe it will lead to success. If they believe that their government is illegitimate and that the cause of their discontent is justified, they will more readily turn to political violence if there are no other means of bringing about change. To this end, it is the responsibility of the government and its institutions to provide peaceful alternatives to violence as a means of change.

This general analysis of violence should not blind us to the differences between types of violent political activity. A riot, for example, involves the spontaneous expression of collective anger and dissatisfaction by a group of citizens. Though riots have long been dismissed as aberrant and irrational action by social riffraff, modern studies have shown that rioters vary greatly in their motivation, behavior, and social background.[15] Most riots in fact seem to follow some fairly clear-cut patterns, such as confining destruction or violence to particular areas or targets. Relative deprivation seems to be a major cause of riots, but the release of the frustrations is not as aimless as is often supposed.

In the 1992 riots in Los Angeles, although the destruction began within hours of the acquittal of Rodney King's assailants, there was consensus among those involved that the trial outcome was only a proximate cause, a "spark" that ignited already volatile ingredients. Violence against the property of Korean shopowners during the riots reflected widely felt ethnic hostility unrelated to Rodney King. There were at least a few who justified looting through comparison with the massive thefts from savings and loans and insider trading in the previous few years. Many more simply felt that society had moved on and left them in poverty and decay; clear examples of relative deprivation abounded. The immediate results made matters worse: more than 50 people dead, mostly African Americans; thousands of businesses destroyed, with a loss of 14,000 jobs; and thousands of people left without access to necessary retail outlets. Although much of the mayhem seems poorly related to effective political action, it was a poignant cry for attention; and the slogan that emerged—"no peace without justice"—was a clear political message.

While deprivation may help fuel the discontent, strikes and obstructions—such as the recent efforts in the United States to block or prevent the blocking of entry into abortion clinics—are typically carried out by well-organized associational or institutional groups. Many violent demonstrations are called "riots" but should not be. Ann Wilner, for example, states that violent protests in Indonesia during the rule of Sukarno were largely stage managed, "instigated, provoked, and planned by one or several members of a political elite," in order to test their strength, gain support from the undecided, frighten others from joining the opposition, and challenge higher authorities.[16]

Historically, the general strike has been used by labor unions to pressure the government or employers on fundamental issues. However, the influence of strikes and obstructions has varied, depending on the legitimacy of the government and coercive pressure from other groups. A massive truckers' strike helped bring down the government in Chile in 1972 and 1973, but student-inspired boycotts in Korea in the 1980s had only a modest impact on the government. Most spectacularly, the strikes, obstructions, and demonstrations in Eastern Europe in 1989 and 1990, like the earlier people's power movement in the Philippines, had massive success against regimes that had lost legitimacy.

Finally, **political terror tactics,** including deliberate assassination, armed attacks on other groups or government officials, and provocation of bloodshed have been used to articulate interests in some societies. The use of terrorism typically reflects the desire of some group to change the rules of the political game. The tragedies in Northern Ireland, the frequent kidnappings, suicide bombings, and attacks by groups in the Middle East seeking to dramatize the situation of the Palestinians, and the assassinations carried out by the Sendero Luminoso (Shining Path) guerrillas in Peru since the mid-1980s demonstrate the use of such tactics.

The use of political terror tactics has seldom been successful without large-scale backing of terrorist groups from the public or an international sponsor. Massive deadly violence may destroy a democratic regime, leading to curtailment of civil rights or even military intervention when many people and leaders feel that any alternative is preferable to more violence. President Fujimori and military leaders in Peru justified their suppression of democratic institutions in April 1992 as necessary to their battle against the Shining Path and cocaine lords. An authoritarian, repressive response often promises quick results against terrorists; however, small-group terrorism usually fails when confronted by united democratic leadership.[17] In a democratic society, violence often forfeits the sympathy that is needed if the group's cause is to receive a responsive hearing.

POLICY PERSPECTIVES ON INTEREST ARTICULATION

As we pointed out in Chapter 2, we need to look at the structures performing political functions from both a process and a policy perspective. If we are to understand the formation of policies, we need to know which groups articulate interests, and what policy preferences they express. Many associational interest groups specialize in certain policy areas. The concerns of other interest groups, such as anomic or institutional groups, may be less easily discerned, but they are equally important for the policy process.

Table 4.3 provides examples of interest articulation for different types of interest groups and different policy areas: extractive, distributive, and regulative policies in the domestic arena, and international policies. The table footnotes indicate when coercive or illegitimate channels were used. Careful examination of each case provides a more precise illustration of the access channels, such as elite representation by African-American members of Congress, use of party channels by the Italian Catholic Church, and use of terror by Palestinians on the West Bank. This table uses examples from many nations in order to suggest the varied possibilities, as well as to fill in all the categories with reasonably obvious cases. If we were studying interest articulation patterns in one nation, of course, we should attempt to build up the table showing the structures, policies, and channels involved during a particular period.

INTEREST GROUP DEVELOPMENT

One of the consequences of modernization is a widespread belief that the conditions of life can be altered through human action. Modernization normally involves education, urbanization, rapid growth in public communication, and in most cases improvement in the physical conditions of life. These changes are closely related to increases in political awareness, participation, and feelings of political competence. Such participant attitudes encourage more diverse and citizen-based interest articulation.

At the same time that participant attitudes emerge in the political culture of modernizing countries, there is a specialization of labor as people work in many types of jobs—a process that leads to the formation of large numbers of special interests. The interdependence of modern life, the exposure provided by mass communications, and the wide-ranging role of government further multiply political interests. Complex processes organized these interests and attitudes into as-

Table 4.3 PROCESS AND POLICY PERSPECTIVES ON INTEREST ARTICULATION

Examples of Interest Articulation in Various Policy Areas

Types of Interest Groups	Domestic Extractive Policy	Domestic Distributive Policy	Domestic Regulative Policy	International Policy
Anomic groups	Nigerian women riot over rumor of taxes (1950s).[a]	Polish workers strike to protest bread prices.	Indonesians demonstrate against dictatorship (1997).[a]	Britons demonstrate against Bosnian policy.
Nonassociational groups	Mexican business leaders discuss taxes with president.	U.S. Black Caucus Congress calls for minority jobs.	Foreign workers in Germany protest citizenship law.	Saudi royal family factions favor oil embargo.
Institutional groups	American universities urge that charitable contributions remain tax deductible.[b]	U.S. Army Corps of Engineers proposes new river locks.	Church leaders ask for an end to apartheid in South Africa.	Chinese politburo faction favors liberal international trade.
Associational groups	French student groups protest government-imposed tuition increases.[b]	British Medical Association negotiates salaries under Health Services.	National Rifle Association lobbies against gun control.	Palestinians launch terror attacks to pressure Israel.[a]

[a] Use of coercive, unconstitutional access channels and tactics.
[b] Use of coercion by some elements or subgroups.

sociational interest groups. The barriers to coordination and cooperation are over-come in many different ways. The emergent interest group systems, pluralist or corporatist, autonomous or controlled, dominated by the better-off or more equally mobilized, are shaped by the history of interest group development during modernization.

Successful democratic development requires that complex interest group systems emerge to express the needs of groups and individuals in the society. Yet, this process is by no means automatic. The problems of organizing large groups for collective action are very large. Societies vary widely in the extent to which people engage in associational activity. One factor explaining participation is the level of trust shared among members of the society. Robert Putnam and his colleagues found that an active associational life in Northern Italian communities was associated with widespread trust in others and that these qualities of political culture were associated with economic growth and a participant political life.[18] Ronald Inglehart has shown similar continuity in social trust across nations.[19] Thus modernization may weaken traditional structures in some societies but fail to foster the development of effective associational groups in others because of the inhibition of social attitudes. A nation's ability to achieve either stability or democracy will be hindered as a result.

In other cases, as we have noted, authoritarian parties and bureaucracies may control and penetrate associational groups and choke off the channels of political access. Eastern Europe offers a situation in which 40 years or more of authoritarian domination suppressed autonomous interest groups. On the one hand, the processes of economic modernization had put great pressure on these authoritarian systems to allow more open organization and expression of political interests. On the other hand, the opening of these societies has led to an expansion of interest articulation activity and a need for associational groups to provide regular and organized expression for citizens' interests. Associational groups are also needed to counterbalance the demands from institutional groups in the civilian and military bureaucracies.

The recent development of organized interest groups in Eastern Europe should not, however, lead us to conclude that every conceivable group now has equal standing. Using the American experience as an example, the articulation of interests is frequently biased toward the goals of the better-off, who are also often better organized.[20] It is often pointed out that the American Association of Retired Persons (AARP) is an effective group that is not counterbalanced by a "Young Taxpayers Group," and that the traditional labor-management competition leaves consumers unrepresented.

We might test this notion more broadly by evaluating systems in terms of their inclusiveness: What proportion of the population is represented to what degree in national-level politics? In South Africa under apartheid, we had the extreme case where the majority were prevented outright from forming associational groups. In the Third World competing interests in the capital rarely involve the interests of rural peasants; sometimes peasant organizations are brutally suppressed, while urban middle- and upper-class groups are able to petition authorities. It seems to be no coincidence that the bias in group inclusion appears greatest where the gap in income and education is widest. We have suggested above that, pushed to the extreme, those excluded from the process will engage in anomic activity or resort to violence, a conclusion supported by statistical studies of inequality and violence.[21] Even in less extreme cases, the presence of different levels of political awareness means that every interest group system is somewhat biased. Democratization involves not only the provision of competitive elections but also the reduction of the bias in interest representation.

Another challenge faces the patterns of interest articulation and representation in advanced industrial democracies. Turnout in national elections has gradually declined over the last few decades. In the United States, for example, turnout in presidential elections averaged 61 percent during the 1950s and 49 percent in the 1996 election. Fewer citizens in the established democracies attend a campaign rally or display their partisan support during a campaign than participated a generation ago. There is evidence that participation in associational groups is also decreasing in the United States, and perhaps in other established democracies.[22] Some scholars argue that it represents a growing social isolation in developed nations, as people forsake social and political involvement for the comfort of their favorite chair and their favorite TV program. If elections are the celebration of democratic politics, fewer individuals seem to be joining in.

Political analysts worry that decreasing political involvement and group activity signals the erosion in the democratic, participatory spirit in the established democracies. This presents a basic puzzle. Why are citizens in established democracies voting *less often* and participating less frequently in democratic elections? At the same time, other peoples around the world are struggling to win their political freedom and the opportunity to participate in democratic politics.

The one thing that can be certain is that democratic politics rests upon a participatory public that uses individual and group methods to express and represent their interests. Thus the development of an active social and political life is an important standard for measuring the political development of a nation.

KEY TERMS

anomic group	controlled interest group systems	nonassociational group
associational group		personal interest contacts
channels of political access	democratic corporatist interest group systems	
		pluralist interest group
civil society	institutional group	political terror tactics
collective action problems	interest articulation	protests
	mass media	

SUGGESTED READINGS

Barnes, Samuel H., Max Kaase, et al. *Political Action: Mass Participation in Five Western Democracies.* Beverly Hills, CA: Sage, 1979.

Dahl, Robert A. *Polyarchy: Participation and Opposition.* New Haven, CT: Yale University Press, 1971.

———. *Democracy and Its Critics.* New Haven, CT: Yale University Press, 1989.

Dalton, Russell J. *Citizen Politics,* 2nd ed. Chatham, NJ: Chatham House, 1996.

Dalton, Russell J., and Manfred Kuechler. *Challenging the Political Order: New Social and Political Movements in Western Democracies.* New York: Oxford University Press, 1990.

Denardo, James. *Power in Numbers: The Political Strategy of Protest and Rebellion.* Princeton, NJ: Princeton University Press, 1985.

Grant, Wyn, ed. *The Political Economy of Corporatism.* New York: St. Martin's, 1985.

Gurr, Ted Robert. *Why Men Rebel.* Princeton, NJ: Princeton University Press, 1970.

Hirschman, Albert. *Exit, Voice, and Loyalty.* Cambridge, MA: Harvard University Press, 1970.

Lichbach, Mark. *The Rebel's Dilemma.* Ann Arbor: University of Michigan Press, 1994.

Olson, Mancur. *The Logic of Collective Action.* Cambridge, MA: Harvard University Press, 1965.

Pateman, Carole. *Participation and Democratic Theory.* New York: Cambridge University Press, 1970.

Powell, G. Bingham, Jr. *Contemporary Democracies: Participation. Stability and Violence.* Cambridge, MA: Harvard University Press, 1982.

Putnam, Robert D. *Making Democracy Work: Civic Traditions in Modern Italy.* Princeton, NJ: Princeton University Press, 1993.

Richardson, Jeremy J., ed. *Pressure Groups.* New York: Oxford University Press, 1993.

Scott, James C. *The Moral Economy of the Peasant: Rebellion and Subsistence in Southeast Asia.* New Haven, CT: Yale University Press, 1976.

Shi, Tianjian. *Political Participation in Beijing.* Cambridge, MA: Harvard University Press, 1997.

Verba, Sidney, Norman H. Nie, and Jae-on Kim. *Participation and Political Equality.* Cambridge, England: Cambridge University Press, 1978.

Verba, Sidney, Kay Schlozman, and Henry Brady. *Voice and Equality.* Cambridge, MA: Harvard University Press, 1996.

Wiarda, Howard J. *Corporatism and Comparative Politics: The Other Great "ism."* Armonk, NY: Sharpe, 1997.

Wilson, James Q. *Political Organizations.* New York: Basic Books, 1973.

NOTES

1. International Studies of Values in Politics Project, *Values and the Active Community: A Cross-national Study of the Influence of Local Leadership* (New York: Free Press, 1971); Sidney Verba, Norman N. Nice, and Jae-on Kim, *Participation and Political Equality* (Cambridge, England: Cambridge University Press, 1978).

2. Samuel Barnes, Max Kaase, et al., *Political Action: Mass Participation in Five Western Democracies* (Beverly Hills, CA: Sage, 1979); Russell Dalton, *Citizen Politics,* 2nd ed. (Chatham, NJ: Chatham House, 1996), ch. 4; M. Kent Jennings, Jan W. van Deth, et al., *Continuities in Political Action* (New York: de Gruyter, 1990); Richard Topf, "Beyond Electoral Participation," in Hans D. Klingemann and Dieter Fuchs, eds., *Citizens and the State* (Oxford, England: Oxford University Press, 1995), pp. 27–51.

3. See Verba, Nie, and Kim, *Participation and Political Equality;* and Barnes, Kaase, et al., *Political Action.*

4. See the data on riots in Charles Taylor and David Jodice, *World Handbook of Political and Social Indicators*, vol. 1, 3rd ed. (New Haven, CT: Yale University Press, 1983), chs. 2–4.

5. Studies of these problems were stimulated by the now classic work of Mancur Olson, *The Logic of Collective Action* (Cambridge, MA: Harvard University Press, 1965). See also Mark Lichbach, *The Rebel's Dilemma* (Ann Arbor: University of Michigan Press, 1994); Mancur Olson, "Dictatorship, Democracy, and Development" *American Political Science Review* 87, no. 3 (Sept. 1993): 567–576; Todd Sandler, ed., *Collective Action: Theory and Applications* (Ann Arbor: University of Michigan Press, 1992).

6. See G. F. Skilling and F. Griffiths, eds., *Interest Groups in Soviet Politics* (Princeton, NJ: Princeton University Press, 1971); the essays by Frederick C. Barghoorn and Skilling in Robert A. Dahl, *Regimes and Oppositions* (New Haven, CT: Yale University Press, 1973); and Roman Kolkowicz, "Interest Groups in Soviet Politics," *Comparative Politics* 2, no. 3 (April 1970): 445–472.

7. Russell Dalton, *The Green Rainbow: Environmental Interest Groups in Western Europe* (New Haven, CT: Yale University Press, 1994); Amrita Basu, ed., *The Challenges of Local Feminism: Women's Movements in Global Perspective* (Boulder, CO: Westview, 1995).

8. Jean Cohen and A. Arato, *Civil Society and Political Theory* (Cambridge, MA: MIT Press, 1992); M. Walzer, ed., *Toward a Global Civil Society* (Oxford, England: Berghahn Books, 1995).

9. Gabriel A. Almond and Sidney Verba, *The Civic Culture* (Princeton, NJ: Princeton University Press, 1963), pp. 300–322; John Pierce et al., *Citizens, Political Communication, and Interest Groups: Environmental Organizations in Canada and the United States* (Westport, CT: Praeger, 1992).

10. Philippe Schmitter, "Interest Intermediation and Regime Governability," in Suzanne Berger, ed., *Organizing Interests in Western Europe* (New York: Cambridge University Press, 1981), ch. 12; Arend Lijphart and Markus Crepaz, "Corporatism and Consensus Democracy in 18 Countries," *British Journal of Political Science* 21, no. 2 (April 1991): 235–246; Wyn Grant, ed., *The Political Economy of Corporatism* (New York: St. Martin's Press, 1985).

11. On the relative success of the corporatist systems in economic performance, see Miriam Golden, "The Dynamics of Trade Unionism and National Economic Performance," *American Political Science Review* 87, no. 2 (June 1993): 439–454; Arend Lijphart, Ronald Rogowski, and R. Kent Weaver, "Separation of Powers and Cleavage Management," in R. Kent Weaver and Bert A. Rockman, *Do Institutions Matter? Government Capabilities in the United States and Abroad* (Washington: Brookings Institution, 1993), pp. 302–344.

12. Kenneth Newton and D. S. Morris, "British Interest Group Theory Reexamined," *Comparative Politics* 7 (July 1975): 577–595.

13. See the essays in Russell J. Dalton and Manfred Kuechler, *Challenging the Political Order: New Social and Political Movements in Western Democracies* (New York: Oxford University Press, 1990).

14. Ted Robert Gurr, "A Comparative Study of Civil Strife," in Hugh David Graham and Ted Robert Gurr, eds., *The History of Violence in America* (New York: Bantam Press, 1969), pp. 462–463.

15. See Mark Baldassare, ed., *The Los Angeles Riots: Lessons for the Urban Future* (Boulder, CO: Westview, 1994); James F. Short and Marvin E. Wolfgang, eds., *Collective Violence* (Chicago: Aldine-Atherton, 1972).

16. Ann Ruth Wilner, "Public Protest in Indonesia," in Ivo K. Feierabend, Rosalind Feierabend, and Ted Robert Gurr, eds., *Anger, Violence, and Politics* (Englewood Cliffs, NJ: Prentice-Hall, 1972), pp. 355–357.

17. On violence and democratic survival, see G. Bingham Powell, Jr., *Contemporary Democracies: Participation, Stability and Violence* (Cambridge, MA: Harvard University Press, 1982), ch. 8; see also the contributions to Juan J. Linz and Alfred Stepan, eds., *The Breakdown of Democratic Regimes* (Baltimore: Johns Hopkins University Press, 1978).

18. Robert D. Putnam, *Making Democracy Work: Civic Traditions in Modern Italy* (Princeton, NJ: Princeton University Press, 1993).

19. Ronald Inglehart, *Culture Shift in Advanced Industrial Societies* (Princeton, NJ: Princeton University Press, 1990), pp. 34–36; see also Almond and Verba, *Civic Culture*, ch. 11.

20. Sidney, Verba, Kay Schlozman, and Henry Brady, *Voice and Equality* (Cambridge, MA: Harvard University Press, 1996); Frances Piven and Richard Cloward, *Why Americans Don't Vote* (New York: Pantheon, 1989).

21. Many of these studies are reviewed by Mark I. Lichbach, "An Evaluation of 'Does Economic Inequality Breed Political Conflict' Studies," *World Politics* 41 (1989): 431–470. More recent references and analysis appear in T. Y. Wang, William Dixon, Edward N. Muller, and Mitchell A. Seligson, "Inequality and Political Violence Revisited," *American Political Science Review* 87, no. 4 (Dec. 1993): 979–993.

22. Robert Putnam, "Bowling Alone," *Journal of Democracy* 6 (1995): 65–78.

CHAPTER FIVE

Interest Aggregation and Political Parties

Interest aggregation is the activity in which the political demands of individuals and groups are combined into policy programs. For example, farmers' desires for higher crop prices, public preferences for lower taxes, environmentalists' demands for natural resource quality, and the interests of businesses often have to be balanced together in determining an economic policy program. A specific program becomes politically significant when it is backed up by substantial political resources, such as popular votes, commitments of campaign funds, seats in the legislature, positions of executive influence, media access, or even armed force.

Interest aggregation can occur in many ways. If an influential party leader or military dictator controls substantial political resources, his or her personal impact on interest aggregation may be considerable. Large nations usually develop more specialized organizations for the specific purpose of aggregating interests and resources behind a policy. Political parties are just such organizations.

Political parties are important in interest aggregation in democratic and in many nondemocratic systems. Each party (or its candidates) stands for a set of policies and tries to build a coalition of support for this program. In a democratic system two or more parties compete to gain support for their alternative policy programs. In authoritarian systems a single party or institution may try to mobilize citizens' support for its policies. In both systems interest aggregation may take place within a political party; for example, party leaders hear the demands of different groups—unions, consumers, party factions, business organizations—and create policy alternatives. In authoritarian systems the process is frequently covert and controlled, and interests are often mobilized to support the government, rather than the government responding to public interests.

The structural-functional approach also highlights the point that political parties may perform many different functions and that different structures may perform the interest aggregation function. Parties frequently perform political socialization, shaping the political culture as they organize thinking about political issues and strive to build support for their ideologies, issue positions, and candidates. Parties are involved in political recruitment as they mobilize voters and select would-be officeholders. They articulate interests of their own and transmit the demands of others. Governing parties are also involved in making public policy and even overseeing its implementation and adjudication. The distinctive and defining goal of a political party, its mobilization of support for policies and candidates, is especially related to interest aggregation. In this chapter we compare the role of parties to other structures in interest aggregation.

PERSONAL INTEREST AGGREGATION

One way in which political interests can be brought together in governing processes is through personal connections. A nearly universal political connection is the **patron-client network**—a structure in which a central officeholder, authority figure, or group provides benefits to supporters in exchange for their loyalty. It was the defining principle of feudalism. The king and his lords, the lord and his knights, the knight and his serfs and tenants—all were bound by ties of personal dependence and loyalty. The American political machines of Boss Tweed of New York or Richard Daley, Sr., of Chicago were similarly bound together by patronage and loyalty. Such networks are not confined to relationships cemented by patronage only. It is usual for a president of the United States to have a circle of personal confidants, a "brain trust" or "kitchen cabinet," bound to their chief by ideological and policy propensities as well as by ties of friendship.

The patron-client network is so common in politics that it seems to be like the cell in biology or the atom in physics—the primitive structure of all politics, the human interactions out of which larger and more complicated political structures are composed. Students of politics in all countries report such networks.

Contemporary patron-client theory was pioneered in studies of Asian politics, where this structure runs through the political processes of countries such as the Philippines, Indonesia, Thailand, Japan, and India.[1] Once these networks were discussed as part of the political process, parallels were found in Europe, Latin America, and most regions of the world. The political process in the kingdom of Saudi Arabia, or the Brunei Sultanate conform to many aspects of the patron-client model. Patron-client relationships involve the recruitment to political office, interest aggregation, policymaking, and policy implementing.

When interest aggregation is predominately performed by patron-client ties, this affects the style of the political process. It typically means a static political system. In such a system it is difficult to mobilize political resources behind unified policies of social change or to respond to crises, because taking action depends on ever-shifting agreements between many factional leaders (patrons).

INSTITUTIONAL INTEREST AGGREGATION

In modern societies, as citizens become aware of larger collective interests and have the resources and skills to work for them, personal networks tend to be regulated, limited, and incorporated within broader organizations. As we see in

Table 5.1   STRUCTURES PERFORMING INTEREST AGGREGATION IN SELECTED CONTEMPORARY NATIONS[a]

| | Extensiveness of Interest Aggregation by Actor | | | | |
Country	Patron-Client Networks	Associational Groups	Competitive Parties	Noncompetitive Parties	Military Forces
Britain	Low	High	High		Low
Brazil	Moderate	Moderate	Moderate		Moderate
China	Moderate	Low		High	High
Egypt	High	Low		Moderate	High
France	Low	Moderate	High		Low
Germany	Low	High	High		Low
India	High	Moderate	Moderate		Low
Japan	Moderate	High	High		Low
Mexico	Moderate	Moderate	Moderate	Moderate	Low
Nigeria	High	Low	Moderate		Moderate
Russia	Moderate	Low	Moderate		Moderate
United States	Low	Moderate	High		Low

[a]Extensiveness of interest aggregation rated as low, moderate, or high. Rating refers to broad-level performance and may vary in different issue areas and at different times. Blank implies not appropriate.

Table 5.1, the extensive reliance upon patron-client networks as a means of aggregating political interests is confined mainly to the less economically developed countries.

The subtle dividing line between interest articulation and aggregation can easily be crossed by organizations with powerful resources. Although often operating merely to express demands and support political contenders such as political parties, **associational groups** can occasionally wield sufficient resources to become contenders in their own right. For instance, the political power of the labor unions within the British Labour Party historically rested on the unions' ability to develop coherent policy positions and mobilize the votes of their members (who were formally represented in the party) to support those positions.

In some political systems, other institutional structures aggregate political interests. For instance, in many democratic countries, there are national decision-making bodies outside the normal legislative channels that possess the authority to make national policy in special areas. As we discussed in Chapter 4, a system of democratic corporatism can effectively aggregate the interests of both labor and business groups into economic policies. These arrangements include continuous political bargaining among organized labor, official representatives of business interests, political parties, and state bureaucracies. Such corporatist systems interconnect organizations that in other political systems play very different, often antagonistic, roles.

Institutional groups like bureaucratic and military factions can also be important interest aggregators. Indeed, the bureaucracy acts as an interest aggregator in most societies. Although established primarily to implement policies set by higher authorities, the bureaucracy may negotiate with various groups to identify their preferences or to mobilize their support. Government agencies may even be "captured" by interest groups and used to support their demands. The desire of bureaucrats to expand their organizations by discovering new problems and policies, as well as increasing their ability to solve problems in their areas of expertise, often leads them to create client support networks.

Military organizations, with their special control of physical force, have great potential power as interest aggregators. If the legitimacy of the government breaks down and all groups feel free to use coercion and violence to shape policies, then a united military can usually be decisive. By one account, around two-fifths of the world's nations have confronted military coup attempts at some time, and these were at least partially successful in changing leaders or policy in about a third of the nations. Less than half of these coup attempts, however, focused on general political issues and public policy. Most coups seemed motivated by grievances and fears that the professional interests of the military would be slighted by civil authorities.[2]

COMPETITIVE PARTY SYSTEMS
AND INTEREST AGGREGATION

In many contemporary political systems, parties are the primary structures of interest aggregation. However, we must keep in mind the critical distinction between **competitive party systems,** which primarily try to build electoral support, and noncompetitive or **authoritarian party systems,** which seek to direct society. This distinction does not depend on the closeness of electoral victory, or even on the number of parties. It depends on the ability of political parties to freely form and to compete for citizen support, and their winning citizen support as a prerequisite for controlling government. Thus a party can win most of the votes in a certain area, or even one national election, but nonetheless still be a competitive party. Its goals involve winning elections, either as a primary objective or as a means for policymaking; its dominance at the polls can be challenged by other parties. In short, its organization and goals aim at finding out what voters want, getting supporters involved, and representing these interests within the political process.

In analyzing the role of competitive parties in interest aggregation, we need to consider not only the individual party but also the structure of parties, electorates, electoral laws, and policymaking bodies that interact together. Typically, interest aggregation in a competitive party system takes place at several stages: within the individual parties, as the party chooses candidates and adopts policy proposals; through electoral competition, as voters give varying amounts of support to different parties; and through bargaining and coalition building in the legislature or executive.

Competitive Parties and Elections

At the first step, individual parties develop policy positions. Typically, the parties believe their positions are backed by a large or cohesive group of voters. In systems with only two parties, it is important for a party to win a majority, so targeting the "center" of the electorate is often strategically necessary to win the most votes.[3] In systems with many political parties, where no one group has much chance of winning a majority, it may be more reasonable to seek a distinctive and cohesive electoral base. Party policy positions may reflect the continuing linkages between a party and specific groups, such as labor unions, business associations, or religious and ethnic groups. Historical issue commitments and ideological traditions also play a role.[4]

In developing their policy proposals parties anticipate the way that election competition brings together party offerings and voter choices. One important element is the election law that determines how voter choices are translated into election outcomes.[5] In the United States, Britain, and many countries once influenced by Britain (such as India, Jamaica, and Canada), the legislative elections rules divide the country into many election districts. In each district, the candidate who has more votes than any other—a *plurality*—wins the election in the district. This simple, **single-member district plurality election rule** is often called "first past the post," a horse racing term, because the winner need only finish ahead of the others but not win a majority of the votes. This system seems obvious and natural to Americans, but it is rarely used in the democracies in Europe or in Latin America.

In contrast to the single-member district system, most democracies use some form of **proportional representation.** In these systems the country is divided into a few, large districts (or kept as a single national district). The competing parties offer lists of candidates, rather than a single candidate. The number of legislative representatives a party wins depends on the overall proportion of the votes it

---

Box 5.1 Duverger's Law

Duverger's Law is one of the best-known phenomena in political science. It reflects the tendency for plurality single-member district election rules to create "two-party" systems in the legislature, while proportional representation electoral systems generate multiple party systems. In single-member district systems, smaller parties that receive a minority of the vote across many districts receive little or no representation in Parliament. This discourages politicians from forming more parties and greatly underrepresents small parties that do compete. In Britain in the 1997 election, for example, 17 percent of the electorate voted for the Liberal Democratic Party, but it received only 7 percent of the seats in Parliament. Duverger's Law is named after the French political scientist Maurice Duverger, who recognized and analyzed it as a general rule.

Source: Maurice Duverger, *Political Parties: Their Organization and Activity in the Modern State,* [1954] trans. Barbara and Robert North, New York: John Wiley, 1963.

receives. If the entire country were a single legislative district, as in the Netherlands and Israel, a party receiving 5 percent of the vote would be awarded 5 percent of the seats in the national legislature.

The procedure that parties use to develop policy positions varies greatly from country to country and from party to party. In the United States the national party conventions held at each presidential election formalize the party's policy positions, both through the development of party platforms and, perhaps more important, through the selection of candidates committed to certain policies. In other countries, parties have more regular congresses, centralized party organizations issue party programs, and the parties develop manifestos for each national election.[6] Whatever the system, the final party position is usually a mixture of strategic electioneering and the aggregation of interests existing within the party.

The parties then offer their chosen candidates and policies to the electorate. They not only present candidates, but they also attempt to publicize them and mobilize electoral support through rallies, media advertising, door-to-door campaigning, and systematic efforts to locate sympathetic voters and get them to the polls. The act of voting by the individual citizen is one of the simplest and most frequently performed political actions. The citizen enters a voting booth and indicates support for a political candidate, party, or policy proposal. Elections are one of the few devices where diverse interests can be expressed equally and comprehensively. By casting ballots and aggregating these votes the citizens can make a collective decision about their future leaders and public policies.[7]

Figure 5.1 shows levels of **election turnout** in a variety of nations in the 1990s.[8] In Britain, Germany, and the United States, as in most of the world's democracies, most citizens are eligible to participate, and they may choose between competing political parties and candidates. In Western Europe at least three-quarters of the citizens usually vote; in the United States about half the electorate goes to the polls in presidential elections, and even fewer participate in most state and local elections.

Despite the simplicity and limitations of the vote, its implications can be profound. Shifts in citizen support can bring to power new coalitions committed to new policies. Citizens thus can influence interest aggregation and policymaking through their role in selecting elites.

In other countries, however, elections have other functions. Elections have been used to legitimate the government, even though the electoral outcome was predetermined, or to select a government, even while excluding many citizens. For instance, nearly all the communist nations of Eastern Europe utilized some form of elections to legitimate their governments. In these nations reported turnout routinely exceeded 98 percent of the electorate. At the same time, the government guaranteed the outcome in advance. Until 1990, voters in the Soviet Union could only vote for one candidate, who was always a nominee of the Communist Party. In some other communist nations, the voters could endorse a government slate of candidates or parties, but the parties had agreed upon the division of seats before the votes were counted. The very high levels of voter participation in these nations reflected government pressure on the public to ex-

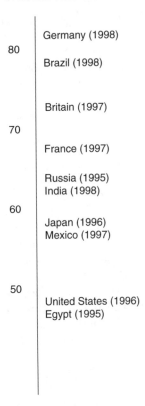

FIGURE 5.1   TURNOUT IN MOST RECENT NATIONAL ELECTIONS   *Source:* Inter-parliamentary Union.

Box 5.2   Election Upset!

Elections can often show that the public's preferences are much different from what political leaders expect. After the Khomeini revolution in 1979, Iran was governed by a conservative religious establishment and its political allies. The regime rolled back civil liberties and followed repressive policies in several areas, while claiming popular legitimacy for its actions. In 1997 Iranians went to the polls to select a president. The choices were between the conservative speaker of parliament and a moderate who few thought would do well. In a stunning upset the moderate, Mohammed Katami, won 69 percent of the vote. Katami has attempted to expand the freedoms enjoyed by Iranians, but he is constrained by the strong conservative and religious forces in Iran.

press their symbolic support for the regime. Elections and voting in these systems, as in national elections in China today, played a role in socializing and shaping citizens' attitudes, but had little to do with interest articulation or aggregation.[9]

Political scientists have shown that voting choices reflect a mix of motivations.[10] Many citizens evaluate past government policies or the future policy promises of the parties; issue-based voting enables the public to express their policy preferences. For other individuals, elections are a simple referendum on government performance; vote the rascals out if times are bad, and reelect them if times are good. In other cases, the charisma of a strong leader, or the incompetence of a weak one, can dominate an election. In each case, however, elections aggregate these diverse concerns to make a collective decision on the composition of government.

Figure 5.2 offers a comparative "snapshot" of interest aggregation by parties and voters in several democratic countries. It uses the device of the left-right scale, which acts as a summary of the issues that voters find most important. The figure shows where experts in each country placed its parties on a scale of numbers, with 1 identified as Left (or liberal in the United States) and 10 identified as Right (or conservative in the United States) in a 1993 survey. The height of the columns above the scale shows what percentage of the electorate voted for each party.

Several interesting patterns of **party-electoral aggregation** are illustrated by Figure 5.2. First, we can see that in the countries at the top of the figure, especially in the United States, most voters support only a few parties. Moreover, the parties are fairly close to the center of the continuum, where the bulk of voters place themselves. Democrats are somewhat to the left and Republicans somewhat to the right, but the left-right "gap" between them, although larger than it was 20 years ago, is still fairly small. If the distribution of voters were displayed in the figure, we would see a lot of overlap in the self-placement of voters supporting different parties. Thus aggregation implies concentration of political resources behind the fairly "centrist" policies of both parties.

In the countries toward the bottom of the figure, many parties received voter support. In France, for example, leftist voters divided themselves between the Communist and Socialist parties, and several other smaller leftist parties. The rightist vote was split between the Gaullist RPR and the more moderate UDF. In addition, there was significant support for an extreme right-wing party, the National Front. There is a very large distance between the left-most party (the Communists) and right-most party (the National Front). The dispersed aggregation of the party-electoral outcomes means that a much more diverse range of ideological interests may be represented in the legislature.

Britain, Germany, and Japan fell between these more extreme cases. Britain looked more like the United States in its pattern of voter support, but the parties were further apart and the smaller Liberal Democratic Party fell between them. The major German political parties were the SPD on the left and the CDU/CSU on the right, a small centrist party between them, an environmentally oriented Green party, and a reformed communist party (the PDS) on the left. Japan in 1993 presents yet another pattern. There was one large party well to the right, the LDP, which had dominated electoral politics in the postwar period, several smaller parties in the center (not all of which appear in the figure), and socialist

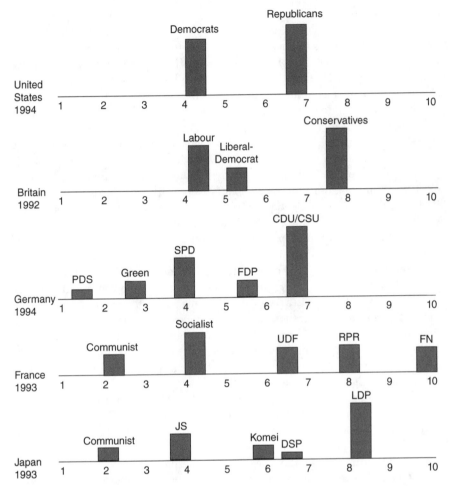

FIGURE 5.2   PLACEMENT OF PARTIES ON THE LEFT-RIGHT SCALE AND THEIR VOTER SUPPORT IN ELECTION *Source:* Party placements on the left-right scale are from the 1993 survey of country experts reported in John Huber and Ronald Inglehart, "Expert Interpretations of Party Space and Party Locations in 42 Societies," *Party Politics* 1 (1995): 73–111. The height of the bar represents the percentage of the vote won by the party in the election closest to the 1993 survey.

and communist parties towards the left end of the political spectrum. The Japanese "snapshot" of 1993 catches the party system at one moment in a decade of remarkable changes, which were to include a partial and temporary unification of the opposition parties, a splintering of the LDP, and its loss and recapture of government control.

Competitive Parties in Government

If a competitive party wins control of the legislature and the executive, it will (if unified) be able to pass and implement its policies. Sometimes this control emerges directly from the electoral process, as a single party wins a majority of the vote. In many countries the election laws are designed to benefit the largest party to help it gain the votes to govern. If these distortions are sufficient, less than 50 percent of the vote may be converted into more than 50 percent of the legislative seats. Such "artificial" legislative majorities have been the rule in countries with "first past the post" electoral systems, such as Britain.[11]

For example, in the 1980s and 1990s none of the legislature majorities won by either the Conservative Party or the Labour Party in Britain were based on support of a majority of voters. Margaret Thatcher's Conservative Party won a solid majority of legislative seats in 1983 and 1987 with the backing of only about 42 percent of the voters. With almost exactly the same level of support in the 1997 elections, Tony Blair and the Labour Party won nearly two-thirds of the seats in Parliament. In all these elections, the quarter of the electorate supporting the smaller parties received only a handful of legislative seats.

In other countries, multiparty competition means that elections do not yield single-party majorities, but party coalitions formed before the election may still offer the voters a direct choice of future governments. During the election, a group of parties may encourage mutual support from their voters, agree to run candidates in different districts in order to maximize their combined vote, or agree to govern together if they jointly win a majority of legislative seats. Preelection coalition governments are similar to majoritarian governments because they can provide voters with clear targets if they choose to reward or punish the incumbents of government. Voters thus possess the ability to choose the direction of government policy through party and electoral aggregation.

Such aggregation of policy preferences through elections is important because parties generally fulfill their electoral promises when they gain control of government.[12] For example, British parties take pride in carrying out their promises while in office. When Socialist and Social Democratic governments have come to power in Europe, they have tended to expand the size and efforts of the governmental sector; conservative parties have generally retarded the growth of government programs. Republicans and Democrats in the United States also have been fairly responsible in keeping their promises. However, parties that have been out of office a long time or that have developed radical programs often find it difficult to implement their programs when they eventually come to power—as reflected, for example, in Margaret Thatcher's inability to implement some of the more conservative elements of her party's program.

When elections do not create a majority party (or preelection coalition), then a new government is formed by postelection negotiations among political parties and their leaders. This is a common aspect of politics in many party systems, such as those in the Netherlands and Belgium.[13] In these nations interests are not aggregated at the level of elections, because the election does not determine the government. Instead, the aggregation of interests occurs at the governmental level when a coalition is negotiated. (Also see the discussion in the Chapter 6, below, and Figure 6.2.)

The aggregation of interests at the governmental level, rather than the electoral level, can have both costs and benefits. On the one hand, when coalitions formed at the elite level determine government policy, voters may be frustrated and disillusioned, feeling that elections do not directly define government outcomes. In addition, because interest aggregation occurs among political elites this means that new elite coalitions can form on different issues. This can be confusing to citizens (and even informed observers). It is difficult for people to assign clear responsibility for government policy when power is shifting and widely shared. This situation lessens the value of the vote as an instrument to shape future governments or to punish parties held responsible for undesirable policy.[14]

On the other hand, the aggregation of interests at the governmental level can mean that voters for all parties, not just the election winners, are represented in policymaking. Such representation can be especially important for minority interests. All citizens hold minority opinions on some issues, and some are minorities on many issues. If the rules of election and representation are fair, the possibility that their representatives can influence policy between elections is a valuable protection for minority interests. Finally, even elected governments that won a majority of votes, which few elected governments have, typically lack majority support for all of their policy proposals. So a flexible pattern of interest aggregation at the legislative level, if based on fair representation, may benefit the nation as a whole. Bargaining between fairly represented groups may even increase the possibility that policies reflect different majorities on different issues. The role of elections as instruments of representation may increase through a system of aggregating interests within the government, even though the role of elections as instruments of accountability may diminish.[15]

Classifying Competitive Party Systems

Figure 5.3 classifies examples of each type of competitive party system. Majoritarian and multiparty systems are distinguished by the number of political parties. The number of parties influences legislative activity and the business of forming government. The **majoritarian party systems** are either dominated by just two parties, as in the United States, or they have two substantial parties and election laws that usually create legislative majorities for one of them, as in Britain. The purely **multiparty systems** have combinations of parties, voter support, and election laws that virtually ensure that no single party wins a legislative majority. Interest aggregation by party bargaining after the election is critical for shaping policy directions. Germany and France, as we have already mentioned, are among the multiparty systems in which voter support of party coalitions at the electoral level has a major impact on forming governments and policies.

The degree of antagonism or polarization among the parties influences the degree of government stability. In a **consensual party system** the parties commanding most of the legislative seats are not too far apart on policies and have a reasonable amount of trust in each other and in the political system.[16] These are typically party systems like those shown toward the top of Figure 5.2. Bargaining may be intense and politics exciting in these systems, but it seldom threatens the system itself.

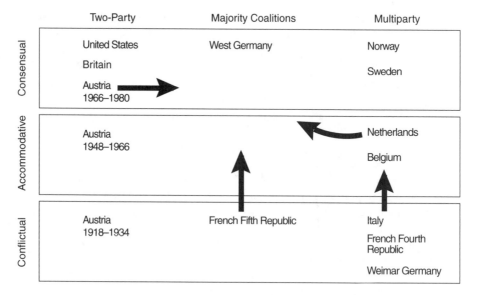

FIGURE 5.3   CLASSIFYING PARTY SYSTEMS BY NUMBER OF PARTIES AND AN-
TAGONISM BETWEEN PARTIES

In a **conflictual party system,** the legislature is dominated by parties that are
far apart on issues or are highly antagonistic toward each other and the political system, such as the Russian party system. If a party system has mixed characteristics of a
certain kind—that is, both consensual and conflictual—we classify it as **consociational,** or accommodative. Arend Lijphart has used those terms to describe party systems in which political leaders are able to bridge the intense differences between antagonistic voters.[17]

The United States and Britain are contemporary examples of relatively consensual majoritarian party systems. They are not perfect two-party systems. In addition to the Labour and Conservative parties, Britain has the Scottish Nationalist
Party, a smaller Welsh party, and the centrist Liberal Democratic Party. However,
in Britain a single party usually wins a legislative majority and controls the legislature and the executive with disciplined party voting. The United States has intermittently had third-party movements and candidates, but they have rarely won
legislative representation. The shifting programs of presidential party candidates
alter the degree of consensus from election to election. Moreover, the looser cohesion of American parties and the frequently divided control of legislature and
executive lead to postelection bargaining that is similar to consensual multiparty
systems. Good examples of consensual multiparty systems are found in Norway
and Sweden. In these countries there are four or five parties—socialists, agrar-
ian/center, liberals, conservatives, small communist movements. A subset of these
parties has usually been able to construct long-lived governments, singly or in
coalition.

Austria between 1918 and 1934 is the best example of a majoritarian conflictual party system. Antagonism between the Socialist Party and the other parties was

so intense that in the mid-1930s it produced a brief civil war. The Austrian experience also illustrates how party systems can change over time. After World War II, the leaders of the two major parties negotiated an elaborate coalition agreement of mutual power sharing—checks and balances—to control its conflicts. After some 20 years of the consociational "Grand Coalition," party antagonism had declined to the point that more normal majority politics could be tolerated, although some consociational elements remained. Later the Austrian party system moved toward a consensual system, with some single-party majorities and some coalitions. Most recently, the Freedom Party, a controversial populist party of the far right, won substantial support by attacking the consensual style of the party system. The party's entry into a coalition government after the 1999 election has damaged Austria's relations with other members of the European Union, because of the party's extreme political views.

France, Italy, and Weimar Germany are good historical examples of conflictual multiparty systems, with powerful Communist parties on the left and conservative or Fascist movements on the right. Cabinets had to form out of centrist movements, which were themselves divided on many issues, thus making for instability, poor government performance, and loss of citizen confidence in democracy. These factors contributed to the overthrow of democracy in Weimar Germany, the collapse of the French Fourth Republic, and government instability and citizen alienation from politics in Italy.

More recently, some of the emerging party systems in Central and Eastern Europe have tended to follow this same course. For instance, in the 1995 parliamentary elections in Russia, 43 parties appeared on the ballot—ranging from unreformed communists on the left to nationalist parties on the right—and seven parties won representation in Parliament. The hope is that this is a transitional period as a new party system is established, not a precursor to the instability that has haunted other polarized party systems.[18]

The mixed consociational system can enable a deeply divided nation to find a way to peaceful democratic development. In the Netherlands, for example, the leaderships of competing movements found bases of accommodation that provide mutual guarantees to the various groups. In Austria and Lebanon after World War II, suspicious and hostile groups—the socialists and Catholics in Austria, and the Christians and Muslims in Lebanon—worked out a set of consociational understandings making it possible for stable governments to be formed. Austria's accommodation was based on a two-party system and Lebanon's on many small, personalistic religious parties. After 1975, however, Lebanon was penetrated and fragmented by the Middle Eastern conflict and fell victim to civil war.

South Africa adopted consociational practices in its transition to democracy. Leaders of the major political parties of the white minority and two major segments of the black majority negotiated (with great difficulty) arrangements for a democratic election and a multiparty coalition government to follow it. A typically consociational feature of the "Interim Constitution" of the transition guaranteed a share in power and government—cabinet posts—to all parties winning over 5 percent of the vote in the election. As the contrasting examples of Austria and Lebanon suggest, such practices (and the ability even to agree to attempt them) offer hope but no guarantees of long-term success to deeply divided democracies.

All this suggests that, although the number of parties affects the degree of political stability, the degree of antagonism among parties is more important. Where multiparty systems consist of relatively moderate antagonists, stability and effective performance seem possible. Where systems consist of highly antagonistic elements, collapse and civil war are ever-present possibilities, regardless of the number of parties. When crises develop, the commitment of party leaders to work together to defend democracy can be critical for its survival. It may be easier, however, to arrange such commitments in a multiparty, representational setting.[19] Some of the new democracies of Eastern Europe and Latin America and Asia, especially those divided by language or ethnicity, face similar challenges.

AUTHORITARIAN PARTY SYSTEMS

Authoritarian party systems are also specialized interest aggregation structures. They deliberately attempt to develop policy proposals and to mobilize support for them, but they do so in a completely different way from competitive party systems. With authoritarian party systems, aggregation takes place within the ranks of the party or in interactions with business groups, landowners, and institutional groups in the bureaucracy or military. The citizens have no opportunity to shape aggregation by choosing between party alternatives.

Authoritarian party systems can be distinguished according to the degree of top-down control within the party and the degree of the party's control over other groups in society. At one extreme is the **exclusive governing party,** which insists on control over political resources by the party leadership. It recognizes no legitimate interest aggregation by groups within the party nor does it permit any free activity by social groups, citizens, or other government agencies. It penetrates the entire society and mobilizes support for policies developed at the top. Its policies are legitimated by an encompassing political ideology that claims to know the true interests of the citizens, whatever their immediate preferences.[20] At the other extreme is the **inclusive governing party** that recognizes and attempts to coordinate various social groups in the society. It accepts and aggregates certain autonomous interests, while repressing others and forbidding any serious challenges to its own control.

Exclusive Governing Parties

Few parties have long maintained the absolute central control, penetration, and ideological mobilization of the authoritarian model. However, the ruling Communist parties of the USSR before 1985, of Eastern Europe before 1989, and of China, North Korea, Vietnam, and Cuba today certainly fall toward the controlling end of the authoritarian party scale. The Chinese regime, for example, typically has not recognized the legitimacy of any large groups within Chinese society. Interest articulation by individuals, within bounds, may be permitted; the mobilization of wide support before the top elite has decided on policy is not permitted.[21]

Even at the stage of authoritarian mobilization, the exclusive governing party may experience more internal aggregation than is commonly recognized or legitimately permitted. Internally, various groups may coalesce around such interests as region or industry, or behind leaders of policy factions. Either openly or covertly, beneath the supposedly united front, power struggles may erupt in times of crisis, with different leaders mobilizing backing for themselves and their positions. Succession crises are particularly likely to generate such power struggles, as demonstrated at the death of Stalin in the Soviet Union and Mao Zedong in China. In addition, the Chinese Communist Party several times has had to rely on the army, even on coalitions of regional army commanders, to sustain its control.

Whether thoroughly authoritarian or merely exclusive, the penetrating and controlling single-party systems can play important roles in mobilizing support for policies. An unchallenged ideological focus provides legitimacy and coherence; the party penetrates and organizes most social structures in the name of that ideology and in accordance with centralized policies.

As a tool designed for unified mobilization, the exclusive governing party has been used by many leaders who were committed to massive social change. A party that successfully mobilized a colonial people behind independence, for example, might be used to change an underdeveloped society. As the experiences of many new nations have shown, however, the creation of an exclusive governing party as an agent for social transformation is extremely difficult. The seduction of power regularly leads to political excesses that are not checked by ideology or competitive democratic politics. The exclusive governing parties in some African states also had limited capacity to control society. Furthermore, the loss of confidence in Marxist-Leninist ideology and in the Soviet model of authoritarian development led all eight of the African regimes that had once invoked it to abandon that approach by the early 1990s.[22]

As exclusive governing parties age, many enter a stage of more "mature" authoritarianism that maintains control but places less emphasis on mobilization. Finally, as shown by the collapse of communism in the former Soviet Union and Eastern Europe, if and when the party leaders lose faith in the unifying ideology, it may be difficult to maintain party coherence.

Inclusive Governing Parties

Among the preindustrial nations, especially in nations with notable ethnic and tribal divisions, the more successful authoritarian systems have seemed to be inclusive. These systems recognize the autonomy of social, cultural, and economic groups and try to incorporate them or bargain with them, rather than control and remake them. In the more successful African one-party systems, such as Kenya and Tanzania, aggregation around personalistic, factional, and ethnic-based groups was permitted within decentralized party organizations.

Inclusive party systems have sometimes been labeled authoritarian corporatist systems. Like the democratic corporatist systems (see Chapter 4), some of these systems encourage the formation of large organized interest groups that can bargain with each other and the state. Unlike the democratic corporatist systems, however, these authoritarian systems provide no political resources directly to the citizens. Independent protest and political activity outside of official channels are suppressed. They permit only limited autonomous demands within the ranks of the party and by groups associated with it.

The degree of legitimate aggregation permitted in the inclusive authoritarian systems may be substantial and take many forms. The party typically tries to gather various social groups under the general party umbrella and negotiate with social groups and institutions outside the party. Some of these inclusive parties have attempted aggressive programs of social change. Others have been primarily arenas for aggregating various social and institutional interests. Some inclusive party governments have even permitted other parties to offer candidates in elections, as long as they have no real chance of winning. The PRI in Mexico has been a typical inclusive governing party.

The relative stability of some inclusive authoritarian party systems should not obscure their frequent failures to build a stable governing structure. In many countries these parties coexist in uneasy and unstable coalitions with the armed forces and the

---

Box 5.3   Mexico's PRI

One of the oldest and the most elaborately inclusive authoritarian parties is the Partido Revolucionario Institucional (PRI) in Mexico. The PRI dominated the political process and gave other parties no realistic chances of winning elections for more than 50 years. The PRI maintained popular support after the creation of a broad coalition within the party by Lázaro Cárdenas in the 1930s; it was also careful to control the counting of the ballots. Its actions were not shaped by electoral competition, at least until recently. However, the party incorporated many social groups within it, with separate sectors for labor, agrarian, and popular interests. While some discontent was suppressed, other dissatisfied individuals were deliberately enticed into the party. The party also gave informal recognition to rather distinct and well-organized political factions grouped behind such figures as former presidents. Various Mexican leaders mobilized their factions within the PRI and in other important groups not directly affiliated with it, such as big business interests. Bargaining was particularly important every six years when the party chose a new presidential nominee. The legal provision that the incumbent president could not succeed himself guaranteed some turnover of elites and may have facilitated more legitimate and open internal bargaining. Recently, however, rising discontent has illustrated the difficulties in coordinating all interests through a single party. The urban and rural poor who have not shared in Mexico's general growth have joined with others who want a more fully democratic system. An armed uprising of peasant guerrillas in early 1994 shocked the political establishment and led to more promises of genuine democratic competition. Legislative elections in 1997 were more open than earlier contests, and ended the 70-year rule of the PRI.

civilian bureaucracy. In some countries the party has become relatively unimportant window dressing for a military regime or personal tyranny.[23] Seldom have these parties been able to solve the economic or ethnic problems that face their nation.

These political systems were often created by unifying struggle against colonialism, and their viability has declined as colonialism has become more distant. As memories of the independence struggle have faded and the leaders of independence movements have departed, the ties of ideology and experience that held these parties together have weakened. This has led to a general loss of legitimacy for the single-party model. In some cases the failure of authoritarian parties has permitted the emergence of party competition. In others the consequence has been a resort to naked coercion by government agencies or private forces, with the military serving as final arbiter.

THE MILITARY AND INTEREST AGGREGATION

After World War II, parliamentary and democratic governments were instituted among most of the nations of the Third World. In many countries the lack of effectiveness and authority of these civil governments led to their breakdown and their replacement by **military governments.** With its control of instruments of force, and in the absence of a strong constitutional tradition, the military was an effective contender for power. Even in those regimes where civilian authority was reestablished, the military generally constituted a significant power contender, and exercised influence in the political process. In Brazil, for example, the military played a crucial interest aggregation role in the democratic processes before 1964 and was the dominant aggregating and policymaking actor for the next 20 years. In many other nations, including Syria, Pakistan, Indonesia, Guinea, Zaire, Paraguay, and Haiti, the military has been the dominant, or at least a major, interest aggregator. In fact, the armed forces are the dominant interest aggregation structure in over one-fifth of the world's regimes, including almost half of those in Africa.

The military's virtual monopoly of coercive resources gives it great potential power. Thus, when agreement fails on aggregation either through democratic or authoritarian party systems, the military may emerge by default as the only force able to maintain orderly government. The soldiers then remain the basic force underpinning the personal tyranny of a civilian president or a military council. Or the armed forces may use their power to further institutional or even ideological objectives. Military rulers may try to create military and/or bureaucratic versions of authoritarian corporatism, linking organized groups and the state bureaucracy with the military as final arbiter of disagreement. They may undertake "defensive" modernization in alliance with business groups or even undertake more radical modernization. In Latin America almost all the corporatist versions of authoritarian aggregation have had a strong military component and only rarely a dominating role for the authoritarian party.

The major limitation of the military in interest aggregation is that their internal structures are not designed to mobilize support across a range of issues or outside their coercive control. The military is primarily organized for the downward processing of commands under threat of coercion. It is not set up to aggregate internal differences, to build a compromise, or to mobilize wide support of

---

Box 5.4   Trying To Make Democracy Work

The military government in Nigeria responded to the democratization wave of the 1990s by initiating state-level elections in 1991, and federal legislative elections in 1992. However, the military mandated a restricted process under which politicians from former civilian regimes were disqualified (as tainted by corruption). Voters were thus left with a choice of only two parties, both created by the government. Turnout was adversely affected by a spreading cynicism about the meaningfulness of the vote. Citizens' doubts were confirmed when the military annulled the presidential election of June 1993, even before the votes were announced, and appointed an Interim National Government to organize new elections. In November 1993 a military coup by Defense Minister General Sani Abacha overturned the Interim National Government, banned all political activity, dissolved the legislature, dismissed the 30 elected state governments, and thus ended even a limited role of elections in interest representation. In spring 1999 the military government allowed an election for president. The victor was a former army general, who is now trying to implement democratic reforms.

---

government policy. Moreover, military organizations are not easily adapted to communicate with social groups outside the command hierarchy. Thus the military lacks many of the advantages in mobilizing voluntary support held by party systems. These internal limitations may be less serious when the military is dealing with common grievances and putting pressure on—or seizing power from—incumbent authorities. These limitations become a major problem, however, when a military government needs to mobilize backing for economic development or other broad government programs. For these reasons military governments frequently prove unstable, are forced to share power with other institutions, or encourage the formation of cooperating authoritarian parties.

TRENDS IN INTEREST AGGREGATION

We have noted in Chapter 4 and elsewhere that the democratic trend in the world gained important momentum with the collapse of authoritarian regimes in Eastern Europe at the end of the 1980s. Figure 5.4 classifies the world's regimes by the predominant interest aggregation structure at three points: the end of the 1970s, the end of the 1980s, and the late 1990s. The percentages should be viewed as estimates, often based on limited information. But the figure provides a rough idea of the frequency of the three major forms: competitive parties, single-party, and military-dominated regimes. The "residual" category of traditional governments consists mostly of small kingdoms in the Middle East, South Asia, and the Pacific.

In 1978 about one-third of the world's 150-plus independent countries had competitive party and electoral systems as their predominant interest aggregation struc-

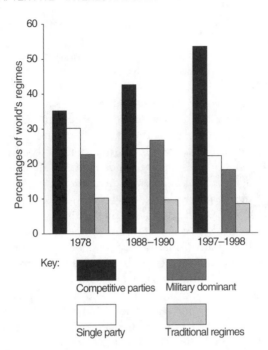

FIGURE   5.4   CHANGE   IN   PREDOMINANT   INTEREST   AGGREGATION STRUCTURE—MOVING TOWARD DEMOCRACY IN THE WORLD? *Source:* Adapted from Raymond D. Gastil, *Freedom in the World 1979, 1988–1989, 1997–1998* (New York: Freedom House, 1979, 1989, 1998).

tures. These regimes were the main form in Western Europe and North America (including the Caribbean), not uncommon in Latin America and Asia, but rare in Africa and the Middle East. Nearly as many countries had some versions of a single-party regime. Single-party systems were the main form in Eastern Europe and relatively common in Africa and Asia. In slightly less than a quarter of the countries the military-dominated interest aggregation, either formally (military governments) or in practice (military-dominated civilian governments). The military-dominated regimes accounted for about a third or more of the countries in Africa and Latin America.

A decade later, the trend was obviously away from single-party governments. Across the world they declined from 30 to 24 percent of the regimes, although still accounting for nearly 40 percent of African nations. As we already know, the decline of exclusive governing party regimes was even more striking. As expected, the democratic trend toward competitive party and electoral systems was notable, with an increase from 36 to 41 percent of the world's political systems (and more experimenting with some competition). The proportion of military governments actually increased slightly, from 23 to 26 percent of the world's countries.

The trend toward democracy took off beginning in 1989 with the dramatic changes occurring in Eastern Europe, and new pressures for democracy in the developing world. The proportion of competitive regimes is now near 60 percent, with declines in the proportions of all other forms. The majority of the remaining single-party systems are loosely corporatist, with a few exceptions such as China and Cuba. The decline of ideological underpinnings for authoritarian governments, as well as the withdrawal of support from the Soviet Union, has contributed to this trend, especially in Africa.

Many African nations moved toward a more democratic and free system during the 1990s. However, several nations remain holdouts against this trend. In Kenya, for example, President Daniel Arap Moi reluctantly gave in to multiparty elections, but was then reelected with less than a majority of the vote against a badly split opposition. Sudan is under a fundamentalist Muslim regime that does not admit to the legitimacy of democratic institutions. Somalia remains divided and undemocratic after a nearly decade-long civil war.

Perhaps in deference to the decline in the legitimacy of authoritarianism, the military is now more likely to dominate from behind the scenes than through direct rule, especially in Latin America. Latin America also has experienced the genuine replacement of military regimes by competitive party regimes in such important countries as Argentina, Brazil, Chile, and Uruguay. Although one-party systems have been opened up in Africa, the proportion of military-dominated governments increased from 36 percent in the 1970s to 46 percent in the 1980s, and an ongoing 30 percent in the late 1990s. Of 13 military regimes enumerated in the world in 1998, 12 were in Africa. The recent casualties to military intervention include competitive governments in Sierra Leone and the Republic of the Congo (formerly Zaire). Although the era of confidence in the military as a solution to development seems to have passed, military domination remains a likely outcome when other types of government are unable to solve internal conflicts.

Where there has been "backsliding" on the road to democracy, such as the temporary shutting down of the Peruvian Parliament by President Fujimori, or the imposition of tight control on political activity in Burma, the military has usually been at least part of the antidemocratic movement. With such examples in mind, we cannot assume that the democratizing trend will continue relentlessly. Multiparty regimes that seem unable to cope with economic and social problems often lose their legitimacy. Such is now the challenge facing the new competitive regimes of Eastern Europe and the former Soviet Union, as well as the Third World.

SIGNIFICANCE OF INTEREST AGGREGATION

How interests are aggregated is an important determinant of what a country's government does for and to its citizens. The factors that most interest us about government and politics—stability, revolution, participation, welfare, equality, liberty, security—are very much consequences of the pattern of interest aggregation. Through interest aggregation, the desires and demands of citizens are converted into a few policy alternatives. The consequence is that many possible policies have been eliminated and only a few remain. In addition, this means that political resources have been accumulated in the hands of the relatively few political actors who decide policy. The policy alternatives that reach this stage are serious matters for political consideration because they have the backing of significant sectors of society. A policy alternative such as the government taking over the steel industry production in the United States has never been "serious," because no group of leaders with major political resources has favored it, even though such policies have been implemented elsewhere.

Narrowing and combining policy preferences are easily seen in the working of competitive party systems. Of the many possible policy preferences, only a few are backed by parties after the parties choose leaders and establish election platforms. In the elections, voters support some of these parties and thus shape the strength of party representation in the legislature. Even at the legislative stage, some further consolidation and coalition building takes place between party factions or party groups. At some point, however, most policy options have been eliminated from consideration. Either they were never backed by parties or the parties supporting them did badly in the elections.

In noncompetitive party systems, military governments, and monarchies, aggregation works differently, but with the similar effect of narrowing policy options. It may be that on some issues, aggregation will virtually determine policy, as when a military government or a faction of an authoritarian party can decide the government's program. In other cases the legislative assembly, military council, or party politburo may contain several factions of similar strength that negotiate to determine policy outcomes.

One characteristic of interest aggregation in all systems is its degree of polarization. In Chapter 3 we discussed consensual and conflictual political cultures. We mentioned that the United States, Germany, and Britain were consensual, with most citizens preferring moderate positions. Italy, France, and Russia were more polarized cultures, with larger concentrations of citizens on the left and fewer in the center.

Ordinarily, we expect polarization in the policymaking body to resemble polarization in the political culture. In a relatively consensual society like Germany, the parliament is made up of mainly moderate and tolerant parties. In more conflictual Italy, the stalemated Parliament was long dominated by two parties very distant from each other—the Communists and the Christian Democrats.

But politics shapes its environment as well as reflecting it. Interest aggregation often alters the amount of polarization that the political culture projects into policymaking. That is one reason why politics is so fascinating. Well-organized and well-led political parties might, at least for a while, be able to dominate politics and limit the strength of extremist groups in the legislature, as in the consociational model we mentioned earlier. Conversely, well-organized extremists might be able to appeal to the fears and prejudices of some groups and get their support at the polls, thus gaining more legislative strength in an otherwise consensual country.

Of course, authoritarian interest aggregation tends to create political power structures that do not reflect popular opinion. In a highly divided and conflict-ridden society, such unrepresentativeness may be viewed as a great virtue. Leaders of military coups in many nations justify their overthrow of party governments by claiming to depolarize politics and rid the nation of conflict it cannot afford. Similarly, heads of authoritarian parties typically claim that their nation must concentrate all its energies and resources on common purposes and that party competition would be too polarizing.

One justification for democracy is that it leads political leaders to act as the people wish. In a polarized political culture, the cost of interest aggregation that reflects division and uncertainty may be seen as too high a price to pay for citizen control. As the frequent instability in authoritarian and military governments indicates, however, it may be easier to do away with the appearance of polarization than the reality. Cultural divisions may end up being reflected through military factions or intraparty groups, instead of through party competition, and the citizens may end up without either freedom and participation or stability.

KEY TERMS

associational groups	election turnout	multiparty systems
authoritarian party systems	exclusive governing party	party-electoral aggregation
competitive party systems	inclusive governing party	patron-client network
conflictual party systems	institutional groups	plurality election rules
consensual party systems	interest aggregation	proportional representation
consociational party systems	majoritarian party systems	single-member districts
	military government	

SUGGESTED READINGS

Converse, Philip E., and Roy Pierce. *Political Representation in France.* Cambridge, MA: Harvard University Press, 1986.

Cox, Gary. *Making Votes Count: Strategic Coordination in the World's Electoral Systems.* Cambridge: Cambridge University Press, 1997.

Downs, Anthony. *An Economic Theory of Democracy.* New York: Harper and Row, 1957.

Gallagher, Michael, Michael Laver, and Peter Mair. *Representative Government in Western Europe,* 2nd ed. New York: McGraw-Hill, 1995.

Jackson, Robert H., and Carl G. Rosberg. *Personal Rule in Black Africa.* Berkeley: University of California Press, 1982.

Kitschelt, Herbert. *The Transformation of European Social Democracy.* New York: Cambridge University Press, 1994.

Laver, Michael, and Norman Schofield. *Multiparty Government.* New York: Oxford University Press, 1990.

Lijphart, Arend. *Democracy in Plural Societies.* New Haven, CT: Yale University Press, 1977.

———. *Electoral Systems and Party Systems.* New York: Oxford University Press, 1994.

———. *Patterns of Democracy.* New Haven, CT: Yale University Press, 1999.

Linz, Juan J., and Alfred Stepan, eds. *The Breakdown of Democratic Regimes.* Baltimore, MD: Johns Hopkins University Press, 1978.

Nordlinger, Eric A. *Soldiers in Politics: Military Coups and Governments.* Englewood Cliffs, NJ: Prentice-Hall, 1976.

O'Donnell, Guillermo, Philippe C. Schmitter, and Laurence Whitehead. *Transitions from Authoritarian Rule: Prospects for Democracy.* Baltimore, MD: Johns Hopkins University Press, 1986.

Perlmutter, Amos. *Modern Authoritarianism: A Comparative Institutional Analysis.* New Haven, CT: Yale University Press, 1981.

Powell, G. Bingham, Jr. *Contemporary Democracies: Participation, Stability and Violence.* Cambridge, MA: Harvard University Press, 1982.

———. *Elections as Instruments of Democracy.* New Haven, CT: Yale University Press, 2000.

Riker, William H. *Liberalism Against Populism.* San Francisco, CA: W. H. Freeman, 1982.

Sartori, Giovanni. *Parties and Party Systems.* Cambridge, England: Cambridge University Press, 1976.

Von Beyme, Klaus. *Political Parties in Western Europe.* New York: St. Martin's, 1985.

Ware, Alan. *Citizens, Parties, and the State.* Princeton, NJ: Princeton University Press, 1988.

NOTES

1. Luis Roniger and Ayse Günes-Ayata, eds., *Democracy, Clientelism, and Civil Society* (Boulder, CO: Lynne Rienner, 1994); S. Eisenstadt and L. Roniger, *Patrons, Clients and Friends* (Cambridge, England: Cambridge University Press, 1984); Lucian W. Pye, *Asian Power and Politics* (Cambridge, MA: Harvard University Press, 1985); Martin Shefter, "Patronage and Its Opponents," in *Political Parties and the State* (Princeton, NJ: Princeton University Press, 1994); see also the studies of the personal networks of leaders in the politics of the former Soviet Union, such as T. H. Rigby and Rokdan Harasimin, *Leadership Selection and Patron Client Relations in the USSR and Yugoslavia* (Beverly Hills, CA: Sage, 1981).
2. William Thompson, *The Grievances of Military Coup-Makers* (Beverly Hills, CA: Sage, 1973).
3. The extensive literature on party strategies owes its largest debt to Anthony Downs, *An Economic Theory of Democracy* (New York: Harper and Row, 1957). More generally, see Dennis C. Mueller, *Public Choice* (Cambridge, England: Cambridge University Press, 1979) and Gary Cox, *Making Votes Count* (New York: Cambridge University Press, 1997.)
4. Russell J. Dalton, Scott C. Flanagan, and Paul Allen Beck, eds., *Electoral Change in Advanced Industrial Societies* (Princeton, NJ: Princeton University Press, 1984); Mark Franklin et al., *Electoral Change* (Cambridge, England: Cambridge University Press, 1992); Herbert Kitschelt, *The Transformation of European Social Democracy* (New York: Cambridge University Press, 1994); Wolfgang C. Mueller and Kaare Strom, *Policy, Office or Votes? How Political Parties in Western Europe Make Hard Decisions* (New York: Cambridge University Press, 1999).
5. Maurice Duverger, *Political Parties: Their Organization and Activity in the Modern State,* [1954] trans. Barbara and Robert North (New York: Wiley, 1963). For more recent discussions of electoral systems and consequences, see Rein Taagepera and Matthew Shugart, *Seats and Votes* (New Haven, CT: Yale University Press, 1989); Cox, *Making Votes Count;* and the references in Note 11 below.
6. Ian Budge, David Robertson, and Derek Hearl, *Ideology, Strategy and Party Change: Spatial Analyses of Post-War Election Programmes in 19 Democracies* (New York: Cambridge University Press, 1987); Richard Katz and Peter Mair, eds., *How Parties Organize: Change and Adaptation in Party Organizations in Western Democracies* (Thousand Oaks: Sage Publications, 1994).
7. Despite their virtues, elections cannot solve perfectly all the complex problems in fairly aggregating interests. For example, giving each citizen one vote does not take account of the varying intensities with which different people may hold their opinions. Moreover, a very large literature in economics and political science has demonstrated various problems, notably that for some distributions of preferences about three or more alternatives, there is no fair rule for aggregating the votes to select a single, unequivocally best, outcome ("Arrow's Paradox"). Important original works in this literature were Duncan Black, "On the Rationale of Group Decision Making," *Journal of Political Economy* 56 (1948) 23–34; and Kenneth Arrow, *Social Choice and Individual*

Values (New Haven, CT: Yale University Press, 1951). For an accessible, although controversial, discussion of some implications for political science, see William H. Riker, *Liberalism Against Populism* (San Francisco: W. H. Freeman, 1982). More recently, see Kenneth A. Shepsle and Mark S. Bonchek, *Analyzing Politics: Rationality, Behavior and Institutions* (N.Y.: W.W. Norton, 1997), Part II.

8. Richard Topf, "Electoral Participation," in H. Klingemann and D. Fuchs, eds., *Citizens and the State* (Oxford, England: Oxford University Press, 1995); Mark Franklin, "Electoral Participation," in Lawrence LeDuc, Richard Niemi, and Pippa Norris, eds, *Comparing Democracies: Elections and Voting in Global Perspective* (Beverly Hills: Sage Publications, 1996), pp. 216–235.

9. However, the initiation of semi-competitive elections for Chinese village leadership positions since 1987 has in some areas had significant impact on the correspondence of opinions between citizens and local leaders. See Melanie Manion, " The Electoral Connection in the Chinese Countryside," *American Political Science Review* 90 (1996): 736–748.

10. Russell J. Dalton, *Citizen Politics: Public Opinion and Political Parties in Advanced Industrial Democracies*, 2nd ed. (Chatham, NJ: Chatham House, 1996); Philip E. Converse and Roy Pierce, *Representation in France* (Cambridge, MA: Harvard University Press, 1986); Michael Lewis-Beck, *Economics and Elections: The Major Western Democracies* (Ann Arbor: University of Michigan Press, 1988).

11. For analyses of the implications of election laws for party representation and government majorities, see Douglas Rae, *The Political Consequences of Election Laws* (New Haven, CT: Yale University Press, 1967); Taagepera and Shugart, *Seats and Votes,* 1989; Arend Lijphart, *Electoral Systems and Party Systems: A Study of Twenty-seven Democracies, 1945–1990* (Oxford, England: Oxford University Press, 1994).

12. Hans-Dieter Klingemann, Richard Hofferbert, and Ian Budge, *Parties, Policy and Democracy* (Boulder, CO: Westview, 1995). See also Richard Rose, *Do Parties Make a Difference?* (Chatham, NJ: Chatham House, 1984), ch. 5.

13. The literature on coalitions, their formation and durability, has now become very large. See especially Michael Laver and Norman Schofield, *Multiparty Government: The Politics of Coalition in Europe* (New York: Oxford University Press 1990); and Wolfgang C. Mueller and Kaare Strom, *Coalition Governments in Western Europe* (New York: Oxford University Press, 2000).

14. For some empirical evidence, see G. Bingham Powell, Jr., and Guy Whitten, "A Cross-National Analysis of Economic Voting," *American Journal of Political Science* 37, no. 2 (1993): 391–444. More generally, see G. Bingham Powell, Jr., *Elections as Instruments of Democracy* (New Haven, CT: Yale University Press, 2000), Chs. 3, 4.

15. For empirical evidence of greater congruence between citizens, governments, and policymakers created in postelection bargaining, see John Huber and G. Bingham Powell, Jr., "Congruence between Citizens and Policymakers in Two Visions of Liberal Democracy," *World Politics* 46, no. 3 (1994): 291–326. More generally, on elections and the representation of votes and preferences, as well as the trade-off with accountability, see Powell, *Elections as Instruments of Democracy,* Chs. 5–10.

16. This classification is adapted from Arend Lijphart, *Democracy in Plural Societies* (New Haven, CT: Yale University Press, 1977); and Arend Lijphart, *Patterns of Democracy* (New Haven, CT: Yale University Press, 1999).

17. Lijphart, *Democracy in Plural Societies.*

18. There is a burgeoning literature on the new party systems of Eastern and Central Europe; see especially Herbert Kitschelt, Zdenka Mansfeldova, and Radoslaw Markowski, *Post-Communist Party Systems: Competition, Representation and Inter-party Cooperation* (Cambridge, England: Cambridge University Press, 1999).

19. See Lijphart, *Patterns of Democracy,* 1999; G. Bingham Powell, Jr., *Contemporary Democracies* (Cambridge, MA: Harvard University Press, 1982), chs. 8 and 10; and Juan J. Linz and Alfred Stepan, eds., *The Breakdown of Democratic Regimes* (Baltimore, MD: Johns Hopkins University Press, 1978).

20. Juan Linz, "Totalitarian and Authoritarian Regimes," in Fred Greenstein and Nelson Polsby, eds., *Handbook of Political Science*, vol. 3 (Reading, MA: Addison-Wesley, 1975), pp. 175–412;

Amos Perlmutter, *Modern Authoritarianism: A Comparative Institutional Analysis* (New Haven, CT: Yale University Press, 1981), especially pp. 62–114.

21. See Franz Schurman, *Ideology and Organization in Communist China* (Berkeley: University of California Press, 1966).

22. On the efforts in Africa, see Crawford Young, *Ideology and Development in Africa* (New Haven, CT: Yale University Press, 1982), ch. 2.

23. See Robert H. Jackson and Carl G. Rosberg, *Personal Rule in Black Africa* (Berkeley: University of California Press, 1982) and Young, *Ideology and Development in Africa.*

CHAPTER SIX

Government
and Policymaking

Policymaking is the pivotal stage in the political process, the point at which bills become law, or edicts are issued by the rulers, whoever they are. Later, policies are implemented and enforced. To understand public policy, we must know how decisions are made. Where is power effectively located in different political systems? What does it take to change public policy: a simple majority vote in the legislature or approval also by an independently elected executive? Or is it a decree issued by the monarch, a signed agreement by military commanders, or a decision by the politburo? Or is it merely the whim of the personal dictator?

This chapter focuses on decision rules and on the policymaking role of government agencies such as legislatures, executives, bureaucracies, and courts. Government agencies are at the core of policymaking. Economic, societal, and personality influences become important when they impinge on decisions made within the institutions of government. Interest group demands for tax relief or for the protection of endangered species cannot become effective unless they are transformed into law or policy by government officials according to some accepted decision rule. Yet, government action does not flow in one direction only. The interaction between government and citizens is a two-way process, including an upward flow of influence and demands from the society, as well as a downward flow of decisions from the government. While parties, interest groups, and other actors may be very active in articulating and aggregating interests, government officials, legislators, and their staffs do most of the actual initiation and formulation of policy proposals.

CONSTITUTIONS AND DECISION RULES

A constitution is the basic rules concerning decision making, rights, and the distribution of authority in a political system. We sometimes use this word to refer to a specific document laying out such principles—for example, the one adopted by the founding fathers of the United States in 1787. But a constitution need not be embodied in a single document and in fact rarely is. We should therefore think of a constitution as a set of rules and principles, whether it is a specific written document, a set of customs or practices, or, as is usually the case, both. Even a military or other dictatorship typically attempts to have set procedures for having decrees proposed, considered, and adopted. Written, or codified, constitutions are particularly important in political systems based on the *rule of law*. This means that government can take no action that has not been authorized by law and that citizens can be punished only for actions that violate an existing law. Under a codified constitution, the constitution is the supreme body of laws.

A constitution contains a set of **decision rules**—the basic rules governing how decisions are made, setting up agencies and offices with specific powers, assigning them territorial and functional jurisdiction, and the like. All governments have decision rules. Decision rules may be simple or complex, and any given political system may have many such rules, or a smaller repertoire of rules that they use in many different circumstances. For example, the U.S. Congress has many different decision rules that apply under different circumstances, whereas the British House of Commons uses a much smaller set of rules (mainly simple majority rule). Decision rules may be more or less formal and precise. Most legislatures have formal and precise decision rules, whereas cabinets at the head of the executive branch often have informal and flexible rules.

Perhaps the most important rules that constitutions establish are those that govern the policymaking process. Policymaking is the conversion of social interests and demands into authoritative public decisions. Constitutions establish the rules by which this happens. They confer the power to propose policies on specific groups or institutions, and they give others the right to amend, reject, or approve such proposals, to make final decisions, or to implement, police, or adjudicate them. The branches of government in modern democracies are largely known by the formal functions they play in this policy process. The legislative branch makes public policies, the executive branch implements and executes them, and the judicial branch adjudicates disputes that arise from them. In reality, however, the functions that different branches of government play are not so easily identified and distinguished from one another. For example, the executive branch is often accountable for most of the policy formulation and initiation (especially in parliamentary democracies), even though officially this function belongs to the legislature.

Knowing what policymaking function a political institution (such as a legislature) plays, however, may still leave us with a very rudimentary understanding of how policies get made. We also need to know how decisions are made within that institution. Within any given branch of government or other political institution, there are numerous rules that affect the policymaking process. The most important of these may be voting rules. In most modern legislative chambers, and in many courts, voting rules are *egalitarian,* which is to say that each member has the same voting power (though presiding officers, such as the Speaker of the British House of Commons, may have the power to break a tie vote). Simply speaking: one person, one vote. That is hardly ever true in government departments (ministries), however. There, decision making is *hierarchical,* and everybody is supposed to defer to his or her superior. In a pure hierarchy, only the vote of a person at the very top (for example, the minister) counts.

When decisions are made through voting, rules are still needed to determine the outcome. Many institutions operate through simple majority voting, which means that in a choice between two options, whichever option gets the larger number of votes wins. An absolute majority means that a winning proposal (for example, a legislative bill) must have the support of a majority of those eligible to vote, including those that might choose to abstain. Qualified majorities of three-fifths, two-thirds, or even three-fourths, are sometimes required for particularly consequential decisions. For example, the U.S. Constitution requires two-thirds majorities in both houses of Congress in order to amend the constitution or override a presidential veto. The most extreme voting rule is unanimity, which means that any one member can block any decision. Different voting rules have different attractions. Qualified majority rules, requiring over 50 percent, can protect against hasty decisions, or against decisions that disadvantage large proportions (perhaps close to half) of the voters. On the other hand, qualified majority rules can give a small minority the power to block proposals favored by a large majority, and the more restrictive voting rules are, the less likely it is that any decision can be made at all.

Decision rules affect political activity because they determine what political resources to seek and how to acquire and use them. Individuals and groups seeking to influence policy have to operate within the framework of these rules. In a federal and decentralized system such as the United States, a pressure group may have to approach both the legislative and the executive branch, and it may have to be active both at the state and the federal level. If instead decisions are made by decree from the commander of the armed forces or the politburo, groups will need to influence these crucial policymakers.

It is important that decision rules be calculable and stable. If they are not, citizens will not know what to expect from government. That may in turn cause them to be less trusting and less willing to invest or make other commitments. It may also lead to serious conflicts, and ultimately government may break down and issues be decided by force. The importance of having predictable decision rules was suggested by Thomas Jefferson in his introduction to the first Manual of the House of Representatives: "A bad set of rules is better than no rules at all."

Making Constitutions

Constitution making is a fundamental political act: It creates or transforms decision rules. Basic constitutional change usually takes place in the aftermath of some significant social change. Most of the constitutions that are in force today were formed as the result of some break, often violent, with the past—war, revolution, or rebellion against colonial rule. New decision rules have to accommodate new internal or external powers. Thus, the defeated powers and the successor states of World Wars I and II all adopted new constitutions or had new constitutions imposed on them. Britain is unusual in having not a formal written constitution but only a long-accepted and highly developed set of customs and conventions, buttressed by important ordinary statutes. This reflects the British record of gradual, incremental, and, on the whole, peaceful political change. Nevertheless, the major changes in British decision rules, such as the shift of power from the Crown to Parliament in the seventeenth century, and the Reform Acts of 1832 and 1867, which established party and cabinet government and vastly extended the right to vote, followed on periods of civil war or unrest.

Perhaps the greatest exception to the association between disruptive upheavals and constitution creation is the peaceful development over the last 40 years of the constitution of the European Union, whose growing powers are altering the decision rules affecting almost 400 million Europeans in 15 countries. But while there has been no violence associated with the formation and growth of the European Union, its origins lie in the bitter lessons of World Wars I and II.

The decades since World War II have seen much constitutional experimentation. After 1945 Japan, Germany, and Italy—the defeated powers—introduced new political arrangements under the active supervision of the Allied victors; and these arrangements have proved to be durable. France has had two constitutions in this period, the second of which—the Fifth Republic of 1958—appears more stable than previous French constitutions. In the last two decades the worldwide trend toward democracy, the end of the Cold War, and the dissolution of the Soviet Union have precipitated a new round of constitutional design. The new constitutional arrangements adopted by democratizing countries such as Spain and Portugal in the 1970s, and the more recent constitutional crafting in Eastern Europe, Russia, and the other Soviet successor states as well as in South Africa and elsewhere, has reignited old polemics about the virtues and faults of different constitutional arrangements, or about the very wisdom of constitutional engineering.[1]

DEMOCRACY AND AUTHORITARIANISM

The most important distinction in policymaking functions is between democratic and authoritarian systems. Democracy means "government by the people." In small political systems, such as local communities, "the people" may be able to share directly in debating, deciding, and implementing public policy. In large political systems, such as contemporary states, democracy must be achieved largely through indirect participation in policymaking. Elections, competitive political parties, free mass media, and representative assemblies are political structures that make some degree of democracy, some "government by the people," possible in large political systems. Such indirect democracy is not complete or ideal. But the more citizens are involved and the more influential their choices, the more democratic the system.

In democratic systems, competitive elections give citizens the chance to shape policy through their selection and rejection of key policymakers. In large societies, competitive elections with full adult suffrage are a necessary condition for meaningful "government by the people." In **authoritarian regimes,** on the other hand, the policymakers are chosen by military councils, hereditary families, dominant political parties, and the like. Citizens are either ignored or pressed into symbolic assent to the government's choices.

Transitions toward democracy have been a major feature of world politics in the last 25 years, beginning in Southern Europe, extending to Latin America and Asia, and more recently to Eastern Europe and the former Soviet Union. This movement toward democracy is a "Third Wave" of worldwide democratization.[2] Both of the previous waves have been followed by reversals, though the overall number of democracies has grown over time. The first wave began in the nineteenth century and culminated with the establishment of many new democracies after the Allied victory in World War I. After World War II, a second democratic wave included many newly independent ex-colonial states, as well as the defeated authoritarian powers. Since about 1975, a third wave has undermined the legitimacy of authoritarian regimes everywhere, especially since the collapse of the Soviet Union in 1991. But note the case of Nigeria, where attempts to establish civilian and democratic regimes have fallen twice to military coups (1966 and 1983), and where a transition toward democracy was again aborted by the military in 1993. Nigeria is not unique. It can be difficult to consolidate stable regimes, especially in poor societies. Today's Third Wave of democratization may well experience many reversals of the sort Nigeria has experienced. In such systems as China and Egypt democracy has not yet taken hold. The democratic opportunities in such societies are often meaningful to educated elites or to those living near the centers of government but less relevant to the average citizen in the countryside.

GEOGRAPHIC DISTRIBUTION OF GOVERNMENT POWER

The basic decision rules of political systems differ along three important dimensions: (1) geographic distribution of authority between the central (national) government and lower levels, such as states, provinces, or municipalities; (2) the separation of powers among different branches of government; and (3) limitations on government authority. We shall discuss these dimensions in order, beginning with the geographic distribution of authority.

According to the geographic division of power, we have confederal systems at one extreme, unitary systems at the other extreme, and federal systems in the middle (see Figure 6.1). The United States under the Articles of Confederation was **confederal.** Ultimate power rested with the states. The central government had authority over foreign affairs and defense but depended on financial and other support from the states. Under the Constitution of 1787, the American government changed from confederal to **federal,** which is to say that both central and state governments had separate spheres of authority and the means to implement their power. Today, the United States, Germany, Russia, India, Nigeria, Mexico, and Brazil are federal systems in which central and local units each have autonomy in particular spheres of public policy. These policy areas and powers are, however, divided among central and local units in varying ways. Britain, France, China, Japan, and Egypt are **unitary systems** with power and authority concentrated in the central government. Regional and local units have only those powers specifically delegated to them by the central government, which may change or withdraw these powers at will.

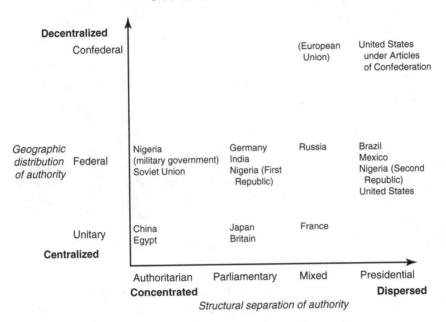

FIGURE 6.1   DIVISION OF GOVERNMENTAL AUTHORITY

Most of the world's states are unitary. In fact, only 18 states are federal, or fewer than one in ten. But whereas the federal states are relatively few in number, they tend to be large and politically important. Thus, federal states account for more than one-third of the world's population and 41 percent of its land area. Generally speaking, the larger and the more diverse a state is, the more likely it is to be federal. Federalism is commonly thought to have a number of advantages. In multinational or otherwise divided societies, it may help protect ethnic, linguistic, or religious minorities, particularly if they are geographically concentrated. It may generally serve as a check on overly ambitious rulers and thus protect markets and citizen freedoms. Moreover, federalism may allow subunits (such as states) to experiment with different policy programs. Governments may thus learn from the experiences of others. In addition, citizens may be free to "vote with their feet" and choose the policy environment that best fits their preferences. However, while federalism promotes choice and diversity, it does so at the expense of equality. Since federalism allows local governments to pursue different policies, the implication is that citizens may get systematically different treatments and benefits from different local governments. Unitary governments may also be in a better position to redistribute resources from richer regions to poorer regions, if that is desirable.

In comparing confederal, federal, and unitary systems, however, we must keep in mind the distinction between formal and actual distribution of power. In unitary systems, in spite of the formal concentration of authority at the center, regional and local units may acquire power that the central government rarely challenges. In the American federal system over the last century, power has steadily moved from the states toward the center. In recent years there has been an effort, under the slogan of a new federalism, to move power from the federal government back to the states. Even in unitary systems there have been efforts to shift some power to provincial and local governments. This has been a response to democratic pressures, demands for greater grassroots influence. Thus, the real differences between federal and unitary systems may be considerably less significant than their formal arrangements suggest. Mexico is an example of the discrepancy between formal and actual federalism. Until recently the Partido Revolucionario Institucional (PRI) had centralized control in this formally federal system. Recent developments in Mexico, with oppositional parties winning ground in some states and the PRI power monopoly under challenge, have produced some "real" federalism to go along with the formalities.

SEPARATION OF GOVERNMENT POWERS

A second aspect of constitutional design has to do with the degree of separation of powers between different branches of the central or regional governments. The theory of **separation of powers** has a long and venerable history going back at least to the work of Locke and Montesquieu.[3] Separation of power, they argued, has the virtue of preventing the injustices that might result from an unchecked executive or legislature. Madison and Hamilton elaborated this theory in *The Federalist*,[4] which described and defended the institutional arrangements proposed by the U.S. Constitutional Convention of 1787. Political theorists in the course of the nineteenth and first part of the twentieth centuries reflecting on the two successful historical cases of representative democracy—Britain and the United States—gradually codified what we may call the "classic" separation of powers theory that dominated the political science of the pre–World War II period. This theory argued that there are essentially two forms of representative democratic government—the presidential and the parliamentary.

The **democratic presidential regime** provides two separate agencies of government—the executive and the legislative—separately elected and authorized by the people. Each branch is elected for a fixed term; no one branch can by ordinary means unseat the other; and each has specific powers under the constitution. Different presidential regimes provide their presidents with a variety of different powers over government appointments and policymaking, such as the authority to veto legislation or to make policy by executive decree under some conditions.[5]

The **parliamentary regimes,** on the other hand, make the executive and legislative branches interdependent. First of all, only the legislative branch is directly elected, whereas the cabinet (the collective leadership of the executive branch) emerges from the legislature. The cabinet is chaired by a prime minister (in Germany called a federal chancellor) who is the head of government and selects the other cabinet members. Typically, neither branch has a fixed term of office. The cabinet can be voted out of office at any time, and most often this is true of the legislature (the parliament) as well.

The critical feature that makes this possible is the **confidence relationship** between the cabinet (the collective leadership of the executive branch) and the parliamentary majority. In a parliamentary system, the prime minister and his or her cabinet must at all times enjoy the confidence of the parliamentary majority. Whenever the parliamentary majority for whatever reason expresses its lack of confidence (through a no-confidence vote), the prime minister and all the other cabinet members have to resign. On the other hand, the prime minister typically has the power to dissolve parliament and call new elections at any time. These two powers, the parliamentary majority's dismissal power and the prime minister's dissolution power, make the two branches mutually dependent. It induces agreement between them by forcing the executive branch to be acceptable to the parliamentary majority. Thus parliamentary democracies do not experience the form of divided government that is common under presidentialism, when the party that controls the presidency does not control the legislature, or vice versa. Instead, the executive (the Cabinet) becomes the agent of the parliamentary majority, and in most parliamentary systems consists largely of members of parliament. Conflicts between parliament and the executive are less likely to occur, and decision making tends to be more efficient than under presidentialism. Since the same party (or parties) controls both branches of government, the cabinet tends to dominate policymaking, and the legislature is typically less influential than under a presidential constitution (see Box 6.1).

Not all democracies fit neatly into the presidential or parliamentary category. Some are hybrid types that are often characterized as "**semi-presidential.**" In some of these mixed types, the president and the legislature are separately elected (as in presidential systems), but the president then has the power to dissolve the legislature (as in parliamentary systems). In such systems, the cabinet may be appointed by the president (as under presidentialism), but subject to dismissal by the legislature (as under parliamentarism). Shugart and Carey identify several types of mixed (or "hybrid") systems with independently elected presidents who have substantial policymaking power but must share control over the executive branch with the legislature. A variety of arrangements exist for such shared control; their consequences are often sharply affected by which party or coalition controls the presidency and legislature. Many of the new constitutions of the emergent democracies of Eastern Europe and the Third World are of this mixed type.

Looking again at Figure 6.1, we see that governments are classified according to the degree of concentration vs. separation of power. In authoritarian governments on the left, executive, legislative, and judicial power are typically concentrated. Two of the twelve countries discussed in this book—China and Egypt—have authoritarian governments not chosen in competitive elections. Mexico and Nigeria are in transition to presidential democracy with competitive party systems. Britain, Germany, Japan, and India are parliamentary systems in which executive and legislative power are concentrated in cabinets representing majorities in popularly elected lower houses of parliament. At the extreme right of Figure 6.1 are pure presidential systems such as the United States and Brazil. In between, we find mixed systems such as France and Russia.

Box 6.1   The Confidence Vote in Parliamentary Democracies

Prime ministers in parliamentary democracies lead precarious political lives. Unlike presidents in presidential systems, prime ministers can be voted out of office at any time, and for any reason, by a parliamentary majority. There are two ways in which this can happen. One is when parliament passes a motion expressing a lack of confidence in the prime minister—a no-confidence motion. The other possibility is when parliament defeats a motion expressing confidence in the prime minister—a confidence motion. No-confidence motions are typically introduced by the parliamentary opposition in the hope of bringing down the prime minister. Confidence motions, on the other hand, are normally introduced by prime ministers themselves, and it is not at all self-evident why they would do so. Since one possible result of a confidence motion is being kicked out of office, it may seem like a form of Russian roulette.

In reality, however, the confidence vote can be a powerful weapon in the hands of the prime minister. It is typically attached to a bill (a policy proposal) that is favored by the prime minister but not by the parliamentary majority. By attaching a confidence motion to the bill, the prime minister forces the members of parliament to choose between the bill and the fall of the cabinet. This can be a particularly painful choice for dissident members of the prime minister's own party. If they vote for the bill, they may bring down their own government, and perhaps immediately have to face the voters to boot. British prime ministers have often resorted to the confidence motion in order to bring rebellious party members into line. In 1993, Conservative Prime Minister John Major faced a parliamentary crisis over the ratification of the Maastricht Treaty, which expanded the powers of the European Union. Major had only a slim majority in the House of Commons, and many "Euro-skeptics" in his own party were opposed to the Maastricht Treaty. About 20 of these Conservative dissidents voted with the opposition and helped defeat the Maastricht Treaty in the House of Commons. Immediately after this embarrassing defeat, however, Major introduced a confidence motion on his Maastricht policy and announced that if he lost this vote, he would dissolve the House of Commons and hold new elections. Many of the Conservative dissidents feared that their party would do poorly in such an election and that they might personally lose their seats. Major's confidence motion passed by a vote of 339 to 299, and the House of Commons approved the Maastricht Treaty. Thus, the confidence vote actually helps explain why party discipline tends to be stronger in parliamentary than in presidential systems.

In the debate over the best system of representative democracy, many political theorists have traditionally favored the British-style parliamentary system. This version of parliamentarism, coupling plurality voting rules that usually create clear party majorities in Parliament with a Cabinet and prime minister responsible to Parliament, results in fairly stable governments responsible to the public will. However, parliamentarism coupled with proportional representation—as in Germany and France between the two world wars—has proved more crisis prone. Such crises occurred because of the emergence of a large number of often extremist political parties, which resulted in cabinet instability and breakdown. On the other hand, the Scandinavian countries demonstrate that parliamentary systems with proportional representation can be quite stable when ideological conflict between the political parties remains moderate. The U.S. presidential system, on the other hand, has often been criticized for periodically producing divided government, which could result in stalemate or "gridlock."

The Third Wave of democratization has reopened this parliamentary-presidential debate. Advocates of parliamentarism, particularly of the continental European variety, argue that it provides a consensual framework in which different ethnic and religious groups can find representation.[6] Since many of the current transitional democracies are ethnically and religiously divided, a parliamentary, proportional representation system may be particularly suitable. Presidentialism, they argue, is more susceptible to social conflict and democratic breakdown. Other scholars point out that while many scholars prefer the parliamentary solution, practical politics is coming out on the side of elected presidents with some political power.[7] Even in the domain of the former British empire (such as in Nigeria) and in most of Eastern Europe and the Soviet successor states, the constitutions provide for powerful presidents. Latin America has been dominated by presidential regimes for more than a century, and a 1993 referendum in Brazil reaffirmed its commitment to presidentialism. And while critics of presidentialism point out that Latin American presidential regimes were prone to coups and breakdowns in the 1960s and 1970s, its defenders reply that parliamentarism suffered its own crises in Europe in the 1920s and 1930s. Presidentialism also offers the citizens a more direct choice of chief executive, and it puts more effective checks on the power of the majority in the legislature.

The relationships between executives and legislatures and between central and local governments are not the only important regime choices. The decades after World War II showed that there were other interesting constitutional options as well. Where cultural and ideological cleavage and conflict were intense (as in the Low Countries and Austria), party leaders mindful of the costs of democratic breakdown and civil war, could agree to disagree on some intractable questions (such as the official language or religious toleration), while they would build broad coalitions on others. They emphasized representation in policymaking by all major social groups, broad elite coalitions, decentralization of decision making and, government by consensus. Arend Lijphart called these stable countries "consociational" democracies.[8] Consociationalism has succeeded in pacifying some previously conflictual societies, but when stability has been attained, politicians have often returned to more competitive politics.

In some smaller European democracies—such as Austria or Sweden—we also find a form of "corporatist" democracy.[9] These are arrangements where the "class struggle" between workers and management, so threatening to democratic stability, could be abated by a social partnership. Through deliberation and bargaining over wages, benefits, prices, and social policy, top leaders from labor, management, and government would attempt to set economic policy (see Chapter 4). Thus often severe and disruptive conflicts could become technical rather than ideological questions, resolvable by deliberation and compromise.

LIMITATIONS ON GOVERNMENT POWERS

Unlike authoritarian regimes, democracies are characterized by some legal or customary limitation on the exercise of power. Systems in which the powers of various government units are defined and limited by a written constitution, statutes, and custom are called **constitutional regimes.** Civil rights—such as the right to a fair trial and freedom to speak, petition, publish, and assemble—are protected against government interference except under specified circumstances.

The courts are crucial to the limitations on governmental power. As illustrated in Table 6.1, governments may be divided into those, at one extreme, in which the power to coerce citizens is relatively unlimited by the courts, and those, at the other extreme, in which the courts not only protect the rights of citizens but also police other parts of the government to see that their powers are properly exercised. The United States and India are examples of systems in which high courts rule effectively on challenges that other parts of the government have exceeded the powers allocated by the constitution. This practice of **judicial review** is authorized to various degrees in about half of the world's democracies and seems to be growing in popularity. But judicial review is often weakened by lack of independence of the appointment or tenure of judges, as in Japan, or by their ineffectiveness in overcoming executive power. Some other constitutional regimes have independent courts that protect persons against the improper implementation of laws and regulations, but cannot legally overrule the assembly or the political executive, as in Britain. The substantive rights of persons in these systems are protected by statute, custom, self-restraint, and political pressure—which are also essential to the effectiveness of courts even where judicial review is authorized. In

Table 6.1   JUDICIAL LIMITATION OF GOVERNMENTAL AUTHORITY

Unlimited		Limited
Nonindependent Courts	Independent Courts	Judicial Review
China	Britain	United States
Egypt	Finland	India
Nigeria		Germany
Mexico		France
		Japan
		Russia

authoritarian systems policymakers do not usually allow courts to constrain their use and abuse of power, even where brave judges attempt to rule against them.

Arend Lijphart characterizes only four of the democratic systems he examines as having "strong" judicial review: Germany, India, the United States, and Canada after 1982.[10] The Supreme Court of India has been singled out as most similar to the United States Supreme Court, having successfully overruled the Prime Minister and assembly by declaring over 100 national laws and ordinances unconstitutional.[11] The German Constitutional Court has also had a substantial impact on national and state policymaking, both through its rulings and through government's anticipation of those rulings. About a quarter of Lijphart's democracies had either strong or medium strength judicial review. In both France and Germany new legislation may be challenged in court by opposition members of parliament even before it takes effect, a process called "abstract" judicial review. Lijhart classified a little over half of his democracies as having "weak judicial review," with the powers of courts constrained by very limited constitutional authority, as in Sweden, or limited independence of government-appointed judges, as in Japan. In the remaining democracies, including Britain, courts enjoyed no power of judicial review of legislation although, as suggested in Table 6.1, they may still protect individuals from government abuse not specifically authorized by law.

In many of the new democracies of Eastern Europe judicial review was proclaimed in the constitution, but proved harder to implement in practice. There have been striking successes in constraining governments in some countries, as in Bulgaria, but failures in others, such as Albania and Belarus. In Nigeria the courts long retained a striking degree of judicial independence under a succession of otherwise undemocratic military regimes, but were shown little respect under the Abacha regime of the mid-1990s, which established special military tribunals to prosecute its perceived enemies. China, on the other hand, after explicit rejection of any limits on "mass justice" from the late-1950s to 1970s, has gradually attempted to introduce a very limited "rule by law," as a way of encouraging stability and economic growth and controlling corruption. But the practice falls far short of the promise of even partial limitation on governmental authority.

All written constitutions provide for amending procedures. Most framers of constitutions have recognized that basic decision rules must be adaptable, because of potential ambiguities, inefficiencies, changes in citizen values, or unforeseen circumstances. On the other hand, if amendments are too easy to make, then important constitutional protections may be jeopardized. Therefore, many constitutions provide that certain arrangements may not be amended—for example, the provision in the U.S. Constitution granting each state equal representation in the Senate. Amending procedures vary widely, ranging from the complex to the simple. Perhaps the simplest case is that of the United Kingdom, where an ordinary parliamentary statute may alter the constitution. Thus the Parliament Act of 1911 reduced the power of the House of Lords to that of proposing amendments and delaying legislation for one parliamentary session. The current effort to eliminate the power of the hereditary peers is similarly taking place through ordinary legislation. Due to the Lords' power to delay legislation, the new reforms may require enactment in two successive parliamentary sessions.

Some constitutions prescribe qualified majorities, such as a two-thirds majority, for constitutional amendments. Others require that an amendment be approved twice with an interval of time between passages. Brazil requires its legislature to vote an amendment in two separate occasions with a three-fourths vote each time. In some cases, constitutional amendments must be approved by a popular vote. The U.S. Constitution has the most difficult formal procedure, requiring initiation by two-thirds of both houses of the Congress (or by the never-employed procedure of a national convention called by two-thirds of the states), and approval by three-fourths of the state legislatures, or three-fourths of specially elected states conventions. Constitutions that have complicated amending procedures, such as the American one, are called "rigid." On average, they tend to be amended less frequently than their "flexible" counterparts.[12]

One of the main points of Figure 6.1 and Table 6.1 is that constitutions may concentrate or disperse government power along several dimensions. There are necessary trade-offs involved in making such constitutional choices. Probably no one who favors democracy and individual liberties would argue for extreme centralization of power in an omnipotent dictator, as in Thomas Hobbes's *Leviathan*. However, constitutional democracies that concentrate power to a somewhat lesser degree, such as the British system, have some important advantages. Their governments tend to be effective and efficient, and by relying on majority rule, they tend to treat all citizens equally. No small group can hold up a decision favored by a solid majority. On the other hand, constitutions that disperse power have their own advantages. They are more likely to check potential abuses of power, such as the tyranny of a majority, and policies will tend to be more stable over time.

In a similar vein, Arend Lijphart divides democratic regimes into two major categories: majoritarian and consensual.[13] The institutions of majoritarian democracy are relatively simple, designed to give power to the representatives of the majority of the voters. Power is concentrated at a single point, not divided as in a separation of powers system. Elections take place in plurality single-member districts and tend to produce two-party systems. Consensual democracies, on the other hand, are designed to break up and constrain the exercise of power. They typically provide for power sharing in the executive, sometimes requiring that ethnic and religious groups be represented in the cabinet. They are also characterized by bicameral legislatures in which one of the chambers represents the states, regions, or ethnic groups. Switzerland is a good example of a consensual democracy, whereas Britain is a classic majoritarian system. Majoritarian systems are typical of homogeneous, culturally unified societies, while consensual democracy is more typical of religiously, linguistically, and ethnically heterogeneous societies. The United States has some majoritarian (plurality elections) and some consensual (federalism and a bicameral legislature with a powerful Senate) features. On the whole, though, constitutional powers in the United States are more dispersed than concentrated.

ASSEMBLIES

In addition to interest groups and political parties, three important types of government institutions are frequently involved in policymaking: (1) the executive, whether elective or appointive; (2) the higher levels of bureaucracy; and (3) the legislative assembly. The distribution of policymaking predominance among these three institutions varies from country to country and from issue area to issue area. Legislative **assemblies** have existed for thousands of years. Ancient Greece and Rome had them, as did many other ancient societies, and indeed the Roman Senate has given its name to modern assemblies in the United States and many other countries. The Icelandic Althingi, first assembled in A.D. 930, is the oldest existing assembly. The British Parliament dates back to the Model Parliament of 1295 and beyond. Almost all contemporary political systems have assemblies, variously called senates, chambers, diets, houses, and the like. Assemblies may also be known as "legislatures" (regardless of what role they actually play in legislating) or as "parliaments" (mainly in parliamentary systems). Their formal approval is usually required for major public policies. They are generally elected by popular vote, and hence are at least formally accountable to the citizenry. Today more than 80 percent of the countries belonging to the United Nations have such governmental bodies. The almost universal adoption of legislative institutions suggests that in the modern world a legitimate government must formally include a representative popular component.

Assembly Functions

Assembly members—ranging from fewer than a hundred to more than a thousand—deliberate, debate, and vote on policies that come before them. Most important policies and rules must be considered and at least formally approved by these bodies before they have the force of law. Assemblies typically also control government spending decisions, so that control of the purse strings (budgeting) is one of their major functions. In addition, some assemblies have important appointment powers, and some (like the British House of Lords in criminal cases) may serve as a court of appeals. Although laws typically need assembly approval, in most countries legislation is actually formulated elsewhere, usually by the political executive and the upper levels of the bureaucracy. When we compare the importance of assemblies as policymaking agencies, the U.S. Congress, which plays a very active role in the formulation and enactment of legislation, is at one extreme. The other extreme is represented by the National People's Congress of the People's Republic of China, which meets infrequently and does little more than listen to statements by party leaders and legitimize decisions made elsewhere. Roughly midway between the two is the House of Commons in Britain. There, legislative proposals are sometimes initiated or modified by ordinary members of Parliament, but public policy is usually initiated and proposed by members of the Cabinet (who are, to be sure, chosen from the members of the parliamentary body). The typical assembly provides a deliberating forum, formally enacts legislation, and sometimes amends it.

Table 6.2   THE ROLE OF ASSEMBLIES IN SELECTED
EUROPEAN COUNTRIES*

Policy Influence	Importance to Citizens
Italy	Britain
Holland	Ireland
Sweden	Germany
Germany	Holland
Britain	France
France	Italy
Ireland	

*Rankings are listed highest to lowest.
Source: Adapted from Philip Norton, "Conclusion: Legislatures in Perspective." *West European Politics* 13 (July 1990), p. 146; and *Eurobarometer* 19 (April 1983), p. 110.

Legislatures differ with respect to both decision-making power and popular perception of their importance. The judgments of academic experts concerning assembly power do not always conform to citizen perceptions as measured in surveys. For example, while the Italian legislature is ranked first in terms of expert estimates of power (see Table 6.2), popular Italian opinion rates its legislative body lowest in importance among the European populations surveyed. Britain, on the other hand, is third from the bottom in the experts' judgments of policymaking influence but ranks high in "importance" in popular opinion. Ireland similarly moves from the lowest expert evaluation to a high public ranking. The legislature's prestige in a nation appears to be less a reflection of its policymaking influence than an expression of the general esteem in which governmental institutions are held. Thus frequent cabinet crises in Italy reduce popular respect for the government, though they create opportunities for parliamentary policy initiatives and a more important legislative role in the making and unmaking of cabinets.

Assemblies should not simply be viewed as legislative bodies. All assemblies in democratic systems have an important relationship to legislation, but not necessarily a dominant role. Their political importance is based not just on this function but also on the great variety of other political functions they perform. Assemblies can play a major role in elite recruitment, especially in parliamentary systems where prime ministers and cabinet members typically serve their apprenticeships in parliament. Legislative committee hearings and floor debates may be important sites for interest articulation and interest aggregation, especially if there is no cohesive majority party. Debates in assemblies can be a source of public information about politics and thus contribute to the socialization of citizens generally and elites in particular. However, as in policymaking, the assemblies of different nations play very different roles in their respective political systems. The British House of Commons ordinarily does not make much of an independent impact on policymaking, because it is controlled by the ruling party's majority. The Commons and its debates are, however, central to public debate, and one of its chief functions is to prepare politicians for executive office. Through its committees, the U.S. Congress plays a major role in making laws and budgets but must share other functions with many other institutions in the decentralized American system. The People's Congress in China plays only a limited socialization role.

Assembly Structure

Assemblies differ in their organization as well as in their powers and functions. Legislatures may consist of one (in which case they are called unicameral) or two (bicameral) chambers. In most bicameral cases, the chambers have different powers and different ways of selecting their members. In Europe, the chambers of parliaments developed out of "estates" (social status groups), bodies intermittently called together by kings or other hereditary rulers for consultation and revenue. In France there were three estates: the clergy, the higher aristocracy, and the so-called third estate, representing other classes. Until 1866, the Swedish parliament had as many as four chambers—it was unique in having a separate chamber for the peasants that made up the bulk of the population. In England in the early period, estates were organized in two chambers: the lords spiritual (the bishops) and temporal (the nobility) in the House of Lords, and knights and burgesses in the House of Commons. Today, the last major hereditary parliamentary chamber, the British House of Lords, is undergoing major surgery that will eliminate the hereditary nobility.

Most democracies, and some authoritarian systems, have bicameral (two-chamber) assemblies. Federal systems normally provide simultaneously for two forms of representation: often one chamber in which representation is based on population, and a second in which representation is based on geographic units. Even in unitary systems (such as France), **bicameralism** is common, but the purpose of the second chamber is to provide a check on policymaking rather than to represent subnational units. The bicameral U.S. Congress grew out of both federalism and the desire to separate the power of the federal government. The House of Representatives directly represents the citizens, with districts roughly equal in population size. In the Senate, on the other hand, the 50 U.S. states are equally represented. The U.S. congressional chambers check and balance one another as well as the other branches of government. Thus the Senate must approve treaties and executive appointments made by the president; both the Senate and the House must consent to a declaration of war; and the House must initiate all measures involving taxation and appropriations.

The American system, in which the two chambers have roughly equal powers, is unusual. In most bicameral systems one chamber is dominant, and the second (such as the Russian Council of the Federation or the French Senate) has more limited powers that are often designed to protect regional interests. Cabinets in parliamentary systems are usually chosen from the majority party or parties' leadership in the more popularly representative chamber. Governments in most parliamentary systems are responsible to only one chamber, which therefore has a more important position in policymaking than the second chamber.

Assemblies also differ in their internal organization, in ways that have major consequences for policymaking. There are two kinds of internal legislative organization: party groups and formal assembly subunits (presiding officers, committees, and the like). There is often an inverse relationship between the strength of parties versus other subunits (such as committees). The stronger parties are, the weaker are committees, and vice versa. British members of Parliament vote strictly along party lines much more consistently than members of the U.S. Congress. As in most parliamentary systems, British members of Parliament rarely vote against the instructions of their party leaders. Because cabinets generally hold office as long as they can command a parliamentary majority, deviating from the party line means risking the fall of the government and new elections. In presidential systems, the president and the legislators are independently elected for fixed terms of office. Thus the fate of the governing party is less directly tied up with voting on legislative measures. In American legislatures, party discipline operates principally on procedural questions, such as committee assignments or the selection of a presiding officer. On substantive policy issues, Democratic and Republican legislators are freer to decide whether or not to vote with their party leaders.

All assemblies have a committee structure, some structural arrangement that permits legislators to divide up their labor and to specialize in particular issue areas. Without such a sublegislative organization, it would be impossible to handle the large flow of legislative business. As we have seen, however, the importance of committees varies. In some legislatures, such as the United States, committees are very influential. This is at least in part because they are highly specialized, have jurisdictions that match those of the executive departments, and have large staff resources. Strong committees tend to have a clear legislative division of labor that matches the executive branch, and they are often arenas in which the opposition can be influential. British committees are much weaker than their opposite numbers in the United States, since they have small staffs, are dominated by the governing party, and get appointed for one bill at a time. Hence, they cannot accumulate expertise in a particular policy area. German and Japanese committees are stronger than those of Britain but weaker than their American counterparts.[14]

POLITICAL EXECUTIVES

In modern states, the executive branch is by far the largest, the most complex, and typically the most powerful branch of government. It is not easy to describe executives in simple ways, but it is sensible to start at the top. Governments typically have a small number of **chief executives,** officials who sit at the very apex of the often colossal executive branch. Such executives have various names, titles, duties, and powers. Some are called presidents, others prime ministers, chancellors, premiers, or secretaries general, and still others are chairmen or chairs. There are even a few kings who still have genuine power. Titles may mislead us as to what functions these officials perform, but they tend to be the main formulators and executors of public policy.

Democratic governments typically feature either a single chief executive (in presidential systems), or a split chief executive of two offices: a largely ceremonial head of state and a more powerful head of government. The two roles are almost always separated in parliamentary systems, which distinguish between the "head

Table 6.3   TYPES OF CHIEF EXECUTIVES IN SELECTED COUNTRIES

Effective	Ceremonial
Individual	
U.S. President	German President
French President	British Queen
French Prime Minister	Japanese Emperor
German Chancellor	Indian President
British Prime Minister	President, PRC
General Secretary, PRC	
Mexican President	
Indian Prime Minister	
Russian President	
Brazilian President	
Collective	
British Cabinet	British Royal Family
Japanese Cabinet	
Chinese Politburo	

of state," who is primarily a ceremonial official, and the "head of government," who makes and implements the decisions. Chief executives can be individual or collective. Table 6.3 distinguishes among executives according to whether they are **individual** or **collective, effective** or **ceremonial.** Political executives are effective only if they have genuine discretion in the enactment and implementation of laws and regulations, in budgetary matters, or in important government appointments. Where they do not have these powers, they are symbolic or ceremonial. In presidential systems the ceremonial and effective roles are almost always held by the same person, the president.

Individual effective executives include the U.S. presidency, an office with very substantial powers. Although the U.S. executive includes collective bodies such as the Cabinet and the National Security Council, they advise the president instead of acting as collective decision-makers. The general secretary of the Central Committee of China's Communist Party is also an individual political executive and is the most powerful political figure.

Sorting out political systems on the individual-collective scale is a bit more complicated. In Britain the prime minister tends to dominate the Cabinet in time of war or emergency. Even in less troubled times strong prime ministers may dominate their Cabinets, but for the most part the British executive is a collective unit. The Cabinet, which consists of the 20 or so most important government ministers, meets regularly and makes important collectively binding decisions. The Federal Council of Switzerland is an extreme example of a collective executive. The Chair of the Federal Council is elected annually and is little more than a presiding officer. Britain's royal family is an example of a collective ceremonial executive. So many occasions call for the presence of the monarch that members of the royal family share the duty.

Although we may speak of the chief political executive as being individual or collective, all executive branches have many members: elective and appointive officials who have policymaking power. A British prime minister makes some 100 ministerial and junior ministerial appointments; a German chancellor may make a similar number. In the United States, an incoming president may have to make as many as 2,000 political appointments, of which 200 are key policymaking positions in the executive branch.

Monarchies are much more rare at the end of the twentieth century than they were at its beginning. Some monarchs, such as the king of Saudi Arabia and some other Arab monarchs, still exercise real power. Most contemporary monarchs, however, have little or no actual political influence. Monarchs like the British queen or the Scandinavian kings are principally ceremonial and symbolic officers with very occasional political powers. They are living symbols of the state and nation and of their historical continuity. Britain's queen may bestow honors or peerages (appointments to the nobility) with a stroke of her wand. She opens Parliament and makes statements on important holidays and anniversaries. When there is an election, or when a government falls, the queen formally appoints a new prime minister. Normally she has no discretion in selecting a prime minister, however, but is required by convention to pick the leader of the majority party in the House of Commons. Recent scandals in the British royal family have lessened its prestige and reduced its capacity to create a sense of cohesion and dignity. The Japanese monarchy has also traditionally been dignified and exalted and played an important role as a national symbol. In contrast, the Scandinavian and Low Country monarchies are more humdrum. Because members of these royal families occasionally use more humble means of transportation, these dynasties are sometimes called "bicycle monarchies" (see Box 6.2).

In republican countries with parliamentary systems, presidents perform the functions that fall to kings and queens in parliamentary monarchies. Thus German presidents give speeches on important anniversaries and designate prime ministers after elections or when a government has resigned. Like parliamentary systems, communist countries have tended to separate the ceremonial and the effective executives. The president of the People's Republic of China, for example, is a ceremonial officer. He greets distinguished visitors and opens and presides over meetings of the People's Congress.

A system in which the ceremonial executive is separated from the effective executive has a number of advantages. The ceremonial executive symbolizes unity and continuity and can be above politics. The U.S. presidency, which combines both effective and ceremonial functions, runs the risk that the president will use his ceremonial and symbolic authority to enhance his political power or that his involvement in politics may make him a less effective symbolic or unifying figure.

The Cabinet

In many political systems, the **Cabinet** is the most important collective decision-making body. Its power is particularly great in parliamentary systems, for several reasons. It typically contains the leaders (often called "ministers" or "secretaries

Box 6.2   Pomp and Circumstance Versus Bicycle Monarchies

Monarchies may be a dying breed, but Western Europe still has more of them than any other region of the world. Britain and Spain are monarchies, as are six of the smaller European democracies (the Netherlands, Belgium, Luxembourg, Denmark, Norway, and Sweden), plus a few microstates such as Monaco. Most of these monarchies have a long history, but two were created in the twentieth century: the Norwegian monarchy in 1905, and the Spanish one in 1975, as Spain transited from the Franco dictatorship to democracy. Monarchies are not all the same. The Spanish king may have more influence than any other European monarch, but few of them have any real power. The Swedish king was even stripped of all his remaining formal powers in a constitutional reform in the 1970s.

Monarchies vary more in style than in power. The British tend toward pomp and ceremony, with decorated horses carrying the Queen to Parliament in a gilded carriage. The Scandinavian and Low Country monarchies are often called "bicycle monarchies." The late King Olav V of Norway (who reigned 1957–1991) was a particularly folksy monarch. An Olympic ski jumper in his youth, he could even in later years often be seen cross-country skiing in the woods around Oslo (the capital of Norway), accompanied only by his dog. During the oil crisis of the 1970s, he insisted on taking public transportation from the royal palace to the ski trails (and on paying for his ticket). When he was still crown prince, he once gave an interview to an American journalist who showed up at the royal cottage without an appointment. While the journalist was interviewing him, the Crown Prince proceeded to do the family dishes.

of state") of all the major departments (sometimes called "ministries") into which the executive branch is divided. The Cabinet also meets frequently—often several times per week—and it is typically selected and led by the head of government: the president in presidential systems and the prime minister in parliamentary ones.

How does the Cabinet get selected? In presidential systems, selecting Cabinet members is typically a presidential prerogative, though sometimes (as with the U.S. Senate), the legislature has to give its approval. The president can typically also dismiss Cabinet members at will, whereas the legislature's ability to do so is most often severely limited.

In parliamentary systems, on the other hand, the process is very different, since the Cabinet needs to maintain the confidence of the parliamentary majority. Therefore, Cabinet formation depends on the result of parliamentary elections and on the composition of Parliament. If a competitive party wins a parliamentary majority by itself, it will (if unified) be able to form a Cabinet of its own members and can then pass and implement its policies. Sometimes who controls the majority is determined directly by the elections. This will always be the case in pure two-party systems, where one party or the other will always have a parliamentary majority. It can also happen in multiparty systems, whenever one party gets more seats than all its competitors combined. But the more parties there are, the less likely it is that one of them will have a majority on its own. We call the outcome in which one party controls a parliamentary majority by itself a majority situation. Whenever majority situations occur in parliamentary systems, the majority party almost always forms a *majority single-party cabinet* by itself.

Far more often, no party wins a majority of votes. In most multiparty countries, the typical election result is that no party has a parliamentary majority by itself—a minority situation. Most commonly under such circumstances, several parties (two, three, or as many as six or seven) join forces and form a *coalition cabinet* in which they are all represented. Sometimes, parties anticipate this need to form coalitions before the election. They may then make a formal agreement with one another and inform the voters that they intend to govern together if they collectively get enough votes. The allied parties thus encourage their voters to mutually support each other and often take advantage of special provisions of voting laws. Many German and French governments have come to power in this fashion. In such cases, the voters can have a direct voice in the choice of the future Cabinet, much as they do in two-party systems. Voters are thus given a major role in choosing the direction of government policy.

But parties often do not make such preelection commitments. Even when they do, they often fail to get the support they would need to control a parliamentary majority. If no party or preelection coalition wins control of the legislature through the election, then parties may bargain after the election, or between elections, to form a new Cabinet.

Whether bargaining takes place before or after the elections, the parties in parliamentary systems typically have a lot of options concerning the composition of the Cabinet. In minority situations, the result can be either a minority government or a majority coalition of several parties. In some cases, a single party decides that it can form a minority cabinet alone, often because the other parties disagree too much among themselves to offer any alternative. Figure 6.2 illustrates these various possibilities. In the minority case, the parties in the Cabinet must continually bargain with other parties to get policies adopted and even to remain in office. In majority coalitions, bargaining will take place primarily among coalition partners represented in the Cabinet.

These complications illustrate two of the problems of combining parliamentary government with electoral systems of proportional representation. Such systems tend to produce minority situations. One problem with this is that the voters are often not given a very clear choice about who will control the executive branch. Instead, the parties may determine this behind closed doors after the election. Sometimes, the results are paradoxical, as when parties that have just lost votes in the elections are able to negotiate their way into a governing coalition. The second problem is that under minority situations, cabinets are sometimes unstable. Italy, for example, has on average had more than one change of govern-

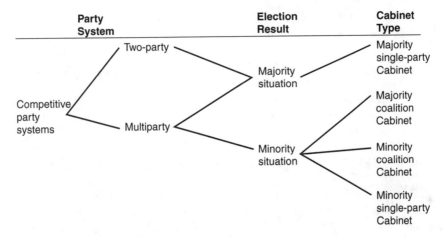

FIGURE 6.2   CABINET FORMATION IN PARLIAMENTARY DEMOCRACIES

ment per year since World War II. Yet, such problems need not always emerge. In Germany, for example, cabinets have been quite stable and the voters have generally been given fairly clear options ahead of elections.

Functions of the Executive

Typically, the executive is the most important structure in policymaking. The executive normally initiates new policies and, depending on the division of powers between the executive and the legislature, has a substantial part in their adoption. In presidential systems, the president very often has veto powers. Thus the chief executive not only has the first word in policymaking, he or she also typically has the last word. In parliamentary systems, on the other hand, the executive is less likely to be able to exercise a veto. The political executive also oversees policy implementation and can hold subordinate officials accountable for their performance. The central decisions in a foreign policy crisis are generally made by the chief executive: the president (George Bush in the Gulf crisis) or the prime minister (Margaret Thatcher in the Falklands crisis). Political initiatives and new programs tend to originate in the executive. A bureaucracy without an effective executive tends to implement past policies, rather than to initiate new ones. Without politically motivated ministers, bureaucracies tend toward inertia.

The decision of a president, prime minister, cabinet, or politburo to pursue a new foreign or domestic policy will usually be accompanied by structural adaptations—the appointment of a vigorous minister, an increase in staff, the establishment of a special cabinet committee, and the like. Where the political executive is weak and divided, as in Fourth Republic France or contemporary Italy, this dynamic force is missing. Initiative then passes to the bureaucracy, legislative committees, and powerful interest groups, and general needs, interests, and problems may be neglected.

In a separation-of-powers system when the presidency and the congress are controlled by different parties, even a strong president may be hampered in carrying out an effective policy. And if the president is hamstrung, the assembly is rarely able to fill the gap. The U.S. system is unique in the extent to which Congress exercises legislative initiative.

Political executives also perform important system functions. Studies of childhood socialization show that the first political role perceived by children tends to be the chief political executive—the president, prime minister, and king or queen. In early childhood the tendency is to identify the top political executive as a parent figure. As the child matures, he or she begins to differentiate political from other roles, as well as to differentiate among various political roles (see Chapter 3). The conduct of the political executive affects the trust and confidence that young people feel in the whole political system and that they carry with them into adulthood.

The role of the political executive in recruitment is obviously important. Presidents, prime ministers, and first secretaries have large and important powers to appoint not only cabinet and politburo members and government ministers but often judges, senior civil servants, ambassadors, and military officers as well. Typically, political executives can bestow honors and distinctions on members of the government and private citizens. The political executive also plays a central role in communication, in explaining and building support for new policies, or in improving performance in various sectors of the society and economy.

THE BUREAUCRACY

Modern societies are dominated by large organizations, and the largest contemporary organizations are government **bureaucracies,** or their systems of public administration. These agencies, by which we mean all the members of the executive branch below the top executive (president/monarch, prime minister, and cabinet) are generally in charge of implementing government policy. The size of government bureaucracies has increased over the course of the twentieth century. This is partly due to government efforts to improve the health, productivity, welfare, and security of their populations. In part, it may also be part of the tendency for government agencies, once they have been established, to seek growth for its own sake. Due to the latter reason, there has in recent decades been a movement to reduce government budgets and to downsize the bureaucracy.

Structure of the Bureaucracy

The most important officials in bureaucracies are the experienced and expert personnel of the top **civil service.** The British "government," which we can think of as its top executive positions, consists of approximately 100 "frontbench" members of Parliament, some 20 of whom serve in the Cabinet, with the remainder named as ministers, junior ministers, and parliamentary secretaries. This relatively small group of political policymakers oversees some 3,000 permanent members of the **higher civil service,** largely recruited directly from the universities. They spend their lives as an elite corps, moving about from ministry to ministry, watching governments come and go, and becoming increasingly important as policymakers as they rise in rank. Below the higher civil service are a huge body of more than half a million permanent public employees, ordinary civil servants, organized into about 20 government departments and a number of other agencies. The total number of British civil servants rose from 100,000 in 1900 to more than 700,000 in 1979, but it then declined by 1991 to about 550,000 under Conservative governments.

The importance of the permanent higher civil service is not unique to Britain, though perhaps it has been most fully institutionalized there. In France, too, the higher civil service is filled with powerful generalists who can bring long tenure, experience, and technical knowledge to their particular tasks. In the United States, many top positions go to presidential appointees rather than to permanent civil servants. Despite this difference and a greater emphasis on technical specialization, there are permanent civil servants in the key positions just below the top appointees in such agencies as the Internal Revenue Service, the Federal Bureau of Investigation, the Central Intelligence Agency, the National Institutes of Health, and all the cabinet departments. These people tend to be specialists, such as military officers, diplomats, doctors, scientists, economists, and engineers, who exert great influence on policy formulation and execution in their specialties. In 1993, the United States had 18.8 million public employees of all kinds, federal, state and local, or about 15 percent of the total labor force. In many European countries, that proportion is even higher.

The Functions of the Bureaucracy

Bureaucracies have acquired great significance in most contemporary societies. One reason is that the bureaucracy is almost alone in implementing and enforcing laws and regulations. In so doing, they may have quite a bit of discretion. Most modern legislation is general and can be effectively enforced only if administrative officials work out its detail and implementation. Policy implementation and enforcement usually depend on bureaucrats' interpretations and on the spirit and effectiveness with which they put it into practice. But the power of bureaucracies is not restricted to their implementation and enforcement of rules made by others. In Chapters 4 and 5 we discussed how bureaucratic agencies may articulate and aggregate interests. Departments like those for agriculture, labor, defense, welfare, and education may be among the most important voices of interest groups. Moreover, administrative agencies in modern political systems do a lot of adjudication. Tax authorities, for example, routinely determine whether citizens have faithfully reported their income and paid their taxes, and these authorities assess penalties accordingly. While citizens may in principle be able to appeal such rulings to the courts, relatively few actually do.

Finally, bureaucracies are involved in communication. Political elites, whether executives or legislators, base many of their decisions on the information they obtain from the public administration. Similarly, interest groups, political parties, the business elites, and the public depend on such information. Most major agencies in modern governments have spokespersons whose job it is to inform and influence the media. With the increasing media power in modern societies, top government executives are eager to present their versions of events. Leaks of secret or confidential information and intelligence have become a veritable flood. Increasingly, however, large parts of the journalistic professions refuse to recognize any limits on the publication of private as well as political information. Thus political executives and bureaucracies can no longer control information in the ways that they formerly did. In dealing with the media, top administrators now must have more complex strategies and professional assistance. The art of "spin control" has replaced their reliance on classification and "executive privilege."

Bureaucracy as a Form of Organization

We commonly use the term "bureaucracy" to refer to all systems of public administration. Strictly speaking, however, bureaucracy refers to a particular way of organizing such agencies, a practice that gained favor in the latter part of the nineteenth century and the beginning of the twentieth century. According to the classical German sociologist Max Weber, bureaucracies have the following features: (1) decision making is based on fixed and official jurisdictions, rules, and regulations; (2) there are formal and specialized educational or training requirements for each position; (3) there is a hierarchical command structure: a firmly ordered system of super- and subordination, in which information flows upward and decisions downward; (4) decisions are made on the basis of standard operating procedures, which include extensive written records; and (5) officials hold career positions, are appointed and promoted on the basis of merit, and have protection against political interference, notably in the form of permanent job tenure. No organization is perfectly bureaucratic in this sense, but professional armies come reasonably close.

These features of bureaucracies have a number of salutary effects. They promote competence, consistency, fair treatment, and freedom from political manipulation. Keep in mind what life could be like without bureaucracies. Before the advent of modern bureaucracy, public officials were often a sorry lot. Some of them inherited their jobs; others got them through family or political connections. Yet others bought their posts and used them either to enrich themselves or gain social status (or both). Many saw them strictly as a sideline and devoted little time to their duties. No wonder, then, that public officials were often incompetent, uninterested in their jobs, corrupt, or all of the above. They often used their powers arbitrarily, to favor friends and neighbors, and to the disadvantage of others. Given the lack of rules and records, aggrieved citizens typically had few recourses.

But the negative connotations that the word "bureaucracy" has taken on suggest that such organizations have liabilities as well. Bureaucratic organizations have a tendency to become stodgy, rule-bound, inflexible, and insensitive to the needs of their clients. In many cases, bureaucrats also have few incentives to be innovative and efficient, or even to work very hard. Although bureaucracies are supposed to be politically and ideologically neutral, in fact they tend to be influenced by the dominant ideologies of the time, to have conservative propensities, and to pursue institutional interests of their own.[15] Bureaucracies may present special problems in periods of major social change. When the Bolsheviks (Communists) took power in Russia in 1917, they had to depend on military officers and officials of the Czarist regime until they could train their own. In post-Communist societies in the 1990s, the resistance and inertia of the old governmental and economic bureaucracies have hampered government reforms and transitions toward democracy and economic freedom.

Many citizens are exasperated with bureaucracy and its propensities for inefficiency and lack of responsiveness. It is reflected in popular cynicism as well as in periodic attempts to reform government. The influence of the British higher civil service has been vividly caricatured in the popular television series, *Yes, Minister,* in which conniving civil servants always seem to get the better of bumbling and self-serving politicians.

Mark Nadel and Francis Rourke suggest a variety of ways that government and societal agencies may influence and control bureaucracies, externally or internally.[16] The major external government control is the political executive. Although presidents, prime ministers, and ministers formally command subordinate officials and may have the power to remove them for nonperformance of duty, executives and bureaucracies actually mutually depend on one another. Top executives typically try to persuade; rarely do they go to the extreme of dismissing or transferring civil servants. Centralized budgeting and administrative reorganization are other means of executive control. The threat to take away resources or authority may bring bureaucratic implementation into greater conformity with the aims of the political executive.

Assemblies and courts also help control the bureaucracy. Legislative committee hearings or judicial investigations may bring bureaucratic performance into line with political desires. Sweden invented the institution of the **ombudsman** to prevent bureaucrats from doing injury or injustice to individuals.[17] This invention has been copied by a number of other states. In the Scandinavian countries, Britain, Germany, and elsewhere ombudsmen now investigate citizen claims that they have suffered injury or damage as a result of government action. Ombudsmen typically have no power of their own, but report to the legislature for remedial action. Their cases rarely lead to criminal conviction, but often government officials change their policies as a result of embarrassing publicity. Thus, ombudsmen offer a more expeditious and less costly procedure than court action. Among the extragovernmental forces that constrain bureaucracies are public opinion and the mass media, as well as interest groups of various kinds.

Not all controls on bureaucracy are external. Internal controls, such as advisory committees, are appointed to oversee the impartiality of their performance. Another way of controlling bureaucracy is to decentralize it, thereby bringing agencies closer to their clients. Finally, the attitudes of the bureaucrats themselves affect their responsiveness and responsibility. The norms and values that bureaucrats bring with them into public service, and the standards and obligations they are taught to respect, have an important bearing on bureaucratic performance.

All such controls on civil servants tend to be less effective outside the advanced industrial democracies. Authoritarian systems lack many of these controls, particularly external ones, such as elected political executives and legislators, independent courts, mass media, and interest groups. Therefore, authoritarian regimes are particularly prone to bureaucratic inefficiency and inertia. In many nonindustrial countries, mass media are neither independent nor influential, few citizens participate in politics, and lower-level government employees are poorly trained and paid—all conditions that encourage bribery, extortion, and bureaucratic mismanagement.[18]

The ills of bureaucracy, including inefficiency and inertia, are pandemic. This is truly a dilemma because we are unlikely to invent any schemes for carrying out large-scale social tasks without the organization, division of labor, and professionalism that bureaucracy provides. Its pathologies can only be mitigated. The art of modern political leadership consists not only of defining and communicating appropriate goals and policies, but also of getting them implemented by a massive and complex bureaucracy—how and when to press and coerce it, reorganize it, reward it, teach it, or be taught by it.

ELITE RECRUITMENT

Political offices have to be filled by human beings, or no functions will be performed. And how those functions are performed depends a good deal on the individuals who actually fill the offices. The ways in which individuals are selected for, or recruited into, political office are therefore a critical part of the ways in which governments are structured.

There are four common mechanisms by which individuals are selected for government office: election, appointment, heredity, and auction. The first two of these are familiar from any contemporary democracy. In fact, the use of the first mechanism, election, is one of the things that makes democracy distinctive. In all democracies, citizens directly elect the assembly, or at least the most powerful chamber of the assembly (e.g., the House of Commons in Britain). In most presidential systems, the chief executive is directly elected as well. And in the United States and many other democracies, there is a variety of other elective offices, from governors and judges down to the proverbial dog catcher. Appointment is the other familiar mechanism. Most executive branch offices tend to be filled by appointment, as are in fact most judicial offices around the world.

Heredity and auction may seem like more curious and somewhat shady ways to select occupants of government offices. They are certainly less democratic. Nonetheless, these recruitment mechanisms have been of great historical importance and continue to be used today. Historically, advocates of the hereditary principle have argued that it gives rulers a longer-term perspective. If a king, for example, expects to be succeeded by his eldest son or another relative, he is more likely to look after the long-term interest of the country than a politician elected for a short term and expecting to be succeeded by a political adversary. Most contemporary monarchs, of course, are hereditary ones (though historically this was far from self-evident), and until the recent reforms most members of the British House of Lords still acquired their right to serve in this way. In the United States, heredity can give you a politically revered (or despised) name, such as Kennedy, Rockefeller, or Bush, but not in itself a political office.

Auction—the selling of government offices to the highest bidder—was widely used through the Middle Ages and up until the introduction of civil service reforms, but would hardly come to mind as a particularly democratic practice today. Nonetheless, all around the world, political offices are filled in ways that smack of auctions. If you want to be the United States ambassador to a small, tropical island nation, for example, a large campaign contribution to the winning presidential candidate may be just the ticket.

Selection mechanisms such as election or appointment are not the only rules that affect who gets to fill different government offices. In addition, constitutions establish eligibility requirements of various sorts. One may be formal educational credentials. Judges, for example, typically need law degrees. So may attorneys general. Another eligibility requirement may be age. In most political systems, government officials must at least be of legal adult age. In the United States, the president must be a minimum of 35 years old. Many countries have formal retirement ages. Other eligibility requirements may include gender (though much less commonly than in the past), religious faith or affiliation (in many countries in which there is an established religion), citizenship, domestic birth, or the lack of a criminal record.

Chief Executives

Historically, finding generally acceptable ways to select the individuals to fill the top policymaking roles has been critical to political order and stability. A major accomplishment of stable democracies has been to regulate the potential conflict involved in leadership succession and confine it to the mobilization of votes instead of weapons. When we refer generally to "recruitment structures," we are thinking of how nations choose their top policymakers and executives. Table 6.4 shows the recruitment structures in the countries selected for this book. The most familiar structures are the presidential and parliamentary forms of competitive party systems. In presidential systems, as in Brazil and the United States, parties select candidates for nomination, and the electorate chooses between these. Russia and France have directly elected presidents but also give an important role to the prime minister, who is appointed by the president but can be removed by the legislature.

Mexico appears similar to other presidential systems, but the Partido Revolucionario Institucional (PRI) has had such control over the electoral process that for half a century the voters merely ratified the party's presidential nominee. That nomination itself has been announced by the outgoing president after complex bargaining between party factions and other powerful groups. Mexico seemed to be moving to give the voters an honest role in choosing between alternative candidates, but until the July 2000 election many voters remained skeptical that a non-PRI president could really come to power.

In both presidential and parliamentary democracies the tenure of the chief executive is limited, directly or indirectly. In the presidential system this happens directly, through fixed terms of office for the chief executive. In the parliamentary system there is a maximum term for the parliament, which then indirectly also limits the life of the cabinet, since the prime minister is accountable to the new parliamentary majority and can be removed by it.

Table 6.4 also illustrates the role of noncompetitive parties. In Mexico, as we have seen, selection has taken place through bargaining within and around the

Table 6.4   RECRUITMENT OF CHIEF EXECUTIVE

Country	Chief Executive Structure	Recruitment Structures	How often has this type of government survived succession?[b]
Brazil	President	Party and voters	Often
Britain	Prime minister	Party, House of Commons, voters	Very often
China	Party secretary[a]	Party and military	Often
Egypt	President	Party and military	Twice
France	President	Party and voters	Often
Germany	Chancellor	Party, Bundestag, voters	Often
India	Prime minister	Party, Lok Sabha, voters	Often (one interruption)
Japan	Prime minister	Party, Diet, voters	Often
Mexico	President	Elites, party, voters	Often
Nigeria	President	Military and voters	Never
Russia	President	Party and voters	Once
United States	President	Party and voters	Very often

[a]"Party secretary" refers to that position or a similar one as head of party in a communist regime.
[b]"Often" means that at least three successions have taken place under that type of government.

PRI and the incumbent president, who cannot succeed himself. Despite the somewhat closed recruitment process, the no-reelection rule forces periodic change in personnel, and often in policy, in response to some popular involvement. The important role so often played by political parties illustrates the great need to mobilize broad political support behind the selection of chief executives. The frequent appearance of parties also reflects, no doubt, the modern legitimacy of popular sovereignty: the promise that the rulers' actions will be in the interest of the ruled.

Authoritarian systems rarely have effective procedures for leadership succession. The more power is concentrated at the top, the riskier it is to transfer it from one person to the next. Very often, authoritarian leaders do not dare to relinquish their power, and leadership succession occurs only when they die. In Communist regimes, the Communist Party long selected the general secretary (or equivalent), who was the controlling executive force. Individual succession was not a simple matter. These systems did not limit the terms of incumbents, who were difficult to oust once they had consolidated their supporters into key party positions. Nonetheless, they always had to be aware of the possibility of a party coup of the type that ousted Nikita Khrushchev from the Soviet leadership in 1964. As a system, however, the Soviet leadership structure seemed quite stable until the dramatic 1991 coup attempt against Gorbachev. Although he was briefly restored to power, the events surrounding the coup stripped the Soviet presidency of power, and legitimacy passed to the presidencies and legislatures of the 15 constituent republics, most importantly to President Boris Yeltsin of Russia. It remains to be seen how soon the Soviet successor republics will have stable procedures for leadership succession. Russia managed its first transition surprisingly smoothly, from Yeltsin to his chosen successor Vladimar Putin, who was elected as the new president in April 2000.

The poorer nations show substantially less stability, and the regimes have usually had less experience at surviving succession crises. Nigeria is typical. It experienced a succession of military coups and governments from 1966 until 1979, then introduced a competitive presidential system, which was overthrown by a military coup shortly after its second election in 1983. The military government again moved toward civilian rule in the early 1990s but then annulled the 1993 presidential election before the results were announced. The military rulers finally allowed a return to civilian rule in 1999.

Many African nations are under military governments; some of them have experienced repeated coups. Military governments, stable or unstable, have also been common in Latin America and the Middle East. The Chinese Communist Party has remained in power for 50 years but has suffered several periods of internal strife, and the army has been involved in recruitment at all levels. India's democracy, having persisted through assassinations and other crises, has been an exception to the rule among poorer nations. It has provided a number of democratic successions with a single interruption (authoritarian emergency rule that postponed elections for several years) in the 1970s.

Representation: Mirroring and Representational Biases

In democratic societies where the idea of popular sovereignty has taken root, citizens tend to think of government officials as their representatives. To the extent that they do, they may be more or less happy with the kind of representation they are getting. It is not obvious, however, what the ideal linkage between citizens and government officials should be. One body of thought holds that government officials should mirror the characteristics of the citizens as far as possible. This principle, also known as *ascriptive representation,* is held to be particularly important with respect to potentially conflictual divisions such as race, class, ethnicity, gender, language, and perhaps age.

The bad news is that political elites hardly ever mirror the citizens they represent on any of these dimensions. Even in democracies such as the United States, Britain, and France, political leaders tend to be of middle- or upper-class background or well-educated and upwardly mobile individuals from the lower classes. There are exceptions. In some countries trade unions or leftist political parties may serve as channels of political advancement for people with modest economic or educational backgrounds. These representatives, however, have usually acquired political skills and experience by holding offices in trade unions or other political groups. Thus the Labour Party delegation in the British House of Commons and the Communist delegation in the French National Assembly have included substantial numbers of workers. And despite the fact that the Norwegian Labor Party held the prime ministership for all but seven years between 1935 and 1981, none of its prime ministers over this period had even completed secondary school. But these are rare and vanishing examples. In most contemporary states, the number of working-class people in high office is small and declining.

Communist countries, despite their ideologies of working-class revolution, have not been able to avoid this class bias. For economic development, they inevitably had to depend on trained technicians. Even running an effective revolutionary party required technical competence and substantial knowledge. In the later decades of its existence, the Central Committee of the Communist Party of the Soviet Union increasingly consisted of well-educated persons recruited from the regional party organizations, the army, and the bureaucracy. When an educated, technically competent, and privileged ruling class emerged in Communist countries, it violated their ideology and caused friction. Thus recruitment policies wavered between emphasizing technical competence versus the "correct" class background. Campaigns to foster the latter were often associated with populistic attacks on bureaucracy and privilege. Nowhere was this more marked than in China, where the Great Proletarian Cultural Revolution of the late 1960s sought to destroy the powers and privileges of party and government leaders and bring power back to the people. However, this campaign resulted in political turmoil and economic disaster. China has later returned to an emphasis on education and technological development.

Women have traditionally also been poorly represented in political leadership positions in most countries. History certainly offers examples of strong and influential female rulers, such as Queen Elizabeth I of England (who ruled from 1558 to 1603). Yet in most countries women did not have the right to vote until well into the twentieth century and have not held many political leadership positions. That has changed significantly in the 1980s and 1990s. In 1980, women on average held fewer than 10 percent of the parliamentary seats in the advanced industrial democracies. By 1990, that figure was up to about 15 percent, and by 1997 women had surpassed 20 percent. Women have also held the chief executive office in a growing number of countries, particularly in Europe and Asia. The most famous female chief executive is probably Margaret Thatcher, who was Britain's longest-serving prime minister (1979–1990) in modern times and a highly effective and influential political leader. But women's advancement has been uneven, and their representation remains low in the developing world. In many Northern European countries, such as Sweden, women by the late 1990s accounted for 30 to 40 percent of the legislators and a similar proportion of cabinet members. In the United States, they had made similar gains in some states—most notably in Arizona, where women held five out of six statewide elective offices after the 1998 elections. But in Russia, Mexico, Brazil, and Japan, women still accounted for fewer than one legislator in ten in the 1990s[19] (see Box 6.3).

Political elites also tend to be unrepresentative with respect to age. In many countries, legislators (much less chief executives) under 40 are a rarity, whereas a large proportion of leading politicians are past normal retirement age. Japan is an extreme example. In 1990, there were about eight legislators over the age of 60 for every one member under 40. In many countries, university graduates—and often lawyers and civil servants in particular—are vastly overrepresented, whereas ethnic, linguistic, and religious minorities are often underrepresented. Representa-

---

Box 6.3   Women as Chief Executives

From about 1970 on, women have gained chief executive office in a growing number of countries. Interestingly, many of them have been from Asian and Middle Eastern countries, where women's roles in public life traditionally has been limited. Sinmavo Bandaranaike of Sri Lanka (1960–1965 and 1970–1977), Indira Gandhi of India (1966–1977 and 1980–1984), and Golda Meir of Israel (1969–1974) were among the pioneers. In the 1980s and 1990s, women also came to power in the Philippines, Pakistan, and Bangladesh, and again in Sri Lanka. In Burma, Nobel Peace Prize winner Aung San Suu Kyi won the elections of 1990 but the military prevented her from taking office.

Women have also made inroads in leadership positions in Europe and North America, though they are still few and far between in Africa and Latin America. The first female leader in a major European country was Prime Minister Margaret Thatcher of Britain (1979–1990). Her strong and decisive leadership made her one of Europe's most influential politicians in the 1980s. Thatcher, who now serves in Britain's House of Lords, was not a conventional feminist, however. She showed little interest in gender issues and appointed very few women to her cabinets. Women have come to power in other western countries as well. Both Ireland and Iceland have had female presidents. Canada, France, and Switzerland have had brief stints with female prime ministers. In Norway, Gro Harlem Brundtland held the prime ministership for a total of about ten years between 1981 and 1996. Brundtland, a physician and environmentalist, now heads the World Health Organization.

The career paths of Asian women leaders have tended to differ from those in Europe. Many of the former have come from prominent political families, such as the Gandhi family in India and the Bhuttos in Pakistan. In several cases, they have been the widows or daughters of important political leaders. In Europe, women leaders are more likely to have made independent political careers, and they can rely on stronger women's interest groups.

---

tional biases are thus numerous and pervasive. And while women's representation is increasing, class biases are getting worse.

Preferences and Competence in Representation

Ascriptive representation is not the only concern in political recruitment, however, and there are reasons for at least some biases in political recruitment. The limits of mirroring were inadvertently expressed by a U.S. senator. In defending a Supreme Court nominee that was accused of mediocrity, the senator lamely contended, "even if he were mediocre, there are a lot of mediocre judges and people and lawyers. They are entitled to a little representation, aren't they?" Most people would probably not go as far as to argue that government officials should mirror the general population in their abilities to do their jobs. Instead, we generally want political elites to be the best possible *agents* for their constituents. In this view, government officials should be selected for their ability to serve the interests of the citizens, whether or not they share the voters' background characteristics.

For politicians to be good agents, they need to have similar *preferences* to the citizens they represent, and they need the appropriate *skills* to do their jobs. In democracies, political parties are the most important mechanism by which the preferences of citizens and leaders get aligned. As far as skills are concerned, education and experience are the most important factors. Political and governmental leadership, particularly in modern, technologically advanced societies, requires knowledge and skills that are hard to acquire except through education and training. Natural intelligence or experience may, to a limited degree, take the place of formal education. Even in leftist parties, however, leadership posts tend to be held by educated professional people rather than by members of the working class.

Hence, it might be a good thing for government officials to be better informed, more intelligent, more experienced, and perhaps better educated than the people they serve. Just as medical patients tend to look for the most capable physician, rather than the one that is most like themselves, so, one could argue, citizens should look for the best qualified officeholder. In this view, selecting government officials is like delegating to experts. Hence, it may be a hopeful sign that citizens in many modern democracies are increasingly willing to select leaders who do not share their background characteristics. In the United States, more and more African-American legislators, such as Julia Carson (a Democrat from Indiana) and J. C. Watts (a Republican from Oklahoma) are elected from districts in which blacks are not in the majority.

As in the case of so many other political choices, there is no obvious or perfect way to choose between mirroring and delegation. This is an old debate, and in many situations it is necessary to make a trade-off between the two. And different offices may require different considerations. Most people would, for example, probably put a higher emphasis on mirroring in their local assembly than in a regulatory agency overseeing nuclear technology.

CONTROL OF ELITES

Elite recruitment is crucial for political stability. Traditional empires and dictatorships, in which self-perpetuation was a major goal of the rulers, seem to have regulated recruitment more carefully than any other system function. Lesser elites were controlled through the careful selection of loyalists to fill military and civilian supervisory roles and through powerful inducements for continuing loyalty. The conquering general or authoritarian dictator mixed rewards to favorites with severe penalties for failure or disloyalty.

Modern authoritarian systems have discovered that they can achieve more efficient and effective control by simultaneously manipulating political socialization, political recruitment, and political communication. Socialization efforts are made to instill loyalty and to limit and regulate information. But if recruitment is made a part of a larger pattern of control, it is hardly neglected. Leadership selection in the former Soviet Union was accomplished through a device called *nomenklatura*. Under this procedure important positions were kept under the direct supervision of a party agency whose officials had the final word on recruitment. Moreover, the party offered a complicated set of inducements to control the behavior of the chosen officials. These inducements made it difficult for any but the topmost officials to have much freedom of action. Soviet leaders used normative incentives, such as appeal to party, ideology, and national idealism; financial incentives, such as better salaries, access to finer food and clothing, better housing, and freedom to travel; and coercive control, such as reporting by police, party, and bureaucrats. They used demotion or imprisonment, even execution, as penalties. To avoid a coup by police or military forces, the varied layers of command and inducement structures were interwoven, so that no layer could act independently.

Impeachment

In many authoritarian systems, there is no legal and institutionalized way to remove political leaders if they become unpopular or overstep whatever bounds they may face. Democratic systems have such tools, but they vary between systems. In parliamentary systems, chief executives can be removed virtually at any time through a vote of no confidence if they lose the confidence of a parliamentary majority. In Germany, Social Democratic Chancellor Helmut Schmidt was ousted by Helmut Kohl of the Christian Democratic Party in October 1982. In Britain Prime Minister Margaret Thatcher's own Conservative Party replaced her with John Major in 1990.

Democratic presidential systems fall somewhere in between. Unlike prime ministers under parliamentary constitutions, presidents have fixed terms of office. However, most presidential systems allow presidents to be removed before their term is up, but typically only if they are guilty of serious criminal or other wrongdoing. The procedure through which this is done is called *impeachment*. In the American system, impeachment procedures can be used against the incumbents in top offices, even the president (as in the cases of Presidents Nixon and Clinton) or a Supreme Court justice, if their activities stray too far beyond legal bounds. Military officers and civil servants are also subject to removal from office or demotion for violating their oaths of office or for failing to perform their duties. These procedures to ensure that the powerful perform their duties are an essential part of political recruitment. Two American presidents in the last 130-odd years have been impeached, which is to say that charges have been raised against them by the House of Representatives. Two presidents have faced impeachment proceedings in recent decades: Nixon in 1974 and Clinton in 1998–1999. However, no president has yet been convicted in the Senate and removed from office, though that fate has befallen other federal officials, such as judges (see Box 6.4).

As written constitutions were adopted in Latin America, Europe, and elsewhere, impeachment clauses that imitated the American practice were often included. While impeachment is associated with constitutions having powerful presidencies with fixed terms of office, it has also been adopted in semi-presidential

---

Box 6.4   Impeachment

Impeachment is often thought of as a procedure that is typical of presidential rather than parliamentary systems. Nevertheless, its modern origins lie in Britain. The framers of the American constitution adopted impeachment from their British institutional heritage. In English constitutional tradition, impeachment was a process affecting top executive and civil officers accused of "high crimes and misdemeanors," for which the penalty was removal from office. Impeachment was quite separate from judicial control over criminal behavior.

An illustrative impeachment case was in process in the British Parliament at the very time that the U.S. Federal Constitution was being drafted, while the *Federalist Papers* were written, and while the states were engaged in ratification. Warren Hastings, Governor General of India (1774–1784), was accused and impeached for "high crimes and misdemeanors" by the Whig Party, which then controlled the House of Commons. The House of Lords tried the case over a seven-year period (1787–1795) but failed to convict Hastings. The institution then fell into disuse in Britain as her system of parliamentary government evolved. In a parliamentary system, cabinet members and ministers hold office only when they have the confidence of a parliamentary majority. A no-confidence vote can bring them down at any time and for any reason. Parliament can therefore much more easily hold the top political elite accountable through the threat of a no-confidence vote rather than impeachment.

---

regimes, and even in purely parliamentary regimes. A limited amount of experience has accumulated with this politico-legal form of control of high civil and judicial officers.

Impeachment typically involves three components: (1) The impeachable offenses are usually identified as presenting unusual danger to the public weal and safety. (2) The sanction is removal from office, and sometimes separate criminal penalties, which may be imposed subsequent to the discharge from public office upon conviction. (3) Impeachment cases are decided by the legislature but require more than ordinary majorities; they may also involve the judiciary in some way.

The establishment of the impeachment power has been associated with the rise of presidential separation-of-powers systems, and with the need in such systems for an extraordinary check against abuse of power on the part of high executive officers. The framers of the American constitution viewed the normal checks and balances as insufficient protection against serious corruptions of power. Impeachment typically combines legislative and judicial powers against an executive out of control (though in the American case it has been employed mostly against offending federal judges). The positive value of impeachment is that it provides a way of mobilizing political power against a threat to the constitutional or legal order. On the other hand, the danger is that it can be used for less pressing purposes. It can be tempting under a separation-of-powers system, when the executive and legislative are controlled by different political parties, and particularly when these parties are hostile to one another, to employ the institution out of primarily partisan motives. To prevent abuse of the impeachment procedure, the odds are typically stacked in favor of the defendant. Impeachment is often a cumbersome procedure, and it typically takes a large majority to convict—in the United States, a two-thirds majority in the Senate.

Brazil, Mexico, and many other Latin American nations have impeachment traditions imbibed from the United States. In Mexico, the president, the state governors, and federal judges are subject to impeachment. Brazil also has an impeachment process similar to that of the United States, except that it takes a two-thirds vote to charge the president and other high civil officers with impeachable offenses. A two-thirds vote is also required in the Senate to convict. The clause was invoked in 1992 when President Collor was impeached on charges of large-scale corruption. He resigned before trial in the Senate.

In the long run the ultimate control of democratic order is periodic and competitive elections. This need to regularly renew their mandates is the fundamental device that leads politicians to respond to the needs and demands of citizens. It is deeply imperfect. It may be difficult to tell when elected officials are incompetent, deceitful, or just unlucky. The complexities of policymaking may baffle the attempt of even trained observers to assign responsibility for successes or failures. The multiplicity of political issues may leave citizens torn between their candidate choices. Or, none of the choices may seem very palatable. Yet, deeply imperfect as it is, this remarkable recruitment structure, through its effects on information, group activity, and party competition, gives every citizen some influence on the policymaking process. For this reason we consider it the most significant democratic structure.

KEY TERMS

assemblies	confidence relationship	judicial review
authoritarian regime	constitutional council	ombudsman
bicameralism	constitutional regime	parliamentary regime
bureaucracy	decision rules	political executive
Cabinet	democratic presidential regime	policymaking
ceremonial executive		semi-presidential regime
chief executives	effective executive	
civil service	federal systems	separation of powers
collective executive	higher civil service	unitary systems
confederal systems	individual executive	

SUGGESTED READINGS

Aberbach, Joel, Robert D. Putnam, and Bert A. Rockman. *Bureaucrats and Politicians in Western Democracies.* Cambridge, MA: Harvard University Press, 1981.

Dahl, Robert A. *Polyarchy: Participation and Opposition.* New Haven, CT: Yale University Press, 1971.

Döring, Herbert, ed. *Parliaments and Majority Rule in Western Europe.* New York: St. Martin's, 1995.

Huber, John D. *Rationalizing Parliament.* Cambridge, England: Cambridge University Press, 1996.

Katzenstein, Peter. *Small States in World Markets.* Ithaca, NY: Cornell University Press, 1985.

Lijphart, Arend. *Democracy in Plural Societies.* New Haven, CT: Yale University Press, 1977.

———. *Democracies: Patterns of Majoritarian and Consensus Government in Twenty-One Countries.* New Haven, CT: Yale University Press, 1984.

———. *Patterns of Democracy: Government Forms and Performance in Thirty-Six Countries.* New Haven, CT: Yale University Press, 1999.

Linz, Juan, and Arturo Valenzuela, eds. *The Failure of Presidential Democracy: Comparative Perspectives.* Baltimore, MD: Johns Hopkins University Press, 1994.

Mainwaring, Scott, and Matthew Shugart, eds. *Presidentialism and Democracy in Latin America.* New York: Cambridge University Press, 1997.

March, James G., and Johan P. Olsen. *Rediscovering Institutions: The Organizational Basis of Politics.* New York: Free Press, 1989.

North, Douglass. *Institutions, Institutional Change, and Economic Performance.* Cambridge, England: Cambridge University Press, 1990.

O'Donnell, Guillermo, and Philippe Schmitter. *Transitions from Authoritarian Rule.* Baltimore, MD: Johns Hopkins Univerity Press, 1986.

Powell, G. Bingham. *Contemporary Democracies.* Cambridge, MA: Harvard University Press, 1982.

Riker, William H. *Federalism: Origin, Operation, and Significance.* Boston, MA: Little, Brown, 1964.

Sartori, Giovanni. *Comparative Constitutional Engineering.* New York: New York University Press, 1997.

Secondat, Charles de, Baron de Montesquieu. *The Spirit of the Laws.* London: Hafner, 1960.

Shugart, Matthew, and John Carey. *Presidents and Assemblies: Constitutional Design and Electoral Dynamics.* Cambridge, England: Cambridge University Press, 1992.

Strom, Kaare. *Minority Government and Majority Rule.* Cambridge, England: Cambridge University Press, 1990.

Tsebelis, George, and Jeannette Money. *Bicameralism.* Cambridge, England: Cambridge University Press, 1997.

Weaver, Kent, and Bert Rockman, eds. *Do Institutions Matter? Government Capabilities in the United States and Abroad.* Washington: Brookings Institution, 1993.

Weber, Max. "Bureaucracy." In H. H. Gerth and C. Wright Mills, eds. *From Max Weber.* New York: Oxford University Press, 1976, pp. 196–244.

Weingast, Barry R. "Political Foundations of Democracy and the Rule of Law." *American Political Science Review* 91, no. 2 (June 1997): 245–263.

NOTES

1. For a skeptical view of constitutional design, see James G. March and Johan P. Olsen, *Rediscovering Institutions: The Organizational Basis of Politics* (New York: Free Press, 1989), pp. 171–172. For a more sanguine argument, see Giovanni Sartori, *Comparative Constitutional Engineering* (New York: New York University Press, 1995).

2. Samuel Huntington, *The Third Wave: Democratization in the Late Twentieth Century* (Norman, OK: University of Oklahoma Press, 1991).

3. John Locke, *Two Treatises of Government*, ed. Peter Laslett (Cambridge, England: Cambridge University Press, 1960); Charles de Secondat, Baron de Montesquieu, *The Spirit of the Laws* (London: Hafner, 1960).

4. *The Federalist: A Commentary on the Constitution of the United States* (Washington: National Home Library Foundation, 1937).

5. On presidential decree powers see John M. Carey and Matthew S. Shugart, *Executive Decree Authority* (New York: Cambridge University Press, 1998); for more general discussions of presidential powers see Matthew S. Shugart and John M. Carey, *Presidents and Assemblies: Constitutional Design, and Electoral Dynamics* (Cambridge, England: Cambridge University Press, 1992); and Scott Mainwaring and Matthew S. Shugart, eds., *Presidentialism and Democracy in Latin America* (New York: Cambridge University Press, 1997.)

6. Juan Linz and Arturo Valenzuela, eds., *The Failure of Presidential Democracy: Comparative Perspectives* (Baltimore, MD: Johns Hopkins University Press, 1994).

7. Donald Horowitz, "Comparing Democratic Systems," in Larry Diamond and Mark F. Plattner, eds., *The Global Resurgence of Democracy* (Baltimore: Johns Hopkins University Press, 1993), pp. 127 ff.

8. Arend Lijphart, *Democracy in Plural Societies: A Comparative Exploration* (New Haven, CT: Yale University Press, 1977).

9. Philippe Schmitter and Gerhard Lehmbruch, *Trends Toward Corporatist Intermediation* (Beverly Hills, CA: Sage, 1979).

10. Arend Lijphart, *Patterns of Democracy: Government Forms and Performance in Thirty-Six Countries* (New Haven, CT: Yale University Press, 1999), p. 226.

11. George H. Gadbois, Jr., "The Institutionalization of the Supreme Court of India," in John R. Schmidhauser, ed., *Comparative Judicial Systems* (London: Butterworth Enterprises, 1987), pp. 111–142.

12. Donald S. Lutz reports that the U.S. Constitution, amended 26 times in 202 years (at the time of his writing in 1991) had been formally changed far less often than the cross-country average of about 2.5 amendments per year. "Toward a Theory of Constitutional Amendment," *American Political Science Review* 88 (1994), pp. 355–370. However, the Japanese constitution, of about average rigidity, had never been amended. Also see Ivo Duchacek, *Power Maps: Comparative Politics of Constitutions* (Santa Barbara, CA: ABC Clio Press, 1973), pp. 210 ff.

13. Arend Lijphart, *Democracies: Patterns of Majoritarian and Consensus Government in Twenty-One Countries* (New Haven, CT: Yale University Press, 1984), Chs. 1 and 2; and Lijphart, *Patterns of Democracy*, 1999. Robert Dahl, *Democracy and Its Critics* (New Haven, CT: Yale University Press, 1989), particularly Ch. 11, reviews and evaluates Lijphart's classification.

14. For a survey of parliamentary committees in Europe, see Ingvar Mattson and Kaare Strøm, "Parliamentary Committees," in Herbert Döring, ed., *Parliaments and Majority Rule in Western Europe* (New York: St. Martin's, 1995), pp. 249–307.

15. See Joel Aberbach, Robert D. Putnam, and Bert A. Rockman, *Bureaucrats and Politicians in Western Democracies* (Cambridge, MA: Harvard University Press, 1981).

16. Mark V. Nadel and Francis E. Rourke, "Bureaucracies," in Fred Greenstein and Nelson Polsby, eds., *Handbook of Political Science*, vol. 5 (Reading, MA: Addison-Wesley, 1975), pp. 373–440.

17. See Frank Stacey, *The British Ombudsman* (Oxford, England: Clarendon Press, 1971); Roy Gregory and Peter Hutchesson, *The Parliamentary Ombudsman: A Study in the Control of Administrative Action* (London: Allen and Unwin, 1975).

18. On the difficulties involved in reducing administrative corruption in developing countries, see Robert Klitgard, *Controlling Corruption* (Berkeley, CA: University of California Press, 1989).

19. See Pippa Norris, "Legislative Recruitment," in Lawrence LeDuc, Richard G. Niemi, and Pippa Norris, eds., *Comparing Democracies* (London: Sage, 1996), pp. 184–215; and Richard E. Matland, "Women's Representation in National Legislatures: Developed and Developing Countries," *Legislative Studies Quarterly* 23, No. 1 (February 1998): 109–125.

CHAPTER SEVEN

Public Policy

In this chapter, we shift our focus to the policies governments pursue. **Public policies** encompass all those authoritative public decisions that governments make. We shall refer to them as the **outputs** of the political system. Policies or outputs are chosen for a purpose; they are meant to promote different end results that we shall refer to as political **outcomes.** Different policy instruments may be more or less efficient ways to reach the outcomes that policymakers ultimately want. We therefore want to know the relationships between political outputs and outcomes. The fact that governments exist to make policy does not necessarily mean that the policies a particular society gets are the ones that its citizens asked for or would have wanted. Whether a certain outcome is good or bad ultimately depends on normative criteria of policy choice that we call *political goods and values.* Though politicians and citizens may legitimately disagree over what social results they want, it is important to keep these goals in mind when studying public policy. Whatever values and goals policymakers and citizens have will surely affect their evaluation of the political outcomes they actually reach. In this chapter, we shall discuss these aspects of public policy in order.

GOVERNMENT AND WHAT IT DOES

Governments do many things. Some of them are timeless, similar in kind to the public policy challenges that existed in the ancient world. In the days of the Roman Empire, for example, military defense was a major government responsibility. It continues to be so in most societies today. In other ways, governments today do things that were unthinkable to rulers in the past. For example, contemporary governments regulate telecommunications and air transportation, policy areas that were unknown until the twentieth century.

Governments as Producers

What governments do can be summarized under several labels. First, governments produce many goods and services. Exactly what governments produce varies a great deal. In most societies, they provide services such as law enforcement and postal services, but in many countries they go far beyond this. In the former Soviet Union and many other communist states, governments owned and operated most major industries and produced everything from military equipment to consumer goods such as clothing and shoes. In a capitalist society such as the United States, the government produces far fewer goods of these kinds, particularly in the consumer goods sector. In other advanced industrial societies, such as much of Western Europe, the government is a larger producer than in the United States, but a far smaller one than in the former Soviet Union. Governments control various industries in many states, but the range is very different. In recent decades, one study shows, governments in the United States employed only 1 percent of the persons engaged in mining and manufacturing and 28 percent of those working for public utilities supplying gas, water, and electrical power; in France, the corresponding figures were 8 percent and 71 percent. Capitalist, free-market societies tend to have governments that are less active as producers than have socialist societies. Yet, there is no society in which the government produces no goods and services, and similarly no state in which all industries are run by the government. Even in the former Soviet Union, part of the agricultural sector was private, as were many simple consumer services such as baby-sitting. On the other hand, even in the United States and similarly capitalist societies, governments provide a range of goods and services, as noted above.

Public Policies

The importance of governments goes far beyond their role as producers of goods and services. Indeed, this may not even be their most important role in most contemporary states. Governments also engage in various forms of public policy, which is the focus of this chapter. Public policies may be summarized and compared according to outputs—that is, according to the kinds of actions governments take in order to accomplish their purposes. We classify these actions or outputs under four headings:

1. the **extraction** of resources—money, goods, persons, and services—from the domestic and international environments;
2. the **distribution**—of money, goods, and services;
3. the **regulation** of human behavior—the use of compulsion and inducement to enforce extractive and distributive compliance or otherwise bring about desired behavior; and
4. **symbolic policies**—the political speeches, holidays, rites, public monuments and statues, and the like—used by governments to exhort citizens to desired forms of conduct, often to build a sense of community (see Chapter 1).

Nightwatchman State, Police State, Welfare State

Political systems have different policy profiles. Some governments produce a lot of goods and services but regulate little. Elsewhere, the government may be heavily engaged in extraction and distribution, but relies on the private sector to produce most goods and services. We can classify states broadly according to their mix of policies and activities. For example, it is customary to contrast the "night-watchman state" of the nineteenth century with the "welfare states" that have emerged in many highly developed societies in the twentieth century, especially in Western Europe, as well as with the police states (under Nazism, fascism, and communism) that have also marked this century. The nightwatchman state is a Lockean state (see Chapter 1), primarily concerned with regulation aimed at preserving law, order, and commerce, and protecting its citizens against foreign attacks. The police state regulates much more intrusively and extracts resources more severely. Fascist and communist governments typically call on their citizens to devote a lot of time to military or other community service. Finally, the welfare state engages itself extensively in distributive activities that seek to provide for the health, education, employment, housing, and income support of its citizens. For this purpose, it also has to extract (tax its citizens) more extensively.

In the first chapter of this book, we discussed three important challenges facing many states in the contemporary world: building community, fostering development, and securing democracy and human rights. Many important public policies are wholly or in part directed at these important challenges. Important public policies are designed to strengthen national identity and community by reinforcing the status of a common language or culture, or by promoting allegiance to a shared political heritage. A host of economic policies aims to promote economic and social development and to distribute the benefits of such developments more or less broadly. Finally, other policies seek to establish or enhance mechanisms that enable citizens to control political decisions. In the past century most Western nations have been transformed from authoritarian, or oligarchic, regimes to democracies. Government policy has increasingly been used to meet popular needs and demands. We cannot infer from that, however, that everything democratic governments do is in the best interest of their citizens.

The data we present in this chapter are intended to provide background for these and other contemporary policy controversies. We will compare the policy performance of different countries across the world, giving an overview of the many policies that states pursue.

EXTRACTION

The first type of public policy is what we call extractive. All political systems extract resources from their environments. When simple societies go to war, individuals of specific age groups (most commonly young men) may be called on to fight. Such direct extraction of services is still found in modern states, in the form of military duty, other obligatory public service like jury duty, or compulsory labor imposed on those convicted of crime. The most common contemporary forms of resource extraction, however, are taxation and borrowing. **Taxation** is the extraction for governmental purposes of money or goods from members of a political system, for which they receive no immediate or direct benefit.

Tax policies are designed to meet a lot of different objectives, which sometimes conflict. On the one hand, governments often want to collect as much tax revenue as possible from their citizens in order to finance various services. On the other hand, they do not want to kill the goose that lays the golden egg. The more governments tax their citizens, the less these people are inclined to work, and if the tax burden becomes too onerous, they may leave the country altogether. Another common trade-off in tax policies is between efficiency and equity. *Efficiency* means extracting the most tax revenue possible at the lowest cost to economic production. *Equity* means taxing in such a way that no one is unfairly burdened, and particularly so that those who have the least are spared as much as possible. In most societies, the tax system is designed to redistribute wealth in favor of the less well-off. Therefore, income taxes are generally progressive, which means that better-off citizens are taxed at higher rates than those who are less well-off. However, highly progressive income taxes can reduce people's incentive to work and hurt capital formation. Therefore, they are often inefficient.

Personal and corporate income taxes and taxes on capital gains and wealth are called **direct taxes,** since they are directly levied on persons and corporations. Such taxes, as well as property taxes, tend to be progressive. But although corporate income taxes are progressive, corporations often avoid them through creative accounting or by moving their operations to countries where taxes are lower. If personal income taxes become too high, the same things can happen. **Indirect taxes** include sales and value-added taxes, excise taxes, and customs duties. Their distributive effects depend on who purchases the relevant commodities and services. Since the poor spend more of their income on food and clothing than do those who are better off, sales (or value-added) taxes on such necessities are regressive. But indirect taxes on luxury goods may be progressive, since the poor rarely purchase yachts, fine jewelry, or private planes. Payroll taxes, which are often used to finance pensions (e.g., social security in the United States), tend to hit the middle class, since the wealthy often receive a larger share of their income in the form of interest or capital gains. Such taxes on wages also penalize people in the labor force relative to retirees and homemakers and can therefore hurt employment. Political systems that rely heavily on sales and payroll taxes are less likely to attain a progressive tax structure overall. On the other hand, sales and payroll taxes are less "visible" than income taxes and seem to generate less resentment and tax avoidance. In many countries, particularly where the government does not have good financial records, indirect taxes are easier to collect. Finally, the more mobile a tax object is, the more difficult it is to tax it. Financial investments tend to be highly mobile, which makes them difficult to tax. Land and its improvements, on the other hand, are not very mobile at all, and many states tax them substantially.

Besides redistribution, tax policies are often designed to promote certain social values, such as charity, energy conservation, or home ownership. For example, many countries stimulate home ownership by making mortgage interest payments tax deductible. The rationale is that home ownership promotes stable families who take an active interest in their neighborhoods. On the other hand, incentives of this kind can, if they are too generous, lead to economic distortions and reduced output. If such tax incentives are too strong, they may lead families to overinvest in housing, so that businesses are starved of capital that might make them grow and prosper. Moreover, mortgage deductions are primarily a middle-class benefit,

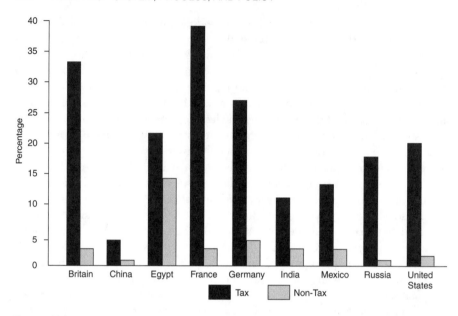

FIGURE 7.1   CENTRAL GOVERNMENT REVENUE AS A PERCENTAGE OF GDP
AND BY SOURCE OF REVENUE FOR SELECTED COUNTRIES 1997 *Source:* World
Bank, *World Development Report, 1999–2000* (New York: Oxford University Press, 2000), table 14,
pp. 256–57.

since truly poor families rarely own their own homes. Thus such policies may ex-
acerbate differences in wealth.

Figure 7.1 shows the central government revenues as a percentage of the
gross domestic product (GDP), the total value of goods and services produced
by a country's residents in a year. For the average country in Figure 7.1, about a
fifth of the GDP is extracted by the central government's taxes, but in some countries the proportion is much higher. Regional and local taxes add to the tax burden. In federal systems, such as Brazil, Germany, India, Russia, and the United
States, these can increase the total tax burden by a third or more.[1]

Governments also derive revenues from non-tax sources (the lighter columns
in Figure 7.1,) such as administrative fees and income from business enterprises
that they run. The total size of government revenue from all these sources in some
advanced capitalist countries is not radically smaller than that of Eastern European countries when they were under Communist control.

Growing tax burdens have led to taxpayer revolts and some scaling back of government extraction. But Sweden still extracts more than 50 percent of its GNP in
taxes and France comes close to the 50-percent mark. Britain and Germany (after
taking account of the subnational governments) are among a number of advanced
industrial societies that collect revenue at around the 40-percent level of GDP,
while the United States and Russia extract about a third. Outside the
European–North American area, central government revenue rarely exceeds 20
percent. Egypt, with its substantial public sector, is an exception. Much of its rev-

enue comes from public enterprises and foreign aid. The central government revenue of India is under 15 percent, which would be increased by about a third if we add state and local governments.

The tax profiles of different states depend on the kinds of taxes imposed, the distribution of income and wealth, the consumption patterns of different population groups, and the mobility of capital and labor. In Germany and Britain most of the revenue comes from social security and income taxes, but Germany relies far more heavily on social security payments and Britain more on income taxes. India and Mexico receive most of their revenue from indirect taxes. Heidenheimer, Heclo, and Adams classify the tax systems of the advanced free-market economies of the **Organization for Economic Cooperation and Development (OECD)** countries into three categories: (1) heavy social security tax systems (including Germany, Austria, the Netherlands, France, and Italy), which receive one-third to one-half of their revenue from social security, which is imposed more or less equally on both employers and employees; (2) the United States and Japan, which fall the farthest below average in total tax burden and rely heavily on direct taxes rather than on sales and consumption taxes; and finally (3) countries such as Sweden and Norway, which impose the highest tax burdens of all the OECD countries and rely on all three types of taxation—direct, indirect, and social security payments but impose particularly burdensome social security payments on employers.[2]

Although overall tax burdens continue to grow, income tax rates have decreased in Western countries since the early 1980s, as there has been a shift from direct income taxes to less visible indirect consumption taxes. From 1975 to 1990 British top marginal income tax rates declined by 43 percentage points, the U.S. rates by 42 points (though they have since risen by about 13 points under Presidents Bush and Clinton), Swedish rates by 35 points, and Japanese rates by 25 points. The average decline in top tax rates for all OECD countries was 18 percent.[3] Tax rates have come down because of the spread of economic views that stress the importance of entrepreneurial incentives for productivity. Lower marginal income tax rates stimulate economic activity and lessen incentives for tax evasion, but they may cause growing income inequalities.

DISTRIBUTION

Government does not only take—it also gives away, and that is what we call distribution. Distributive policies include the allocation by governmental agencies of various kinds of money, goods, services, honors, and opportunities to individuals and groups in the society. It can be measured and compared according to the quantity of whatever is distributed, the areas of human life touched by these benefits, the sections of the population receiving these benefits, and the relationship between human needs and governmental distributions intended to meet these needs.

Figure 7.2 reports central governmental expenditures as a percentage of GDP in the spending categories of health, education, and defense. Clearly, central government expenditures depend a great deal on the level of economic development. Developed countries generally allocate from one-half to two-thirds of their

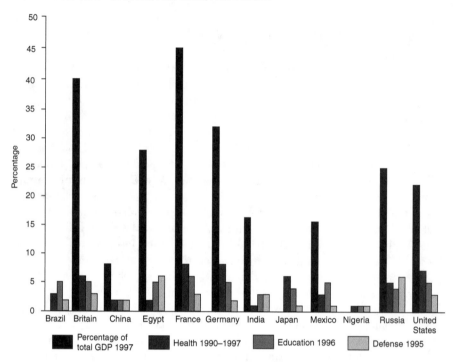

FIGURE 7.2   CENTRAL GOVERNMENT EXPENDITURES AS A PERCENTAGE OF GDP AND BY OBJECT OF EXPENDITURE 1990–1997 *Source:* World Bank, *World Development Report: 1999–2000* (New York: Oxford University Press, 2000), able 14, pp. 256–257; Table 7, pp. 242–243; Table 6, pp. 240–241; Table 17, pp. 262–263.

central government expenditures to education, health, and welfare. France, Germany, and Britain spend more than two-thirds of their budgets here, as compared with just under one-half of all state and local expenditures in the United States. Developing countries such as India and Nigeria spend very little on health, but typically a little more on education. Low-income countries face a tragic quandary: While they urgently need to upgrade the skills of their workforces, their commitments in education and health are insufficient to make rapid headway. The government in a country such as Nigeria seems hardly to touch its people. India's efforts are only slightly greater. Sadly, the countries that "need" it the most have the least to spend on education and health.

National security spending shows a different pattern. Particularly among less-developed countries, spending varies as much with the international environment as with overall economic means. Some states that are locked in tense international confrontations, such as in the Middle East, or that are trying to exert international influence, make extraordinary defense efforts. Because of its worldwide security commitments, the United States is by far the heaviest military spender, though in recent years U.S. defense spending has decreased substantially. Relative to the size of the national economy, however, Egypt spent more on defense in 1995 than did the United States. Japan, which spends as much as most Western countries on health and education, was very low in defense efforts. Prior to the watershed year of 1989, the Soviet Union and the Communist countries of Eastern Europe spent less on education, health, and welfare than the democracies of Western Europe. As the successor countries of the former Communist bloc introduce market economies, their government revenue and expenditure patterns may become more similar to the West.

Harold Wilensky's study of welfare efforts in some 64 widely divergent countries confirms that poor nations, with limited budgets and many pressing demands, cannot easily spare the resources for these programs.[4] In both absolute and relative terms, social security expenditure in poor nations tends to be limited. But in these societies the aged and the infirm typically receive some care through the extended family. Just as our GNP measures fail to include the subsistence economy and therefore underreport the wealth of the poorest countries (see Chapter 1), our measures of educational and health expenditures may underreport the efforts of the poorest states. Most developing societies still have a preindustrial welfare safety net. Wilensky also found that larger welfare programs were associated with centralized governments, well-organized working-class parties and movements, and low military expenditures.

The Welfare State

The twentieth century has witnessed a vast increase in the scope of distributive policies in industrial societies. This has largely been associated with the growth of the **welfare state.** The welfare state generally refers to a set of government, and sometimes private, policies in the areas of old age pensions (known in the United States as social security), health, sickness, and accident insurance, unemployment benefits, and the like. Over time, welfare state policies have come to include such benefits as housing subsidies, child and childcare benefits, and other distributive policies. The first modern welfare state programs were introduced in Germany in the 1880s. In response to Germany's rapid industrialization and urbanization, the government began offering social insurance programs that protected workers against unemployment, accidents, sickness, and old age poverty. During the twentieth century, most industrialized states have adopted and greatly expanded welfare state policies, particularly in the period from the Great Depression of the 1930s until the 1970s.

Figure 7.3 shows that the welfare state in advanced capitalist (OECD) countries has continued to grow during the 1980s and 1990s, albeit at a somewhat slower rate. As the figure shows, welfare state spending consists of two major categories: cash transfers to individuals and families, and direct government spending on services. Though both categories have grown, the transfer programs remain the largest. Among the individual programs that make up the welfare state, old-age pensions (social security) and health care loom particularly large. In many European countries with jobless rates of 10 to 15 percent, unemployment benefits are another major government outlay.

Not all welfare states are alike. Even among the advanced industrial countries, some welfare states are more extensive than others, and different political

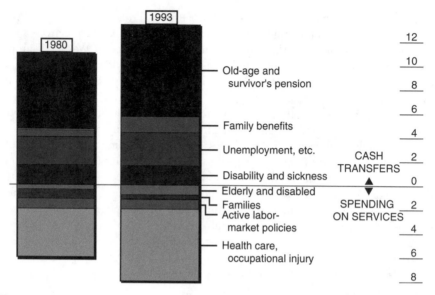

FIGURE 7.3 THE WELFARE STATE IN OECD COUNTRIES (OECD AVERAGE TRANSFERS AND SPENDING AS PERCENT OF GDP) *Source:* "Privatising Peace of Mind," *The Economist,* (October 24, 1998), p. 4.

systems emphasize different programs and benefits. All the wealthier nations make efforts to assist the aged, the disabled, and the unemployed; however, differences in expenditures reflect policy and historical experience. The U.S. model stresses equality of opportunity through public education. In contrast, on the European continent, social security and health programs have taken precedence over education. The United States made a much greater effort, and much earlier, in mass education than did most European nations. On the other hand, Americans began spending on social insurance and public services much later, and still do less in this area. Americans have historically put much more emphasis on equality of opportunity and less on welfare obligations than Europeans.

Also, it is important to keep in mind that many welfare services in the United States are provided by private foundations, churches and other religious organizations, and individuals. In 1997 Americans made private donations of $143 billion to nonprofit organizations. More than three-fourths of these gifts came from living individuals, many of them persons of very limited means. The nonprofit sector of the U.S. economy accounts for 8 percent of the gross domestic product, more than twice as much as in 1960. It employs close to 10 percent of the American workforce, more than the federal and state governments combined.[5] The nonprofit sector exists in other developed states as well, but generally on a much smaller scale.

At the same time, governments have greatly expanded their spending on other benefits. Education is one of the most important of these. Developing societies have made large efforts to provide at least primary education for all of their citizens, while in most of the more developed societies there has been a huge increase in secondary and university enrollments. A few decades ago, fewer than 5 percent of young adults in many European countries were able to pursue a university or college education. Today, those numbers have risen to 40 percent or more (as will be later shown in Table 7.5). In most of these countries, the majority of colleges and universities are public. Consequently, government spending on secondary and higher education has risen very substantially.

As government expenditures have grown to between one-third and one-half of the national product in most industrial democracies, a number of problems have arisen. In some countries the increasing cost of the welfare state in taxes has caused serious concern about the costs of these programs and the ability of future generations to pay for them. One of the most serious problems is that at the same time that senior citizens are qualifying for greater pension benefits and health care costs are rising rapidly, the ranks of the elderly are swelling relative to those in the workforce. Figure 7.4 shows that over the next decades, dependency ratios will increase in all advanced industrial societies, and particularly in such countries as Japan. The dependency ratio is the proportion of those outside the workforce (because they are too young or too old) to those in the working-age population. That means that fewer and fewer working people will have to pay higher and higher taxes to support existing health and welfare programs. In the United States, there have been concerns that Medicare and Social Security may incur large deficits in the future. In other countries, social welfare programs are already costing more than their designated taxes are bringing in.

Another problem with some welfare state policies is that they give citizens few incentives to behave responsibly. For example, generous unemployment or sick leave policies may give people little incentive to work. The unusually generous sick leave benefits in Norway give workers 100 percent of their pay from the first day that they miss work. While Norwegian workers thus enjoy a lot of income security, the country also has one of the highest absenteeism rates in the world. In many Norwegian industries, the average worker is absent one out of eight working days. In neighboring Sweden, which has less generous sick leave benefits, workers are "sick" much less often.

These widely perceived problems with the welfare state have stirred efforts to prevent further increases in spending obligations (entitlements) and to contain the costs of those already in effect. Conservative parties in particular have stressed setting limits on public expenditures and labor costs.[6] The size of the government budget and its effects on savings, investment, inflation, and employment have been the central issue in the politics of advanced industrial societies in recent years. Thus the gradual expansion of welfare benefits, which characterized the earlier decades of the twentieth century, can no longer be taken for granted.

REGULATION

Regulation is the exercise of political control over the behavior of individuals and groups in the society. There are many ways in which governments can regulate the lives of their citizens. Although we usually associate regulation with legal coercion or its threat, there are other ways to regulate as well. Governments may control

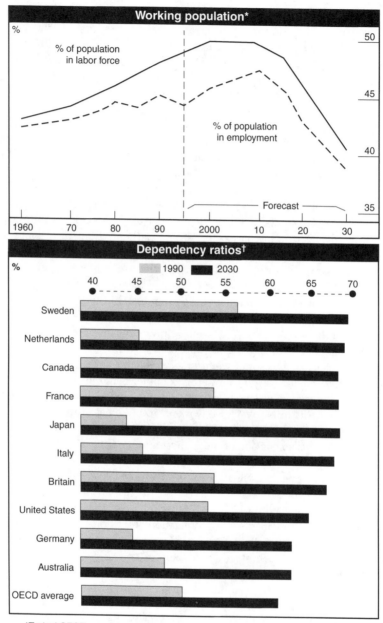

*Typical OECD country
†Population aged 0–14 and 65 and over as percentage of working-age population

FIGURE 7.4   THE SHRINKING WORKING POPULATION   *Source:* "Privatising Peace of Mind," *The Economist,* (October 24, 1998), p. 9.

behavior by offering material or financial inducements or by persuasion or moral exhortation. For example, many governments try to reduce tobacco use by a combination of methods: (1) bans on smoking, sales, or advertising, (2) sales ("sin") taxes, and (3) information campaigns to convince citizens of the hazards of tobacco use.

Regulation occurs for a number of reasons, as we have discussed in Chapter 1. As social contract theorists such as Hobbes and Locke realized, government regulation can facilitate many beneficial social activities. Economic production and commerce, for example, relies on government regulation to establish and protect property rights and to enforce contractual obligations. At the same time, citizens and consumers often demand regulations that protect them against fraud, manipulation, and obnoxious externalities such as environmental degradation. Increasingly, governments and international organizations, such as the European Union, have been involved in setting product standards, particularly for such products as pharmaceuticals and food. Governments also regulate to protect their citizens, and often particularly children and women, against physical and other abuse, and some such protections are extended to animals and the natural environment as well.

Government regulative activities have proliferated enormously over the last century or so, due to new objective needs as well as to new demands by the citizens. Industrialization and urban concentration have caused problems in traffic, health, and public order. Industrial growth has created problems with monopolies, industrial safety, labor exploitation, and pollution. Moreover, the growth of science and the development of the attitude that humanity can harness and control nature have led to increased demands for governmental action. Finally, changes in citizen values can lead to demands for new kinds of regulation. Thus, in recent decades regulation in the United States has extended to include gun control, protection of voting rights, prohibition of discrimination in employment, control of pollution, and the like. At the same time, in most modern nations regulation of birth control, abortion, divorce, and sexual conduct has lessened.

But even though there are many similarities in regulative policies across the world, states often differ substantially in their policy profiles. Patterns of regulation vary not only with industrialization and urbanization, for example, but also with cultural values. In the study of public policy, we describe and explain such differences between political systems by asking the following questions:

1. What aspects of human behavior and interaction are regulated and to what degree? Does the government regulate such domains as family relations, economic activity, religious activity, political activity, geographic mobility, professional and occupational qualifications, and protection of person and property? These questions have to do with the *domain* of government regulation.
2. What sanctions are used to compel or induce citizens to comply? Does the government use exhortation and moral persuasion, financial rewards and penalties, licensing of some types of action, physical confinement or punishment, or other forms of coercion? These questions help us map the *instruments*, or *mechanisms*, of regulation.
3. What social groups are regulated, with what procedural limitations on enforcement and what protections for rights? Are these sanctions applied

uniformly, or do they affect different individuals or groups differently? Are there rights of appeal? Such questions help us identify the *subjects* of regulation.

All modern states use sanctions in varying degrees, reflecting different values, goals, and strategies. Yet, one aspect of regulation is particularly important for political purposes: government control over political participation and communication. Recall from earlier chapters that the presence of political competition defines whether a political system can be democratic. Countries vary all the way from authoritarian systems that prohibit party organization, voluntary associations, and freedom of communication, to democratic ones, where such rights are protected. Government regulation in this area therefore has a crucial effect on democracy.

Regulation is not always negative, however, as in the suppression of rights. Our civilization and amenities depend on governmental regulation. Such matters as safety of persons and property, prevention of environmental pollution, provision of adequate sanitation, safe disposal of toxic wastes, maintenance of occupational safety, and equal access to housing and education are commonly covered by governmental regulation.

Table 7.1 shows the political rights and civil liberties ratings for the countries included in this book, based on expert judgments. Political rights refer to the opportunities people have to participate in the choice of political leaders— voting rights, the right to run for office, and the like. **Civil liberties** refer to the protection of substantive areas of human behavior, such as freedom of speech, press, assembly, and religion, as well as procedural protections, such as those of trial by jury and against arbitrary and cruel treatment. There is an important

Table 7.1 POLITICAL RIGHTS AND LIBERTIES RATINGS FOR SELECTED COUNTRIES 1999–2000

Country	Political Rights	Civil Liberties
Brazil	3	4
Britain[a]	1	2
China	7	6
Egypt	6	5
France	1	2
Germany	1	2
India	2	3
Japan	1	2
Mexico	3	4
Nigeria	4	3
Russia	4	5
United States	1	1

[a]Rating for Britain explicitly excludes Northern Ireland, which was rated 3, 3.
Source: Expert ratings of political rights and civil liberties for each country on 1 (highest) to 7 (lowest) scale, provided by Freedom House from their website, www.freedomhouse.com. Ratings are as of January 1, 2000.

correspondence between political and civil rights. No country that scores high on participatory rights is very low on civil liberties, and no country low on participatory rights is high on civil liberties. This suggests a strong relationship between popular participation and the rule of law and equitable procedure. The developed democratic countries all have ratings of 1 or 2 for both political and civil rights. At the other extreme, China and Egypt strongly suppress both political rights and civil liberties. China in particular has tried to exercise comprehensive control over the media and sets few limits on government regulation vis-à-vis the individual. Brazil, Mexico, Nigeria, and Russia were rated in the middle. These rankings, of course, vary over time. Nigeria's military governments of the 1990s were repressive and frequently brutal, earning scores of 7 and 6 before power was turned over to an elected civilian president in 1999. Rights and liberties in the United States have improved since the civil rights movement of the 1960s.

In a cross-national study of governmental repression in 153 countries during the 1980s, Steven C. Poe and C. Neal Tate concluded that democratic political institutions and conditions of peace and social order best explained positive civil and political rights records. Authoritarian states and those involved in internal or international war were the most frequent civil rights violators. A high level of economic development also helped explain a strong rights record.[7]

COMMUNITY-BUILDING AND SYMBOLIC POLICIES

A fourth type of output is symbolic policies. Much communication by political leaders takes the form of appeals to history, courage, boldness, wisdom, and magnanimity embodied in the nation's past; or appeals to values and ideologies, such as equality, liberty, community, democracy, communism, liberalism, religious tradition, or promises of future accomplishment and rewards. Political leaders appeal to such values for different reasons—for example, winning elections or getting their own pet projects legislated. But many symbolic appeals and policies have the purpose of building community—for example, by boosting people's national identity, civic pride, or trust in government.

Symbolic outputs are also intended, however, to enhance other aspects of performance: to make people pay their taxes more readily and honestly, comply with the law more faithfully, or accept sacrifice, danger, and hardship. Such appeals may be especially important in times of crisis. Some of the most magnificent examples are the speeches of Pericles in the Athenian Assembly during the Peloponnesian War or those of Franklin D. Roosevelt in the depths of the Great Depression, or of Winston Churchill when Britain stood alone after the fall of France in World War II. But symbolic policies are also important in less extreme circumstances. "Jawboning"—exhorting business executives and labor leaders to go slow in raising prices and wages—is a frequently employed anti-inflation measure. Public buildings, plazas, monuments, holiday parades, and civic and patriotic indoctrination in schools all attempt to contribute to the population's sense of governmental legitimacy and its willingness to comply with public policy.

OUTCOMES: DOMESTIC WELFARE

While we can describe the policies that different governments pursue in the areas of extraction, distribution, and regulation, it is not always clear what their consequences will be. How do extractive, distributive, regulative, and symbolic policies affect the lives of citizens? Unexpected economic, international, or social events may frustrate the purpose of political leaders. Thus a tax rebate to increase consumption and stimulate the economy may be nullified by a rise in the price of oil. Increases in health expenditures may have no effect because of rising health costs, or health services may not reach those most in need. Sometimes policies have unintended consequences that may be undesirable. Consequently, we have to look into the actual welfare outcomes as well as governmental policies and implementation, in order to estimate the effectiveness of public policy.

Table 7.2 compares a number of welfare indicators for our selection of countries. The first two columns report measures of economic well-being or its lack: growth in private consumption and percent of the population living on less than $2 per day. The severe problems of Nigeria are particularly notable: not only do we see the vast majority of the population living on less than $2 a day, which is also true in India, but private consumption spending actually declined in the 1990s. The latter columns report availability of critical public facilities: safe water and sanitation. Table 7.3 reports on a number of health outcomes, including life expectancy, infant mortality, the health of children, and fertility. Table 7.4 tells us about access to com-

Table 7.2   WELFARE OUTCOMES FOR SELECTED COUNTRIES 1990–1998

Country	Growth in Private Consumption per Capita % Annual 1980–1997[a]	Population Below $2 per Day %, Late 1990s	Access to Safe Water (%), Mid-1990s	Access to Sanitation (%), Mid-1990s
Brazil	0.2	17.4	72	67
Britain	1.8	ND	100	100
China	4.5	53.7	90	21
Egypt	1.3	52.7	64	11
France	1.1	ND	100	96
Germany	ND	ND	ND	ND
India	1.9	86.2	81	16
Japan	ND	ND	96	100
Mexico	0.0	42.5	83	66
Nigeria	−2.6	90.8	39	36
Russia	ND	25.1	ND	ND
United States	1.1	ND	ND	ND

[a]Corrected for distribution.
Source: World Bank, *Entering the 21ˢᵗ Century: World Development Report 1999–2000* (New York, Oxford University Press, 2000), pp. 232–233; World Bank, *World Development Indicators 2000,* Tables 2.4, 2.15. Retrieved May 12, 2000 from *http://www.worldbank.org/data/wdi2000*/pdfs/tab2_4.pdf,2_15.pdf

Table 7.3 HEALTH OUTCOMES FOR SELECTED COUNTRIES 1990–1998

Country	Public Health Expenditure as % of GDP	Physicians per 1000 Citizens	Life Expectancy at Birth, 1998	Infant Mortality per 1,000 Live Births	Infant Health: % Malnutrition Under Age 5	Fertility Rate
Brazil	3.4	1.3	67	33	6	2.3
Britain	5.9	1.6	75	6	ND	1.7
China	2.0	2.0	70	31	16	1.9
Egypt	1.8	2.1	67	49	15	3.2
France	7.1	2.9	78	5	ND	1.8
Germany	8.3	3.4	77	5	ND	1.4
India	0.6	.4	63	70	53	3.2
Japan	5.9	1.8	81	4	ND	1.4
Mexico	2.8	1.2	72	30	14	2.8
Nigeria	0.2	.2	53	76	39	5.3
Russia	4.5	4.6	67	17	3	1.2
United States	6.5	2.6	77	7	ND	2.0

Source: World Bank, Entering the 21st Century: World Development Report 1999–2000 (New York, Oxford University Press, 2000), pp. 232–233; World Bank, World Development Indicators 2000, Tables 2.14, 2.16, 2.18. Retrieved May 12, 2000 from http://www.worldbank.org/data/wdi2000/pdfs/tab2_14.pdf,2_16.pdf,2_18.pdf

Table 7.4 COMMUNICATION AND INFORMATION, 1995–1998

Country	Newspapers	Televisions	Telephones, Main Lines	Personal Computers
Brazil	40	316	121	30.0
Britain	329	645	557	263.0
China	ND	272	70	8.9
Egypt	40	122	60	9.1
France	218	601	570	207.8
Germany	311	580	567	304.7
India	ND	69	22	2.7
Japan	518	707	503	237.2
Mexico	97	261	104	47.0
Nigeria	24	66	4	5.7
Russia	105	420	197	40.6
United States	215	847	661	458.6

Note: Per 1,000 people unless otherwise indicated.
Source: World Bank, *World Development Indicators 2000,* Tables 5.10, 5.11, 5.12. Retrieved May 12, 2000 from *http://www.worldbank.org/data/wdi2000*/pdfs/tab5_10.pdf,5_10.pdf,5_12.pdf

munication and information, such as telephones, newspapers, television, and personal computers. Table 7.5 compares countries at various levels of economic development in terms of their educational efforts and the extent to which they succeed. These data show how governmental and private efforts, in societies at different levels of economic development and of differing social structures and cultures, affect human life chances. Although the natural resources and the socioeconomic structure constrain these outcomes, government and private efforts can make a big difference.

In Chapter 1, we saw how income distribution tends to be most unequal in medium-income developing societies, such as Brazil, and more equal in advanced market societies as well as in low-income developing societies, such as India (Table 1.4.) In his studies of European economic history, Simon Kuznets showed that in the early stages of industrialization income distribution became more unequal. In the later stages of industrialization, however, income distribution came closer to equality again.[5] The "Kuznets curve" is explained by the common trends of economic and political modernization. In the early stages of modernization, the large rural sector is left behind as industry and commercial agriculture begin to grow. At higher levels of economic attainment, the rural agricultural sector is reduced in size compared with the industrial and service sectors. In addition, when trade unions and political parties develop in democratic countries, they bring about legislation that affects income distribution through taxation, wage policy, and distributive policies.

Economic development affects economic prosperity, public health facilities such as sanitation and availability of potable water, health expenditure and outcomes, and access to the outside world through telephone and television, roads, and other infrastructure. During the 1990s, the average public health expenditure per capita for the economically developed countries was $2505, compared with $182

Table 7.5 EDUCATION AND LITERACY, 1997–1998

Country	Public Education Expenditure As Percent of GDP, 1997	Percentage of Relevant Age Group Enrolled—Secondary, 1997	Percentage of Relevant Age Group Enrolled, Tertiary, 1997	Percentage 15 Years and Above Illiterate, All, 1998	Percentage 15 Years and Above Illiterate Female, 1998	Female Share of Labor Force, 1998
Brazil	5.1	66	15	16	16	35
Britain	5.3	92	52	ND	ND	44
China	2.3	70	6	17	25	45
Egypt	4.8	75	23	46	58	30
France	6.0	99	51	ND	ND	45
Germany	4.8	95	47	ND	ND	42
India	3.2	60	7	44	57	32
Japan	3.6	100	43	ND	ND	41
Mexico	4.9	66	16	9	11	33
Nigeria	0.7	33[a]	4	39	48	36
Russia	3.5	88	41	1	1	49
United States	5.4	96	81	ND	ND	46

[a]"Gross," rather than "net," enrollment.
Source: World Bank, World Development Indicators 2000, Tables 2.9, 2.10, 2.12, 2.3. Retrieved May 12, 2000 from http://www.worldbank.org/data/wdi2000/pdfs/tab2_9.pdf,2_10.pdf,2_12.pdf,2_3,pdf; total literacy from http://www.worldbank.org/data/databytopic/ILIT.pdf

for the developing countries. The average number of physicians per 1000 persons in the developed world was 2.8, as compared with 1.3 in the developing world. While most of the people of the developed world had access to safe water, this was true for only about half of the population of the less-advantaged areas. The relationship between economic level and health is dramatically demonstrated in the figures for Nigeria: only 39% of the population has access to safe water. In addition the country has a high birth rate of 5.4 and its citizens have at birth a life expectancy of just over 50 years (compared with 70 to 80 years in advanced industrial countries). On the average there is only a single physician per 20,000 inhabitants; almost one out of ten infants fails to survive the first year of life; and more than one-third of Nigerian children under five years of age suffer from malnutrition.

The importance of culture for public policy is suggested by the figures for China and India. With a similarly low GNP per capita, Chinese average life expectancy is 70 years and infant mortality is 31 per 1,000 live births, while those of India are 63 years and 70 per 1,000, respectively. China has five times as many physicians as India relative to its population. Half of India's children under five were undernourished, as compared to a fifth of those in China.

While the incidence of infant mortality and malnutrition is much lower in advanced economies, these problems are still serious among the poor in advanced industrial countries such as the United States. Although Table 7.3 does not show this (because it shows only government, not private, health spending), the United States spends the largest proportion of its GNP on health care of any state (approximately 16 percent). At the same time, however, the United States has a somewhat higher infant death rate than Japan and Western Europe, due to more widespread poverty, drug abuse, and unequal access to health care. As Table 7.3 shows, Japan has an exceptional record in health outcomes. It has the longest life expectancy and the lowest infant mortality rate among all our countries; and its fertility rate of 1.4 means a declining population. (A fertility rate of approximately 2.1 results in a steady-state population. Anything over that rate results in population increase, which in poor countries reduces the impact of economic growth.)

Table 7.4 provides a brief picture of the communications infrastructure. In the developed countries on the average there is a telephone for every two persons; in Nigeria there are as few as four to a thousand. Television has become widely available even in countries at middling development levels (e.g., Brazil and Mexico). Personal computers, however, are much more rare outside the advanced industrial economies. Whereas the relative incidence of television sets is less than three times higher in the United States than it is in Brazil, the relative frequency of personal computers is 15 times higher.

Table 7.5 provides us with a picture of educational attainment in our selected countries. The first column, showing public education expenditure as a percentage of GDP, gives a rough measure of the "priority" given to education. Remember, however, that private schools, which in some countries are very common, are not counted here. Countries such as Egypt devote similar percentages of their GNP to education as do the advanced industrial societies. Hence we may say that they are making proportionally similar efforts to educate their populations. But the differences in dollar expenditures per student are very large. China and India spend less generously on education, even relative to the size of their economies. Nigeria spends the least of all and requires only children from ages 6 to 12 to attend school. The outcomes are largely what we might predict from these differences in output. Nigeria had only a third of the appropriate age cohort in secondary education, by far the poorest record of these countries. India's figures are double that. The figures for Egypt are even better—75 percent in secondary schools, and 23 percent in colleges, universities, and other postsecondary educational and training institutions. At the high end in educational outcomes, France, Germany, Japan, and Britain have virtually all of their primary and secondary school-age children in schools, and about half of the college-age population is in some form of advanced education. In the United States, college education is even more common.

The figures on literacy are a crude measure of skill and competence. Here the payoffs of development and investment in education are clear. Nearly half of the Egyptian, Indian, and Nigerian populations are unable to read or write. On the other hand, China, with a similarly low GNP and small investment in education, is only 17 percent illiterate. Women in developing countries are especially likely to lag behind in literacy. Surprisingly, however, about only a quarter of Chinese women were reported to be literate. These figures must, of course, be treated with caution, because they are often based on the number of school years completed, not on actual reading ability. The high official literacy figures in the United States, for example, conflict with studies showing substantial functional illiteracy among American adults.

The discrepancy between male and female literacy rates tells us something of the status of women. Those countries in which women make up a smaller proportion of the labor force (as shown in the last column in Table 7.5) also tend to be the ones in which female illiteracy is most common. Modernizing the status of women generally makes them better informed, which in turn may mean that they make choices that are more likely to lead to a more stable and healthy population. Faced with poverty, disease, and the absence of a safety net, parents in Third World countries traditionally want to have many children, to ensure that some survive and can support them in old age. The self-interest of parents in having large families comes into conflict with the national interest in population control and economic development. As women are educated and/or enter the labor force, they recognize the advantages of smaller families and become more aware of the importance of education and adequate health care.

Table 7.5 thus reveals the sobering difficulties of trying to change societies, even in an area such as literacy, where modern methods and technology are available. It is hard for a poor country to spend a high percentage of its GNP on education, because sacrifices must then be made elsewhere. The country's revenue is generally limited by the fact that much of its productive effort has to go into feeding a rapidly growing population. And no matter how large the country's effort may be, it does not translate into much per child, because the resource base is small and the population is growing rapidly. Moreover, since most older people are illiterate, the net effect on literacy is slow.

DOMESTIC SECURITY OUTCOMES

As Thomas Hobbes would remind us, maintaining domestic law and order and protecting persons and property are the most basic responsibilities of government. Without them the conduct of personal, economic, and civic life are impossible. Until recently crime rates have been on the increase in many advanced industrial countries, as well as in the developing world. Thus in the United States the crime rate increased by almost 15 percent between 1982 and 1991. In France the 1990 incidence of crimes against persons and property was almost twice that of 1975. In Russia the crime rate doubled between 1985 and 1993, as that country experienced the collapse and remaking of a moral and legal order. Crime rates have recently begun to come down in the United States and some other countries. The number of murders per 100,000 population in the United States peaked at 9.4 in 1994, and declined to 6.8 in 1997 (see Figure 7.5). Violence in Russia has skyrocketed, so that the country now has a murder rate three to four times as high

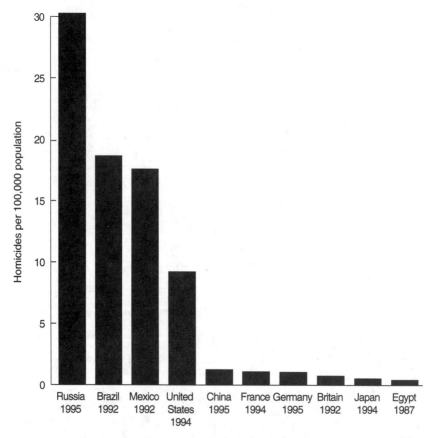

FIGURE 7.5   HOMICIDES PER 100,000 POPULATION IN SELECTED COUNTRIES, 1987–1995 *Source: United Nations Demographic Yearbook, 1996* (New York: United Nations, 1996).

as the United States. Brazil and Mexico also have murder rates that are considerably higher than the United States, while those of such European countries as England, France, and Germany are a small fraction of the American numbers. (All were at the 1 percent or below level in the early 1990s.) China has similarly low murder rates, whereas Japan and Egypt are even lower.

The high crime rate is primarily a problem of the larger urban areas where much of the population of modern countries resides. What these figures suggest is that in modern and modernizing societies over the last decades, despite increasing expenditures on law enforcement, the physical safety of our persons and possessions has been declining. Wealth and income may increase rapidly, but the liabilities of modernization include the anxiety over personal safety that is so common in urban life.

In a sense, the inner cities hold the outer cities in a state of siege. The United States is the primary example here, though the phenomenon is familiar though throughout the advanced industrial world. The reasons for this are complex, involving material, structural, cultural, and moral changes. Greatly increased migration into the inner cities of advanced industrial countries, or in the rapidly developing ones, either from the domestic countryside, or from foreign countries at lower levels of economic development, has increased diversity and conflict. The weakening and even the breakdown of the nuclear family have impaired the capacity of modern cultures to transmit effective standards of conduct to the young. Also, inequality of income and wealth, unemployment, and the hopelessness of life prospects in the inner city lie behind this general decline in public order and safety. In the former Communist countries the situation is compounded by the fact that these states have simultaneously undergone or are undergoing a major legal and moral revolution. In developing societies, such as Mexico and Nigeria, urban growth has been even more explosive than in the advanced capitalist states, and the problems of poverty and infrastructure are far more severe.

There are several reasons that crime rates have recently come down in the United States and elsewhere. One is a strong economy, in which more young people have been able to find jobs. A second reason is stricter law enforcement. According to a recent study, the United States now imprisons more people than any other country in the world—perhaps half a million more than communist China. The total prison population in the United States is around 1.8 million, including more than 1 million in custody primarily in state prisons, and 600,000 in local jails, awaiting sentencing or serving short sentences. This population has been increasing at a rate of more than 50,000 per year. Both federal and state governments seek to reduce crime by increasing the length of imprisonment. By removing the criminally prone from the streets, these authorities do succeed in cutting the crime rate, but at the cost of an exploding prison population. To meet these rising costs many prisons have been privatized, and prison labor employed for profit by private corporations. Similarly, in France the prison population almost doubled between 1983 and 1990.[9] Some impression of the different efforts in policing crime and disorder is reflected in the number of police officers relative to total population. The range is from the high of one police officer for every 350 persons in the United States, to 820 in India, and 1,140 in Nigeria. A third cause of lower crime rates has been a decrease in the number of youth at the age at which most crimes are committed. Given the rising 15–25-year-old male population in the United States in current years, we can expect violent crime to increase once again.

INTERNATIONAL OUTPUTS AND OUTCOMES

States typically engage in a great variety of international activities in order to enhance their welfare and security. Such economic, diplomatic, military, and informational activities may result in prosperity and depression, war and peace, the spread of ideologies and religions, and the like. Peter Gourevitch in his book *Politics in Hard Times* analyzes the policy responses of five Western industrial nations—Britain, France, Germany, Sweden, and the United States—to the three world depressions of 1870–1890, 1930–1940, and 1975–1985.[10] Gourevitch shows how these crises affected business, labor, and agriculture differently in each country; consequences for political structure and policy varied greatly. Thus the world depression of the 1930s resulted in a conservative reaction in Britain (the formation of a "National" government), a moderate left reaction in the United States (the "New Deal"), a polarization and paralysis of public policy in France ("Immobilisme"), a moderate social democratic reaction in Sweden, and a radical right and left polarization in Germany, leading to a breakdown of democracy and the emergence of National Socialism. While the causes of World War II were complex, the pacifism of Britain, the demoralization and defeatism in France, the isolationism of the United States, and the nihilism and aggression of Germany were all fed by the devastating worldwide economic depression of the 1930s.

The most costly outcome of the interaction among nations is warfare. Table 7.6 reports the numbers of deaths from international and internal collective violence

Table 7.6   DEATHS FROM COLLECTIVE CIVILIAN-MILITARY VIOLENCE FOR SELECTED COUNTRIES, 1900–1995

Country	Civilian Deaths	Military Deaths	Unspecified Deaths	Total Deaths
Brazil	—	1,000	2,000	3,000
Britain	131,000	1,350,000	—	1,481,000
China	4,047,000	2,671,000	818,000	7,536,000
Egypt	51,000	28,000	—	79,000
France	490,000	1,830,000	—	2,320,000
Germany	2,232,000	7,150,000	—	9,382,000
India	889,000	71,000	37,000	997,000
Japan	510,000	1,502,000	—	2,012,000
Mexico	125,000	125,000	10,000	260,000
Nigeria	1,005,000	1,000,000	6,000	2,011,000
Russia/USSR	12,028,000	11,901,000	96,000	24,025,000
United States	—	524,000	—	524,000
TOTALS	21,508,000	28,153,000	969,000	50,630,000

Sources: Adapted from Ruth Leger Sivard, "Wars and War Related Deaths, 1900–1995," *World Military and Social Expenditures 1996* (Washington: World Priorities, 1996), pp. 18–19. U.S. deaths add Korean and Vietnam war totals, from U.S. Department of State figures, to Sivard report of World War I and II deaths.

for our twelve selected countries for the greater part of the twentieth century (1900–1995). These are mostly civilian and military deaths occurring in the course of interstate warfare, but they also include the slaughter of civilians in the course of implementation of ideological goals as in the Soviet Union, the holocaust of European Jewry carried out by the Nazi's in the course of World War II, the many "ethnic cleansing" episodes in Europe and in Africa, and chronic and endemic civil wars in all parts of the world. The table shows the people of USSR-Russia, by a margin of more than two-to-one, to be the great victims of the tormented history of the twentieth century. The enormous casualties suffered by the Russians on the Eastern Front in the earlier years of World War I destroyed the legitimacy of the Czarist regime. The collapse of Czarism was followed by the Bolshevik Revolution, the Civil War, and the Terror, each of which cost the lives of millions. Soviet Russian suffering climaxed in World War II with a total of seventeen million civilian and military dead. The Soviet Union/Russia suffered more than 24 million civilian and military war dead in the course of the wars and other great disturbances of the twentieth century.

Germany has the second largest total of deaths from collective violence in the twentieth century. More than three million of them occurred in the First World War and these mostly military. In World War II Germany suffered almost five million military deaths and another one and three-quarter million violent civilian deaths for a total of almost nine and one-half million. These are casualties experienced by Germany, not including those caused by Germany and reported in figures for other countries.

Other countries with huge losses include Japan, which experienced over two million deaths in war, mostly in World War II, including half a million civilian losses. The suffering of the French and British was of roughly similar magnitude, with the cost to France somewhat higher than to Britain. The United Kingdom had more than a million war dead in World War I and France, half again as many. In World War II France lost more than 650,000; Britain, almost half a million. In World Wars I and II the United States, operating away from home and joining late, had fewer losses, but still over 120,000 in World War I and under half a million in World War II. In the Korean and Vietnam wars, while America suffered only moderate losses by these terrible standards, Korean and Vietnamese military and civilian dead were in the millions.

In the second half of the twentieth century, the most devastating conflicts have occurred in the Third World. Many African countries, newly independent in the decades after World War II, and consisting of ethnic components arbitrarily put together by colonial powers, have serious problems of national cohesion and have suffered from chronic civil war. Large-scale civil war in Nigeria in the late 1960s and early 1970s took more than two million lives. As British India settled into its (current) three parts of India, Pakistan, and Bangladesh, there have been numerous deadly conflicts within and between the three countries. Some two million lives, mostly civilian, have been lost, half of them, as shown in Table 7.6, in India. The territorial and power changes of the post–Cold War period brought another wave of ethnic slaughter, called "cleansing," religious clashes, and struggles for power in new nations between power factions and warlords. The breakup of the Soviet Union and Yugoslavia has resulted in bloody border wars and secessional conflicts (e.g., in Croatia, Bosnia, Kosovo in the old Yugoslavia, and Chechnya in Russia).

The Uppsala Conflict Data Project reports 103 armed conflicts (defined as involving at least 25 deaths) in the world from 1988 through 1997. Only six of these, including the continuing clashes between India and Pakistan, were interstate conflicts; most were within current state boundaries. In 1997, a fairly typical year, 33 of these conflicts were in progress, of which seven involved more than 1000 persons killed.[11] Although in 1998 this declined to 27 conflicts, of which only two were international, nuclear weapons tests conducted by India and Pakistan heightened fears of far deadlier consequences of their territorial dispute over Kashmir. Even aside from the horrors of nuclear conflict, the deadly costs of international warfare have gradually escalated. One authority estimates that more than 90 percent of the war deaths since 1700 have occurred in the twentieth century. Civilian deaths caused by war have increased even more rapidly than military ones. In the last decades of the century, more than three-quarters of the war deaths have been civilian.[12]

The United Nations in the post–Cold War world has intervened in some of these conflicts by providing peace-keeping missions when the parties to conflicts are ready to accept these mediations; more rarely as peace-makers when the conscience of the world cannot blink at cruel events transmitted by television. A case in point was the UN intervention in the Serbian invasion of Bosnia, and in the Serbian ethnic cleansing in Kosovo; or more recently in the transformation of the peace-keeping mission of the UN in the civil war in Sierra Leone into a peace-making effort in that African country. The UN's effectiveness in controlling collective violence both domestic and international depends on the maintenance of consensus among the great powers. How tenuous this consensus can become is illustrated in the troubled efforts of the UN to implement the disarmament and inspection agreements attending the conclusion of the Gulf War of 1990–1991.

The economic costs of national security are also quite high. Hidden in the national debts of most major countries in the form of large interest obligations are the deferred costs of borrowing for earlier wars and the maintenance of national defense in a world of nation-states still governed by the "security dilemma"—the mutual assumption among nations of the probable aggressive intent of their neighbors. Current defense expenditures, plus the interest costs of past conflicts, are "opportunity costs," funds that might have been spent on more constructive public objects or left in the private sector for consumption or investment. While military expenditures in the world have declined since the collapse of the Soviet Union, there is no promise that this reduction will continue, or that the sense of international safety that began to spread in the late 1980s and the 1990s will be justified by events.

POLITICAL GOODS AND VALUES

If we are to compare and evaluate public policy in different political systems, we need to consider the political goods that motivate different policies. That leads us back to the issues we discussed in Chapter 1, to the purposes that governments serve. There are at least three important criteria that most of us would agree that government policy should meet. The first is *fairness*. If government undertakes some public policy, we would like that policy to be fair. The problem is that people often disagree over what is fair. In some situations, and according to some people, fairness requires that all people are treated equally (as when family members attempt to divide a tempting pie). In other situations, fairness demands that individuals be treated according to their dessert or contributions (as when grades are given in a college course). And in yet other situations, fairness seems to mean that people are treated according to their needs (for example, in cases of medical treatment). Thus fairness can imply *equal treatment* in some cases, *just desserts* (reward in proportion to merit or contribution) in others, and *treatment according to need* in yet others. Many distributive policies—for example, pension systems such as social security/medicare in the United States—rely on some combination of these criteria. But the debate over these various conceptions of fairness is never settled. In most cases, however, fairness would rule out practices that are *arbitrary* or *partial*. Few of us would find it fair if government officials threw dice to determine who would be imprisoned or given pensions, or if they made such decisions solely on the basis of their personal prejudices or connections.

Government policy should also be *effective* and *efficient*. A preference for effectiveness means that we prefer policies that actually lead to their desired purpose to those that do not. Efficiency means that government policies should attain their objectives at the lowest possible cost. If two alternative policies would lead to the same result but at very different costs, we would prefer the policy with the lower cost. In designing government agencies, most of us would prefer institutions that are lean and inexpensive to bloated agencies that produce no better results. A final criterion is the promotion and preservation of *freedom*. As anarchists, libertarians, and other government skeptics would remind us, public policies should promote and protect freedom and basic human and political rights. If two policies are equally efficient and fair, then we would prefer the one that respects the rights and liberties of the citizens to the greater extent.

There is no simple way to say which value should prevail when they conflict. But it is different preferences between such values as freedom, fairness, and efficiency that set different cultures, parties, and political philosophies apart. One society or group of citizens may value fairness over liberty; another may make the opposite choice, as in the statement, "Give me liberty or give me death!"

This book is organized around the concepts of system, process, and policy. We can think about values as "political goods" related to each of those levels of analysis. A long tradition in political analysis has emphasized order, predictability, and stability. Citizens are most free and most able to act rationally when their environment is stable and predictable. We call these conditions "system values" since they reflect the functioning and effectiveness of the whole set of political institutions. Some people want change and new opportunities. Others dislike change and prefer stability. Political instability—constitutional breakdowns, frequent cabinet changes, riots, demonstrations, and the like—upsets most people and can cost lives and material destruction.

Another school of thought emphasizes goods associated with the political process—citizen participation and free political competition. Democracy is good and authoritarianism bad, according to this school of thought, because of the way citizens are treated in the process, and not so much because democracy, for example, produces better economic results. But a third and final focus is on policy goods, such as economic welfare, quality of life, and personal security. A political system that improves welfare, decreases inequalities, enhances public safety, and cleans up its environment becomes the model, whatever the political process that produced these results. Without taking sides in this discussion, we hold each of these goods to be important.

Table 7.7 draws on our three-level analysis of political systems to present a checklist of political goods or values. We cannot deal with these items at great length, only emphasize a few of the ideas involved. *System goods* have to do with the regularity and predictability with which political systems work and with their ability to adapt to environmental challenges. Regularity and adaptability are typically somewhat in conflict. There are times when order and stability are at the top of the agenda. In the United States, the administration of Warren Harding after World War I was such a period, called "a return to normalcy." There was a similar withdrawal from mobilization after World War II and the Korean War. On the

Table 7.7   POLITICAL GOODS

Levels of Political Goods	Classes of Goods	Content and Examples
System level	System maintenance	Regularity and predictability of processes in domestic and international politics
	System adaptation	Structural and cultural adaptability in response to environmental change and challenges
Process level	Participation in political inputs	Instrumental to domestic and foreign policy; directly produces a sense of dignity and efficacy, where met with responsiveness
	Compliance and support	Fulfillment of citizens' duty and patriotic service
	Procedural justice	Equitable procedure and equality before the law
Policy level	Welfare	Growth per capita; quantity and quality of health and welfare; distributive equity
	Security	Safety of person and property; public order and national security
	Liberty	Freedom from regulation, protection of privacy, and respect for autonomy of other individuals, groups, and nations

other hand, the 1930s and the 1960s were periods of change and adaptation, in which the reach of governmental powers was extended. But the stress on change and adaptation can also be a call for reductions in the scope in government, as in the Thatcher administration in Britain or in the Republican "Contract with America" of 1994–1995.

Process goods include participation, compliance, and procedural justice. We value participation not merely as a means to responsive government, but for its own sake, as it enhances citizen competence and dignity. Compliance with authority can also be a good, as individuals respond to the impulse to serve others, which can be one of humanity's most gratifying experiences. President John F. Kennedy in his inaugural address called on such impulses to serve and sacrifice when he said, "Ask not what your country can do for you; ask what you can do for your country." Procedural justice (trial by jury, habeas corpus, no cruel and unusual punishment) is another crucial process value, without which citizens would have much greater reasons to fear their governments.

Policy goods include welfare, personal and national security, and freedom from interference in a life of reasonable privacy. The right to bear arms, protected in the Second Amendment to the U.S. Constitution, has recently become a hotly contested issue. Liberty is sometimes viewed only as freedom from governmental regulation and harassment. Freedom is more than inhibition of government action, however, because private individuals and organizations may also commit infractions of liberty and privacy. In such cases, liberty may be fostered by government intervention. Much legislation against racial segregation and discrimination generally has been impelled by this purpose. Liberty to act, organize, obtain information, and protest is an indispensable part of effective political participation. Nor is it irrelevant to social, political, and economic equality. Prior to the breakdown of communism in Eastern Europe and the Soviet Union, it was a common view that the communist countries were trading liberty for equality, by contrast with capitalism, which was said to trade off equality for liberty. One important thing that has come to light after the collapse of communism is the extent of corruption and privilege, as well as economic stagnation, in communist societies. While they had surely traded off liberty for a basic security of employment, it was primarily the economic failures and moral decay that demoralized the communist bloc.

STRATEGIES FOR PRODUCING POLITICAL GOODS

All political systems embody strategies for producing political goods. Different kinds of political systems represent different institutional choices intended to produce different combinations of political goods. The framers of the U.S. Constitution believed that separation of powers would protect liberty; Karl Marx believed that the "dictatorship of the proletariat" would lead to a just and harmonious society; Mussolini believed that a strong leader would increase national power and glory; the Ayatollah Khomeini believed that a state and society modeled after the Koran, and administered by the clergy, would achieve justice on earth and eternal salvation.

Since the collapse of the Soviet Union in 1991, democracy has seemed to be "the only game in town." Earlier in the twentieth century there have been several political ideologies in competition with political democracy—communism, democratic socialism, fascism, corporatist authoritarianism, and the like. Fascism went down in flames in World War II. Communism all but collapsed in the late 1980s, drained of credibility by the failure of its promises and by its corruption. Most of its successor regimes are trying to democratize and establish free markets. The bureaucratic authoritarian regimes of Latin America, discredited by their cruelties and economic failures, have turned to the market and democracy. The postcolonial regimes of Sub-Saharan Africa, after a brief interlude of populist democracy in the "liberation" enthusiasm of the 1960s, turned to authoritarian regimes of one kind or another. Then in recent years some of them have begun to experiment once again with democracy. Social democracy and democratic corporatism have survived in Western Europe, somewhat tarnished by their association with the socialism of Eastern Europe.

Although democracy and the free market economy have been the wave of the immediate past, other strategies may very well become credible once again. Below we spell out the major political-economic alternatives in the world today. Political systems exist in preindustrial, industrializing, industrial, or postindustrial economies. We saw in Chapters 3, 4, and 5 that socioeconomic development brings increased political awareness and participation. In the industrial nations political input structures must be developed to deal with this potential for citizen participation. One strategy is for a single authoritarian party to contain, direct, and mobilize citizens under government control. The other is to permit competing parties that represent different goods and strategies. We refer to the first strategy as authoritarian and the second as democratic. We further classify systems by the degree to which they limit the role of the government in the economy. Thus we have the following varieties of political systems:

   I. Industrial nations
      A. Democratic
         1. Market-oriented
         2. Social Democratic (regulation-oriented)
      B. Authoritarian
         1. Conservative
         2. Radical
  II. Preindustrial and Industrializing Nations
      A. Authoritarian
         1. Neotraditional
         2. Personal Rule
         3. Clerico-mobilizational
         4. Technocratic-repressive
         5. Technocratic-distributive
         6. Technocratic-mobilizational
      B. Democratic Transitional

Industrialized Democratic Nations

The industrialized democratic nations must reconcile pressures to maintain or increase government services and personal income with the need to accumulate resources for investment in economic growth. Many contemporary democratic industrial nations are challenged by unemployment and/or relatively slow rates of growth. The classic capital-labor confrontation has been complicated by the rise of the service economy and the emergence of environmental challenges. The service economy complicates the class structure and reduces the power of trade unions. Industrial pollution of land, air, and water divides nations differently, with a substantial part of the middle classes opposing growth that implies environmental degradation, and a substantial part of the working classes making the opposite choice. These dilemmas—both the old capital versus labor issues, and the newer service economy and environmental issues facing all advanced democracies—may be dealt with in a market-oriented fashion as in the Britain of Margaret Thatcher, and the United States of the Reagan era, or in a social democratic fashion as in Norway and Sweden.

But though there are policy differences between the market-oriented and social democracies, both types of democratic regimes have in the last decades reconsidered taxing, welfare, and regulative activities. The size, cost, and inefficiencies of government have become major political issues. In the United States both major political parties are embarked on efforts to limit and restructure government—the Republicans leading a campaign to reduce spending and return powers to the state governments; and the Democrats with their program of "reinventing government." The environmental issue divides both conservative and left parties. In some European countries "Green," ecologically oriented, parties have emerged. In 1998, the German Greens became the first such party to win control of the executive branch of a major country, albeit as a junior partner, when it formed a coalition government with the Social Democrats.

Industrialized Authoritarian Nations

Industrial authoritarian nations come in radical and conservative varieties. Prior to the collapse of communism in Eastern Europe, the Soviet Union, Poland, and Hungary were radical industrialized authoritarian regimes. Though many of these countries have now moved toward market economies and democracy, anti-Western groups in Russia and in states such as Belarus may have sufficient vitality to reinstitute repressive politics and preserve much of the command economy of the pre-1989 era. The more serious the ethnonational conflict and the more severe the economic failures, the more likely such a scenario will be. But this is unlikely to be justified in the rhetoric of Marxism-Leninism. It is more likely that such repression would be justified in ethnonationalist terms. In the Islamic parts of the old Soviet Union, clerico-authoritarian trends seem to be on the rise.

Franco Spain (1938–1975), Greece under the military dictatorship (1967–1974), the Chile of Pinochet (1973–1988), and the Brazil of "the generals" (1964–1985) are examples of conservative authoritarianism. The military authoritarian regimes of Southern Europe and Latin America of the 1960s and 1970s suppressed popular political organization but granted considerable freedom to private enterprise. They sought to foster economic growth, though at the expense of increasing inequality of wealth and income.

In general, and across different regime types, the credibility of socialism and of high welfare expenditures has declined in the last decades, while that of the market economy has risen. It is still to be seen whether this is a pendular move, or whether the power of the state reached a historic high point in the 1980s. The democratization of the Latin American and Eastern European countries may hinge on their economic success. Economic failure may trigger an authoritarian return. Thus, while there are currently few industrialized authoritarian regimes (whether radical or conservative), it would be a mistake to think that the category is no longer relevant.

Preindustrial Nations

The preindustrial nations face common challenges of modernization. There are some seven strategies of political development followed by preindustrial countries—one democratic and the six authoritarian regimes that follow.

Neotraditional Political Systems

Neotraditional political systems emphasize stability, the maintenance of an established order. The best exemplars are Saudi Arabia and the sheikdoms of the Persian Gulf. Since these regimes are oil rich, they have so far been able to modernize selectively (for example, the military) and buy off opposition and discontent. But as they develop economically through their oil royalties, and as they provide health, educational, and other amenities to a substantial part of their populations, some kind of political modernization may follow. This may in turn lead to the development of a political opposition and stronger demands for reform.

Personal Rule

Most of the regimes of Sub-Saharan Africa are not neotraditional, though they may contain traditional structures such as kingdoms or chiefdoms. The colonial regimes out of which most of the Sub-Saharan countries emerged were artificial constructs that often included many different languages, ethnicities, and religions. The formally democratic regimes that were established after independence soon gave way to various versions of "personal rule."[13] The "personal ruler" is not simply a governor in the limited political sense; he has a "proprietary" relation to the regime, its institutions and agencies, and exploits it for his personal purposes. Rent seeking is thus a serious problem in such countries, as the case of President Mobutu of Zaire illustrated in Chapter 1. Where these systems stabilize, the rulers maintain control through police suppression, patronage, spoils, and privileges distributed through clientelistic networks. Many of the personal rule regimes in Sub-Saharan Africa are characterized by low (or even negative) growth, low life expectancy, low literacy, and low health standards. Since these regimes are economically unproductive, they have little legitimacy and are susceptible to military coups.

Clerico-Mobilizational Regimes

In the last decades, and principally in Islamic countries, a clerico-authoritarian mobilizational ideology has emerged. Clerico-mobilizational regimes are built on a religious authority for which they try to mobilize active support. They are antisecular in social matters (for example, regarding the status of women and family policies) and they restrict civil society through media censorship and by suppressing secular opponents. They are authoritarian, but neither traditional nor technocratic. They want to control the modern media, use it for their own purposes, and clean it of its moral corruption. They are ambivalent in economic policy, urging market intervention from the point of view of Koranic precepts, but in practice they do not seriously interfere with banks and other economic institutions. They are nationalist and anti-Western.

This "fundamentalist" religious movement is represented in both branches of Islam—Shia and Sunni. The Shia version is exemplified in Iran, which is dominated by clerics and Islamic legislators and judges. Sunni Islam has similar radical theocratic movements, not only in the Middle East but in Afghanistan, Pakistan, and in the Islamic areas of the former Soviet Union. Movements of this kind are threatening to take power in Algeria and Egypt. The Hamas in Gaza have resisted a peace settlement in Palestine and favor a clerico-authoritarian Palestinian government. The fate of these new movements is still unclear. They may not be very effective in mounting an international coalition. Nationalism and the split between Shia and Sunni Muslims may impede collaboration. Collaboration across religious boundaries—between Islamic, Jewish, and Christian fundamentalist movements—is even less likely.

Technocratic Repressive

The **technocratic repressive** approach promoted economic growth previously in Indonesia and in parts of South America, where a coalition of military and civilian technocrats and business interests suppressed participation and pursued a growth-oriented investment policy at the cost of growing economic inequality. Such Middle Eastern countries as Iraq, Syria, and Egypt still pursue this strategy. In other countries that have gone democratic, economic or democratic failures may lead to reversions to technocratic repressive strategies.

Technocratic-Distributive

There also is a distributive, and more egalitarian, version of the modernizing authoritarian regime. One example is South Korea prior to its democratization. South Korea suppressed participation but encouraged some income redistribution along with growth. Early land reforms, rapid development of education, labor-intensive, export-oriented industrialization, and substantial American advice, support, and pressure marked the Korean experiment. Its economic success seems to have led to effective democratization.

Technocratic-Mobilizational

The last category, the authoritarian technocratic-mobilizational strategy, has been exemplified primarily by preindustrial Communist countries, and in a milder form by Taiwan. There is a single political party mobilizing and involving citizens in the political process. Competitive participation is suppressed or limited. There are few such states today, but we cannot rule out the possibility that they may return. China, Vietnam, North Korea, and Cuba are the last remaining Communist societies, dominated by single mobilizing political parties. China, Vietnam, and even Cuba have opened their socialist economies to market forces. North Korea may be on the brink of such a policy shift. China has seen enormous growth (see Chapter 13), and there is much speculation about how long it can avoid some political pluralism.

The non-Communist mobilizational systems vary substantially in success and in their emphasis on growth versus distribution. Taiwan has combined growth and distributive equity, and in recent years politics has become increasingly competitive. Mexico has been dominated by the Partido Revolucionario Institucional (PRI), which incorporates the major interest groups of labor, business, and agriculture into its internal structure, for more than a half-century. The PRI seemed to be securely in power until the last few years, but Mexico is now on the brink of a genuinely competitive and pluralist system.

Democratization in Developing Countries

Just as democracy has become the "only political game in town," democratization and its consolidation have become the main preoccupations of many contemporary political scientists. Current understandings of transitions to democracy emphasize the importance of leadership, choice, and bargaining, whereas they tend to play down the importance of economic and social factors. Many scholars argue that democratization can occur wherever the leaders, pressured or influenced by democratization elsewhere, begin moving in the democratic direction. The recent literature very persuasively emphasizes the uncertainty and unpredictability of democratic transitions.[14] If democratization is therefore uncertain, tentative, and reversible, "democratic consolidation" is a condition in which the main elites have accepted democracy and in which participatory behavior has been widely adopted among the general population. Thus the new literature implies the presence of a "civil society" based on free media and a lively associational life. These conditions in turn are associated with widespread literacy and rising economic standards. From this perspective a great many contemporary Third World democracies are not consolidated institutionally or culturally.[15] Yet, the democratic emergence of Taiwan and South Korea suggests that industrialization, urbanization, education, and communication can indeed foster consolidated democratization.[16] On the other hand, India, a democracy for almost its entire existence since independence in 1947, demonstrates that a relatively underdeveloped country can sustain a democracy even without these economic, social, and political conditions.

TRADE-OFFS AND OPPORTUNITY COSTS

One of the hard facts about political goods is that though all may be desirable, they cannot be pursued simultaneously. A political system often has to trade off one value to obtain another. Spending funds on education is giving up the opportunity to spend them on welfare, or to leave them in the hands of consumers for their own use. These **trade-offs** and **opportunity costs** are also found in complicated decisions about investment for the future as opposed to consumption today. Even more difficult are the trade-offs between security and liberty, or stability and adaptation, where the very concepts imply giving up some of the one for some of the other. Extreme liberty, as Hobbes would tell us, would make a highly insecure world where the strong might bully the weak and where collective action would be difficult to arrange. Yet, without liberty, security is of little value, as the prisoner is too well aware. Not only do political goods have trade-offs, but the trade-offs are not the same under all circumstances. Under some conditions increasing liberty somewhat will also increase security—for example, because riots against censorship will end. Under some conditions investment in education will be paid back many times in health and welfare, because trained citizens can care better for themselves and work more productively.

One of the important tasks of social science is to discover the conditions under which positive and negative trade-offs occur. Regrettably, political science has no way of converting units of liberty into units of safety or welfare. And because politics may involve violence on a large scale, we must acknowledge that we can never calculate the value of a political outcome gained at the cost of human life. People act as though they know how to make such conversions, but as political scientists we can only point to value judgments that people have been willing to make. The weight given to various goods differs across cultures and contexts. The advantage of a clear-cut ideology is that it provides people with logical schemes for telling how much one value should be traded against another, and thus offers orderly bases for choice. Such schemes may be invaluable for those pressed to action in the terrible circumstances of war, revolution, and famine. However, there is no ideology, just as there is no political science, that can solve all these problems objectively.

KEY TERMS

central government revenues and expenditures

civil liberties

direct vs. indirect taxes

distribution

extraction

gross domestic product (GDP)

neotraditional political system

opportunity cost

Organization for Economic Cooperation and Development (OECD)

outcomes

outputs

public policies

regulation

symbolic policies

taxation

technocratic

trade-off

welfare state

SUGGESTED READINGS

Berger, Suzanne, ed. *Organizing Interests in Western Europe.* Cambridge, England: Cambridge University Press, 1981.

Castles, Francis G., ed. *The Comparative History of Public Policy.* Cambridge, England: Polity Press, 1989.

Dahl, Robert. *Democracy and Its Critics.* New Haven, CT: Yale University Press, 1989.

Di Palma, Giuseppe. *To Craft Democracies.* Berkeley: University of California Press, 1990.

Diamond, Larry, ed. *Democracy in Developing Countries.* Boulder, CO: Lynne Rienner, 1992.

Flora, Peter, and Arnold Heidenheimer. *The Development of Welfare States in Europe and America.* New Brunswick, NJ: Transaction Books, 1981.

Goldthorpe, John, ed. *Order and Conflict in Contemporary Capitalism.* Oxford, England: Clarendon Press, 1984

Gourevitch, Peter. *Politics in Hard Times.* Ithaca, NY: Cornell University Press, 1986.

Heidenheimer, Arnold, Hugh Heclo, and Carolyn Teich Adams. *Comparative Public Policy,* 3rd ed. New York: St. Martin's, 1990.

Huntington, Samuel. *The Third Wave: Democratization in the Late Twentieth Century.* Norman, OK: Oklahoma University Press, 1991.

Jackson, Robert, and Carl Rosberg. *Personal Rule in Black Africa.* Berkeley, CA: University of California Press, 1982.

Katzenstein, Peter. *Small States in World Markets.* Ithaca, NY: Cornell University Press, 1985.

Lindblom, Charles E. *Politics and Markets.* New Haven, CT: Yale University Press, 1978.

Lijphart, Arend. *Patterns of Democracy.* New Haven, CT: Yale University Press, 1999.

Marks, Gary, and Larry Diamond, eds. *Reexamining Democracy.* Newbury Park, CA: Sage, 1992.

Mainwaring, Scott, Guillermo O'Donnell, and Arturo Valenzuela. *Issues in Democratic Consolidation.* Notre Dame, IN: University of Notre Dame Press, 1992.

Olson, Mancur. *The Rise and Decline of Nations.* New Haven, CT: Yale University Press, 1982.

Putnam, Robert D. *Making Democracy Work.* Princeton, NJ: Princeton University Press, 1993.

Schmitter, Philippe, and Gerhard Lehmbruch, eds. *Trends Toward Corporate Intermediation.* Beverly Hills, CA: Sage, 1979.

Wilson, James G. *The Politics of Regulation in the United States.* New York: Basic Books, 1980.

NOTES

1. See World Bank, *Entering the 21ˢᵗ Century: World Development Report 1999–2000* (New York: Oxford University Press, 2000), Table A.1, pp. 216–217.
2. Peter Flora and Arnold Heidenheimer, *The Development of Welfare States in Europe and America* (New Brunswick, NJ: Transaction Books, 1981); Arnold Heidenheimer, Hugh Heclo, and Carolyn Teich Adams, *Comparative Public Policy,* 3rd ed. (New York: St. Martin's, 1990).
3. Heidenheimer, Heclo and Adams. *Comparative Public Policy,* pp. 211–219.
4. Harold Wilensky, *The Welfare State and Equality* (Berkeley: University of California Press, 1975); Harold Wilensky, Gregory Luebbert, Susan Hahn, and Adrienne Jameson, *Comparative Social Policy: Theories, Methods, Findings* (Berkeley, CA: Institute of International Studies, 1985).
5. *The Economist* (May 30, 1998), p. 19.
6. See, for example, Samuel Brittan, *The Economic Consequences of Democracy* (London: Temple Smith, 1977); Michael Boskin, *The Crisis in Social Security* (San Francisco: Institute for Con-

Index